# Getting Started with Containers in Google Cloud Platform

## Deploy, Manage, and Secure Containerized Applications

Shimon Ifrah

Apress®

*Getting Started with Containers in Google Cloud Platform*

Shimon Ifrah
Melbourne, VIC, Australia

ISBN-13 (pbk): 978-1-4842-6469-0                    ISBN-13 (electronic): 978-1-4842-6470-6
https://doi.org/10.1007/978-1-4842-6470-6

Managing Director, Apress Media LLC: Welmoed Spahr
Acquisitions Editor: Celestin Suresh John
Development Editor: Laura Berendson
Coordinating Editor: Aditee Mirashi

Cover designed by eStudioCalamar

Cover image designed by Freepik (www.freepik.com)

Distributed to the book trade worldwide by Springer Science+Business Media New York, 1 New York Plaza, Suite 4600, New York, NY 10004-1562, USA. Phone 1-800-SPRINGER, fax (201) 348-4505, email orders-ny@springer-sbm.com, or visit www.springeronline.com. Apress Media, LLC is a California LLC, and the sole member (owner) is Springer Science+Business Media Finance Inc (SSBM Finance Inc). SSBM Finance Inc is a **Delaware** corporation.

For information on translations, please e-mail booktranslations@springernature.com; for reprint, paperback, or audio rights, please e-mail bookpermissions@springernature.com.

Apress titles may be purchased in bulk for academic, corporate, or promotional use. eBook versions and licenses are also available for most titles. For more information, reference our Print and eBook Bulk Sales web page at http://www.apress.com/bulk-sales.

Any source code or other supplementary material referenced by the author in this book is available to readers on GitHub via the book's product page, located at www.apress.com/9781484264690. For more detailed information, please visit http://www.apress.com/source-code.

Printed on acid-free paper

# Table of Contents

# About the Author

**Shimon Ifrah** is an IT professional with more than fifteen years of experience in the design, management, and deployment of information technology systems and networks. In the last few years, Shimon has been specializing in cloud computing and containerized applications on Microsoft Azure, Amazon AWS, and Google Cloud Platform (GCP). Shimon also holds more than twenty vendor certificates from Microsoft, AWS, VMware, and Cisco. During his career in the IT industry, he has worked for the largest managed services and technology companies in the world, helping them manage systems for the largest enterprises. He is based out of Melbourne, Australia.

# About the Technical Reviewer

 **Jaivish Kothari** is an open source enthusiast with a wide range of experience in the tech industry. He has worked on a variety of projects in storage and networking, spanning multiple cloud domains and using different programming languages.

# Acknowledgments

I would like to thank my loving family for supporting me during the writing of this book, as well as the previous two.

A special thank you goes to my publisher, Apress, for believing in me and giving me all the support needed to write my books.

# Introduction

In early 2018, I decided to write a series of three books about deploying container services, with each book tackling one of the major public cloud providers. Almost three years later, that mission has been completed with the release of this book. The primary goal of this book is to help new and existing Google Cloud Platform (GCP) administrators, engineers, developers, and architects get started with GCP's container services and build strong foundations on the platform. The secondary goal of this book is to help AWS and Microsoft Azure administrators, engineers, developers, and architects cross-skill their knowledge from other platforms and get going with GCP.

If you read the previous two books in the series, you will find that this book follows the same format of deep dives and hands-on demonstrations. I have tried to make this book as hands-on as possible with many learn-by-doing examples, followed by high-level explanations. Since GCP has a great command-line tool (gcloud) to manage its services, I added a command-line option to most demos, and in many demos I started with the command-line option rather than the management console.

I really hope you enjoy this book and, most important, learn something new that will help you get going. These days, knowledge is power, and I hope you find this book empowering.

# CHAPTER 1

# Get Started with Google Cloud Platform (GCP)

In this chapter, we will get started with Google Cloud Platform (GCP) by covering the following topics:

- Get introduction to GCP

- Learn the benefits of a GCP free tier account

- Understand projects in GCP

- Use Cloud Shell to deploy workloads

- Secure the GCP account

- Learn about GCP container services

## Introduction

Google Cloud Platform (GCP) was launched in November 2011 as a public cloud computing platform offering computing, storage, networking, database, Big Data, security, and identity services. The seed that grew into GCP was the 2008 release of the Google App Engine, which offered runtime and platform as a service (PaaS) web services to developers inside Google data centers. GCP is also part of the Google Cloud, which includes the business productivity suite, also known as G Suite. As of writing this book, GCP has a presence in twenty countries across sixty-one datacenters.

Currently, GCP offers around ninety products and cloud services in the following categories:

© Shimon Ifrah 2021
S. Ifrah, *Getting Started with Containers in Google Cloud Platform*,
https://doi.org/10.1007/978-1-4842-6470-6_1

- **Compute Services:** App Engine, Compute Engine (virtual machines), Kubernetes, Cloud Functions, Cloud Run

- **Storage and Databases:** Cloud storage, SQL, BigTable, Spanner

- **Networking:** VPC, load balancing, Armor, CDN, Interconnect, cloud DNS

- **Big Data:** Big Query, cloud dataflow, Dataproc, Composer, Datalab, Dataprep, Pub/Sub, Data StudioAutoML

- **Cloud AI:** AutoML, TPU, Machine Learning Engine, Job Discovery, Dialogflow Enterprise, natural language, speech-to-text, text-to-speech, Translation API, Vision API, Cloud Video Intelligence

- **Management Tools:** Stackdriver, Deployment Manager, Cloud Console, Cloud Shell, Console Mobile App, APIs

- **Identify and Security:** IAM, Identity-Aware Proxy, Data Loss Prevention API, Key Enforcement, Key Management Service, Resource Manager, Security Command Center, Security Scanner, Access Transparency, VPC Service Controls

- **IoT:** IoT Core, Edge TPU, IoT Edge

- **API Platform:** Maps Platform, Apigee API Platform, API Monetization, Developer Portal, API Analytics, Apigee Sense, Endpoints

GCP also offers professional certifications for engineers, developers, and architects.

# Get Started with Google Cloud Platform (GCP)

We will get started by building the fundamentals needed to deploy services and applications to GCP, which is an integrated cloud platform. Our focus will be on GCP's container services, but at the same time we will set up all the support services that are needed to run production workloads securely and reliably.

# The Benefits of a GCP Free Tier Account

The GCP free tier account comes with a number of free services that you will never be asked to pay for, regardless of whether the twelve-month period has passed. Having access to always-free services can help with the testing of applications, scripts, and many more tasks you might need to test during the lifecycle of your application.

## GCP Free Tier

To help engineers, developers, and architects get started with GCP, Google offers a free tier subscription for new users that provides the following:

- $300 credit for twelve months
- Always-free GCP services that include:
    - Free monthly use of an f1-micro virtual machine instance
    - 5GB per month of cloud storage
    - Access to free Cloud Functions (serverless)
    - No cluster management fee for Google Kubernetes Engine (GKE) cluster (you will pay for nodes only)
    - Access to run free web applications on App Engine
    - 60 minutes of free speech-to-text service
    - 120 minutes of Cloud Build service

## Sign Up for GCP Free Tier account

To sign up for a free tier account and use the $300 free credit, perform the following steps:

- Go to the following URL: `https://cloud.google.com/free`
- Click on the Get Started for Free button to start the registration process, as shown in Figure 1-1.

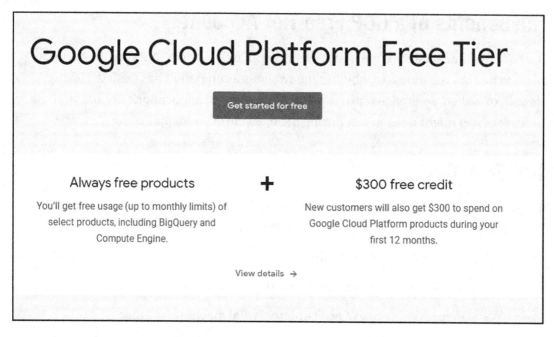

***Figure 1-1.*** *Get started with GCP*

- Follow the registration and verification process, and you will see the free credit notice, as shown in Figure 1-2. You will also need to provide a credit card during the process; however, it will not be charged until you activate billing on your account.

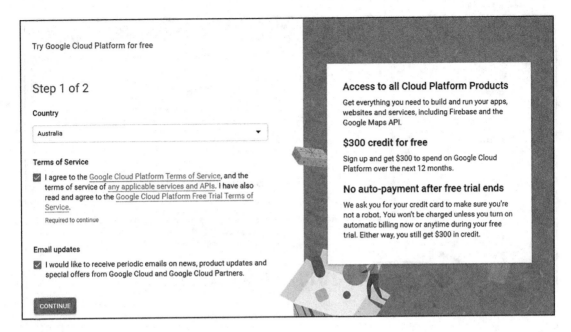

***Figure 1-2.*** *$300 credit for free*

- On completion, you will see the Google Cloud console, as shown in Figure 1-3. The left navigation menu offers access to all the services available on the GCP platform. The Dashboard offers access to the actual selected service. You can access the GC console directly using the following link: `https://console.cloud.google.com/`

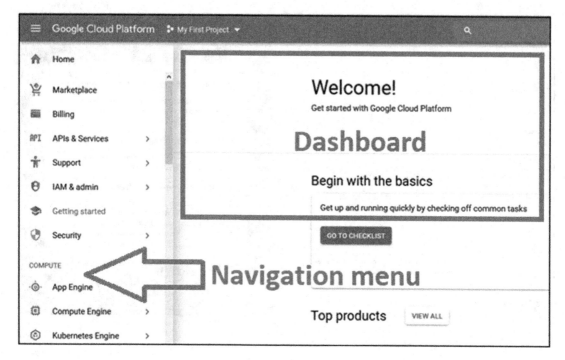

**Figure 1-3.** *Google Cloud console*

To check the status of your GCP billing and how much free credit is left, do the following:

- From the GC Console's Navigation menu, click on Billing.

- The Billing dashboard will display the current free credit left on the account, as shown in Figure 1-4. For instance, I have $447 AUD, which is equivalent to $300 USD.

*Figure 1-4.* *Promotional credits*

# Understanding GCP Projects

Before we go deeper into the GCP platform, I would like to explain an essential and fundamental concept that you should know. Everything in GCP is based on a project; a project is a logical unit that organizes resources like storage, compute, API, permissions, and billing. Each project is a separate entity, which means that resources in one project cannot access resources from other projects. Once a project is deleted, all resources inside the project except users are removed, which makes it cost-effective and efficient.

A common reason for using projects in GCP is to separate production and development workloads into different projects. By doing so, we prevent the breakdown of our production environment as a result of mixing it with non-production workloads.

## Creating a Project

To understand the concept a bit better, let's go ahead and create a project that will host a Linux instance. GCP will create a default project and make things a bit easier for you to get started. The default project is called My First Project, as shown in Figure 1-5.

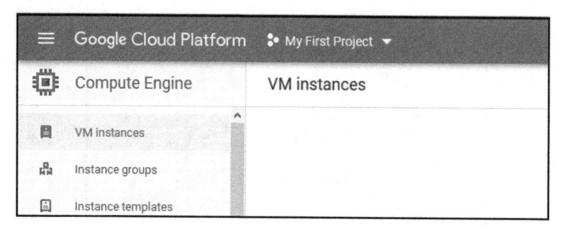

***Figure 1-5.***  *My First Project*

In our case, I will create a new project and place my virtual machine instance in it. To do so, I will use the GCP Resource Manager console; to access the console, click on IAM & Admin from the Navigation menu and select "Manage resources," as shown in Figure 1-6.

---

**Note**    You can also access the Resource Manager console from the top search box by searching for "manage resources."

---

***Figure 1-6.*** *Manage resources*

To create a new project, click on the Create Project button on the top menu, as shown in Figure 1-7.

---

**Note**   You can also delete an existing project from the same console.

---

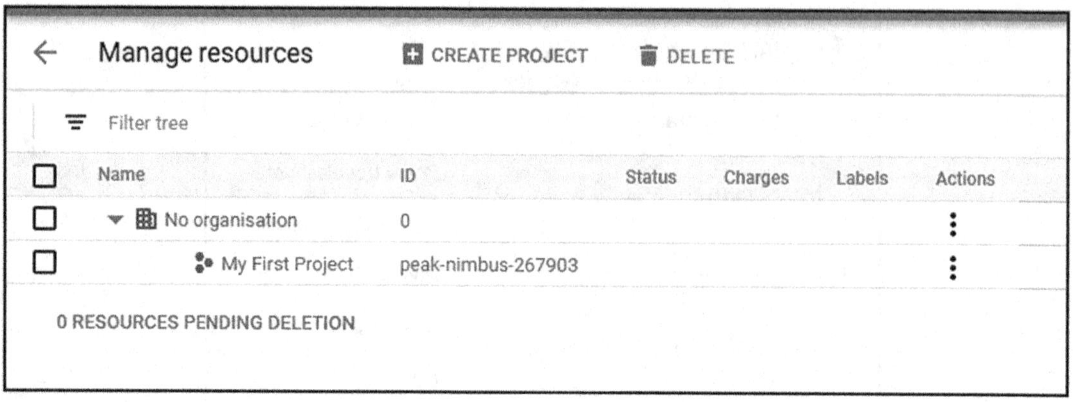

| | Name | ID | Status | Charges | Labels | Actions |
|---|---|---|---|---|---|---|
| ☐ | ▼ 🏢 No organisation | 0 | | | | ⋮ |
| ☐ | ஃ My First Project | peak-nimbus-267903 | | | | ⋮ |

← Manage resources        ➕ CREATE PROJECT        🗑 DELETE

☰ Filter tree

0 RESOURCES PENDING DELETION

*Figure 1-7.*  *Create a new project*

On the New Project page, fill in the project name details and click Create, as shown in Figure 1-8.

**Note**    By default, each GCP tenant can create twenty-five projects; if you need to create more than twenty-five projects, you will need to contact support and request a quota increase. The process to request a quota increase is straightforward and involves filling in a form and waiting for GCP to increase the quota. This process helps GCP manage their resource allocation strategy and ensure the platform is not over-utilized.

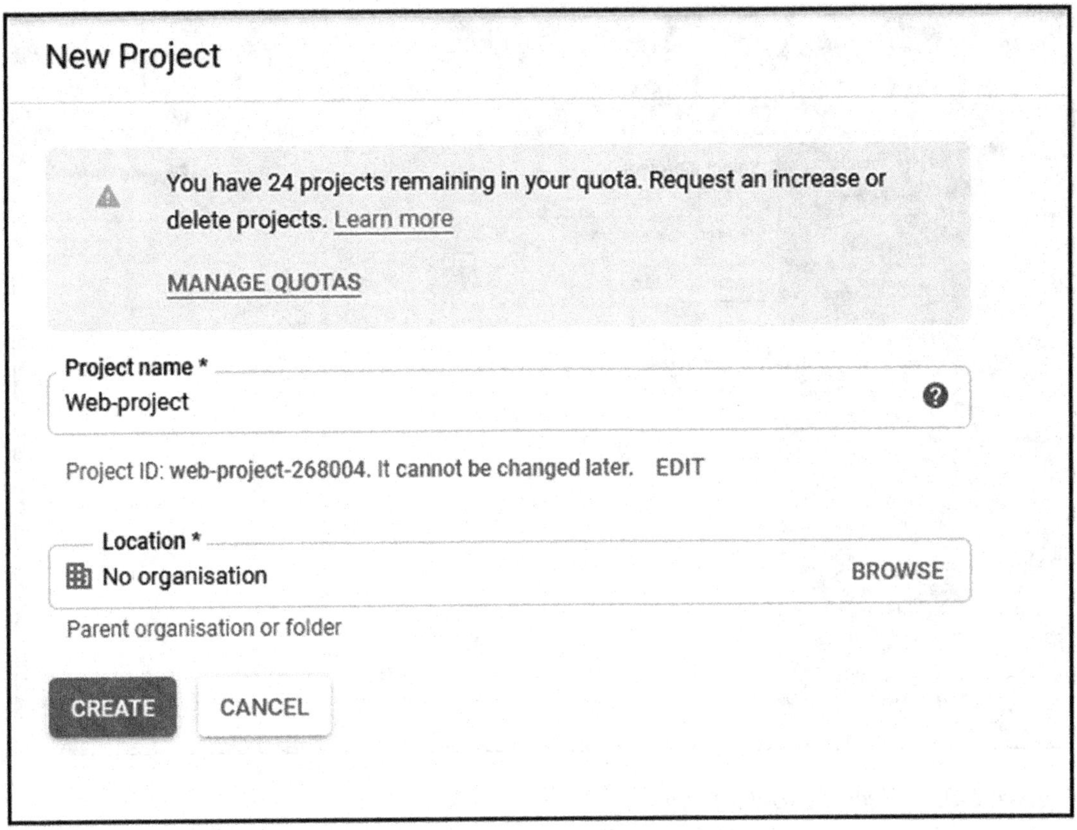

New Project

⚠  You have 24 projects remaining in your quota. Request an increase or
   delete projects. Learn more

   MANAGE QUOTAS

Project name *
Web-project                                                                    ❓

Project ID: web-project-268004. It cannot be changed later.    EDIT

Location *
🏢 No organisation                                                      BROWSE

Parent organisation or folder

CREATE     CANCEL

**Figure 1-8.**  *Create a new project*

It will take GCP thirty seconds to create the project, at which point it becomes
available to us. After the project is ready, we can access it from the projects drop-down
list located at the top-left corner, as shown in Figure 1-9. To open my new project, I will
click on the arrow and select my project from the Select a Project page.

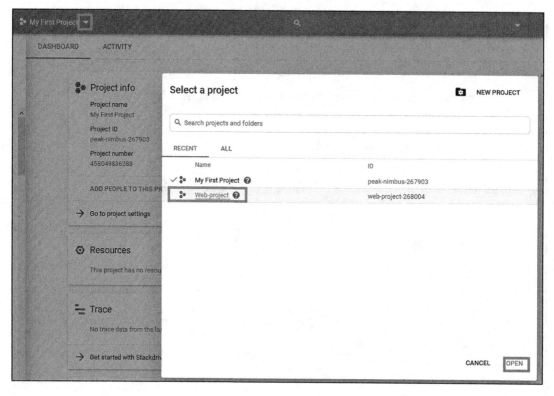

***Figure 1-9.***  *Select a Project page*

# Create a VM Instance

To create a new virtual machine instance, use the Navigation menu, click on Compute Engine, and select "VM Instances" from the list. The first time you access VM Instances, you will see a message telling you that "Compute Engine is getting ready . . . ," which means GCP is preparing the backend infrastructure needed to provision VMs. While the GCP prepares the infrastructure, the Create button is grey, and you cannot create instances. When the process is completed, go ahead and click Create. The getting ready message is shown in Figure 1-10.

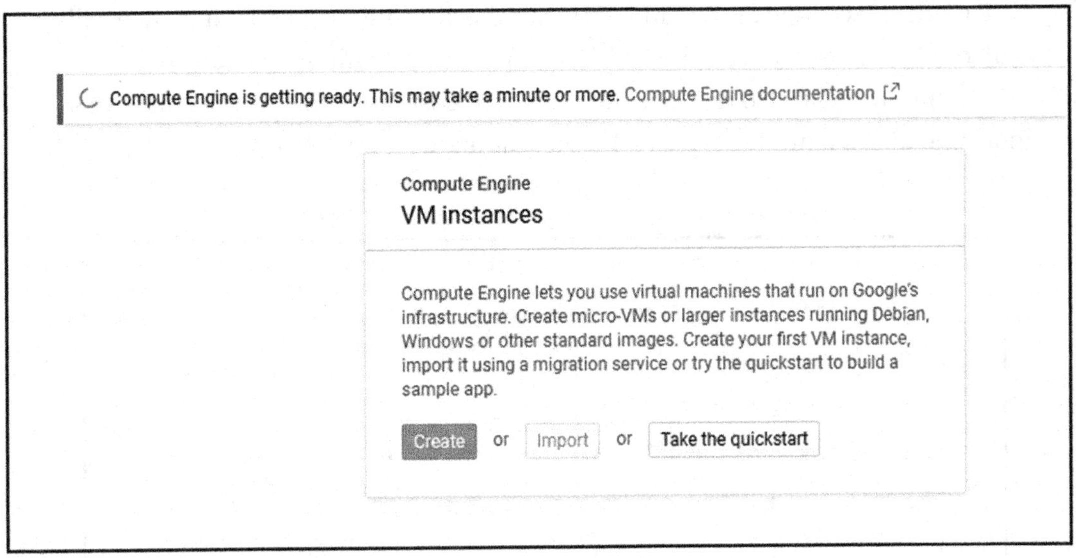

***Figure 1-10.*** *VM Instances*

After clicking on Create, you will see the Create an Instance page with all the options. The GCP VM creation process is very straightforward and is available in a single-page wizard, which makes the process simpler and faster.

To create an instance, fill in the Name, Region, Zone, Image, and Instance Size fields. The Create an Instance page is shown in Figure 1-11.

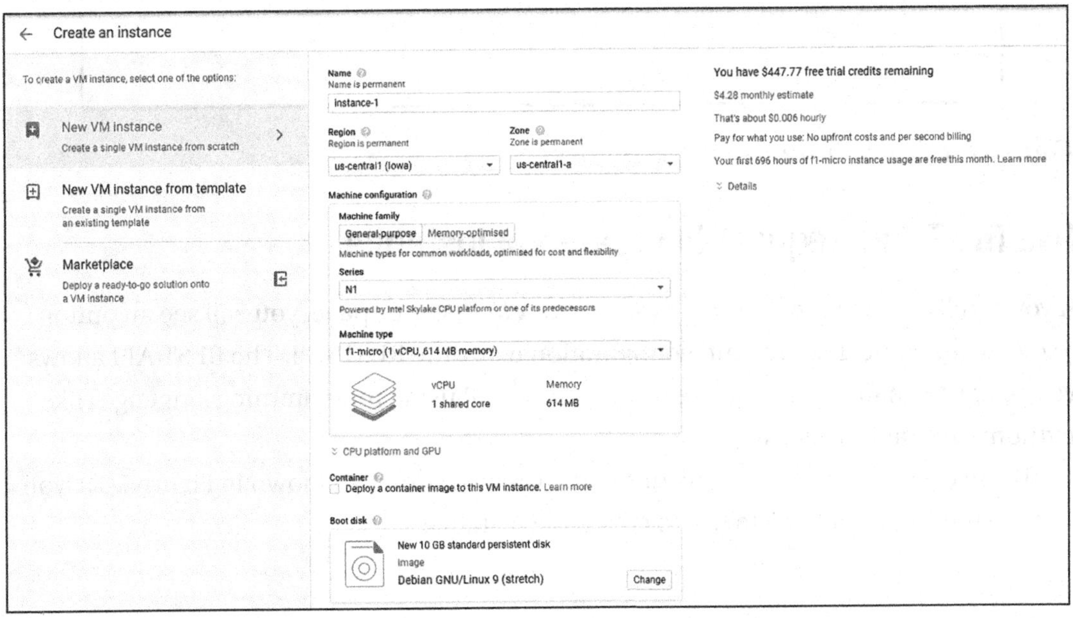

***Figure 1-11.*** *Create an instance*

GCP made the costing of the VM very clear; the monthly cost of the instance will show up on the left. In my case, the VM will cost me $4.28 a month, which comes out to $0.006 per hour. GCP also displays the estimated cost breakdown, which includes compute and disk. Figure 1-12 shows the cost estimate for my VM instance.

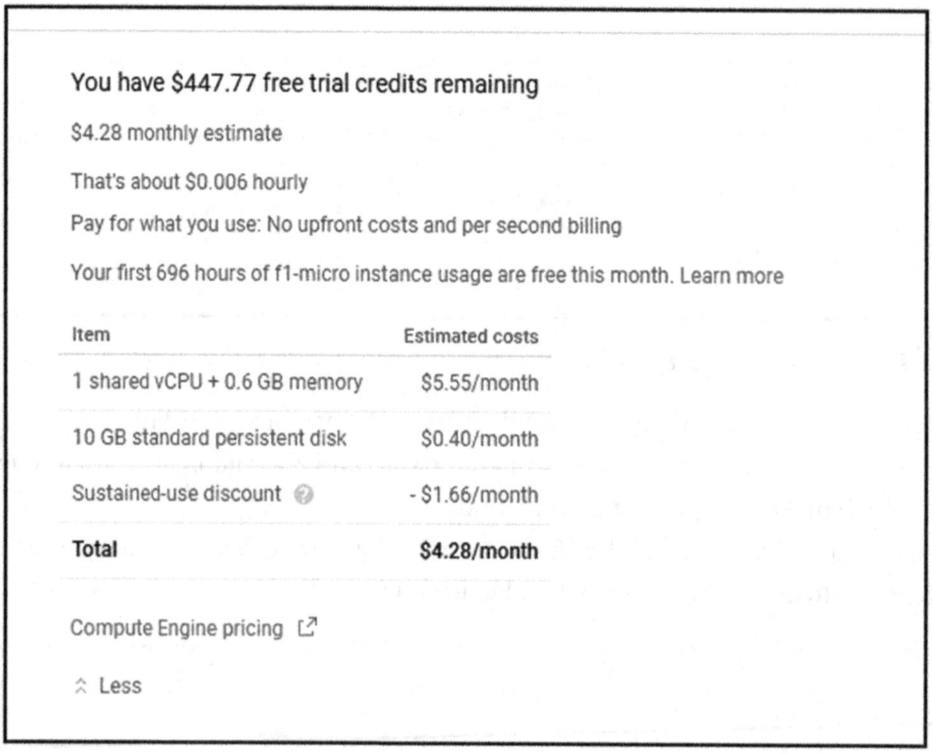

**You have $447.77 free trial credits remaining**

$4.28 monthly estimate

That's about $0.006 hourly

Pay for what you use: No upfront costs and per second billing

Your first 696 hours of f1-micro instance usage are free this month. Learn more

| Item | Estimated costs |
|------|-----------------|
| 1 shared vCPU + 0.6 GB memory | $5.55/month |
| 10 GB standard persistent disk | $0.40/month |
| Sustained-use discount ⊘ | - $1.66/month |
| **Total** | **$4.28/month** |

Compute Engine pricing ⬏

⌃ Less

***Figure 1-12.*** *VM instance cost estimates*

# Use REST API Request to Create VM Instance

If you scroll down to the bottom of the Create VM Instance page, you will see an option to create the same instance and configuration using the REST API. The REST API allows you to create, manage, and delete resources in GCP using programming languages like Python, .NET, and Node.js.

If you click on the "REST" link under the Create button, as shown in Figure 1-13, you will see the code you need to use to create the instance.

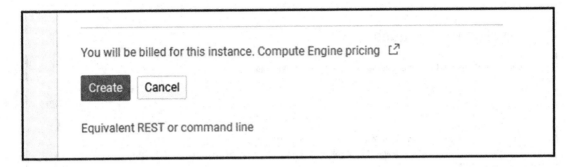

***Figure 1-13.*** *REST API command*

In Figure 1-14, you can see the REST API requests required to create the instance. For more information about accessing and using the GCP REST API, please visit the following URL:

https://cloud.google.com/compute/docs/apis?hl=en_GB

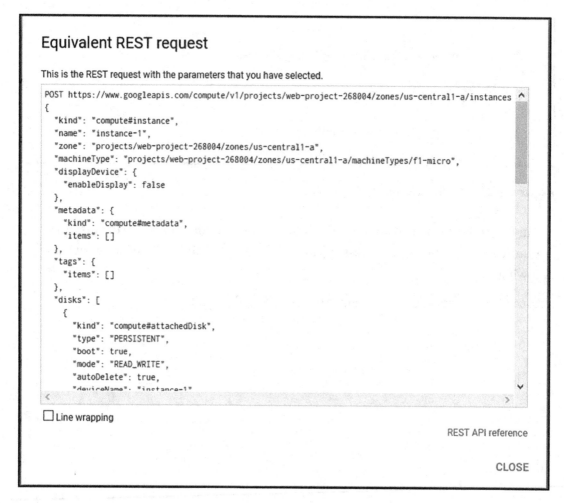

*Figure 1-14.* *REST API request*

## Use gcloud Command Line to Create VM Instance

You can also use the gcloud command-line utility to create the same instance. If you click on the "Command Line" link shown in Figure 1-13, you will see the gcloud command you need to run to create the VM instance, shown in Figure 1-15.

In a later section, we will explore Cloud Shell and gcloud commands.

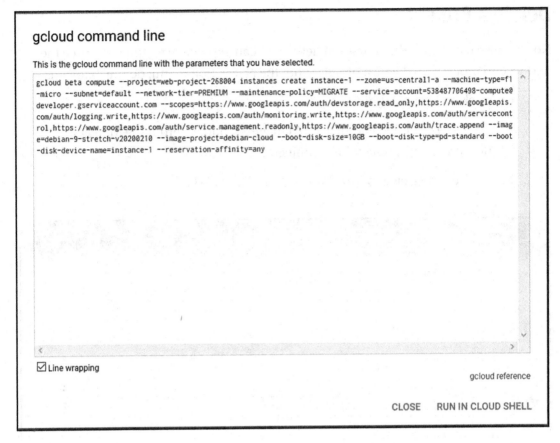

**Figure 1-15.** *gcloud Command Line*

Once the VM has been created, you can see the VM Instances page, as shown in Figure 1-16.

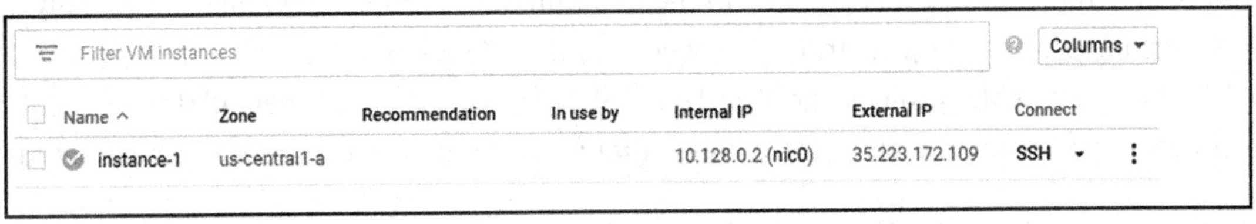

**Figure 1-16.** *VM instances*

# Delete a Project

Now that we have created our first VM, let's go ahead and delete a project and see the end-to-end process. To delete a project, from the Navigation menu, do the following:

- Click on IAM & Admin

- From the extended list, click on Manage Resources. From the Manage Resources page, select "Web-project."

- Click on the Delete button, as shown in Figure 1-17.

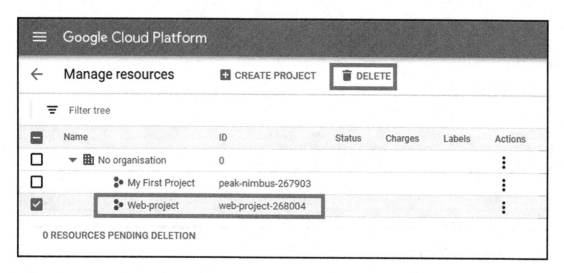

***Figure 1-17.*** *Delete project*

After you click Delete, you will be presented with the "shut down project" message that is shown in Figure 1-18. To confirm the deletion of the project, you need to actually type the name of the project, and not just copy and paste the name.

Once you type the project name and click Shut Down, GCP will keep all the resources inside the project for thirty days, after which point all resources will be deleted.

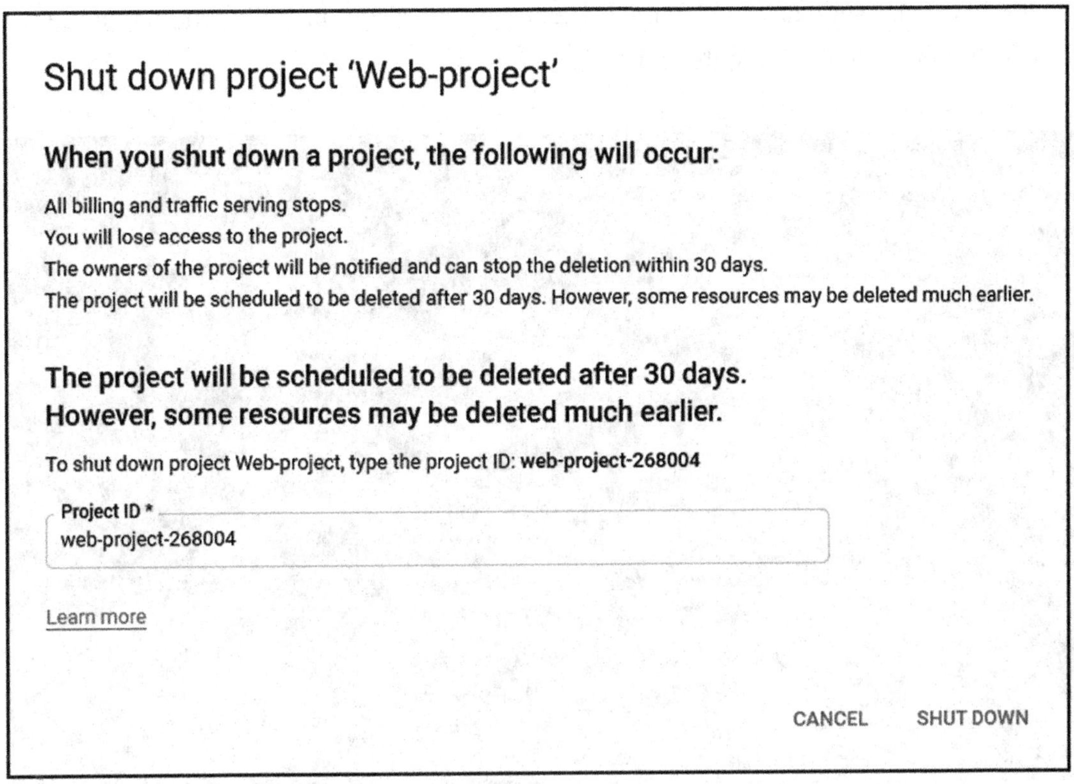

Shut down project 'Web-project'

**When you shut down a project, the following will occur:**

All billing and traffic serving stops.

You will lose access to the project.

The owners of the project will be notified and can stop the deletion within 30 days.

The project will be scheduled to be deleted after 30 days. However, some resources may be deleted much earlier.

**The project will be scheduled to be deleted after 30 days. However, some resources may be deleted much earlier.**

To shut down project Web-project, type the project ID: **web-project-268004**

Project ID *
web-project-268004

Learn more

CANCEL    SHUT DOWN

*Figure 1-18.  Shut down project*

After removing the project, you will see the "pending deletion" message that is shown in Figure 1-19.

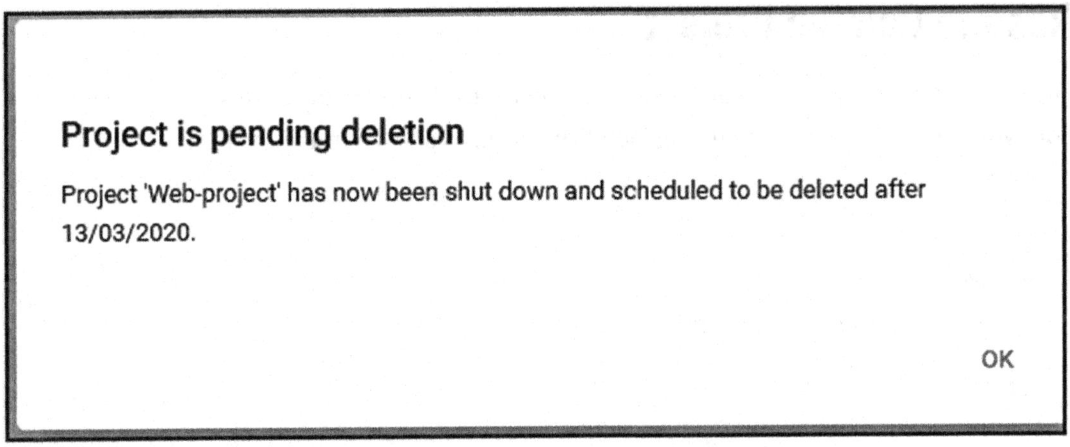

**Project is pending deletion**

Project 'Web-project' has now been shut down and scheduled to be deleted after 13/03/2020.

OK

*Figure 1-19.  "Pending deletion" message*

GCP will also send an email to the owner of the subscription, telling them that the project has been deleted (Figure 1-20).

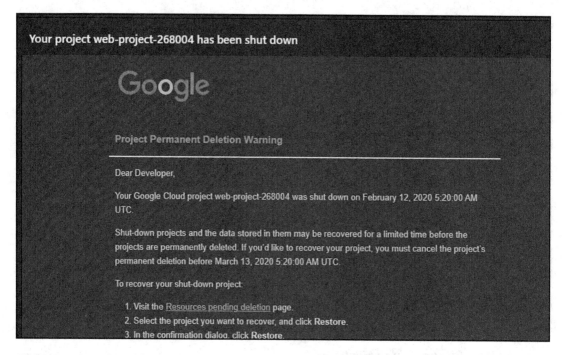

**Figure 1-20.** *Email message regarding project deletion*

What if you change your mind and want to restore the project and all resources in it?

## Restore Deleted Project

GCP has made this process very simple. If you look on the "Manage Resources" page, you will see the "Resource Pending Deletion" link, as shown in Figure 1-21.

| | Name | ID | Status | Charges |
|---|---|---|---|---|
| ☐ | Name | ID | Status | Charges |
| ☐ | ▼ 🏢 No organisation | 0 | | |
| ☐ | 🔹 My First Project | peak-nimbus-267903 | | |

1 RESOURCE PENDING DELETION

**Figure 1-21.** *Projects pending deletion*

If you click on the link, you will see all projects pending deletion; in my case, I will see Web-project, as shown in Figure 1-22. To restore my project, I will simply select the project and click Restore.

---

←     **Resources pending deletion**      RESTORE

---

| ☑ | **Name** | ID |
|---|---|---|
| ☑ | •• Web-project | projects/web-project-268004 |

*Figure 1-22.* *Restore project*

# Understanding Cloud Shell

Google Cloud Shell is a web-based interactive shell environment running inside GCP cloud. With it, we can manage our cloud environment via the gcloud command-line utility.

Cloud Shell runs inside a Linux Debian g1-small compute engine VM that is provisioned on a per-usage basis. Once the session is terminated, the instance is deleted; however, the $HOME directory is kept in persistent storage, so you can access it again when you next start Cloud Shell. The $HOME directory has a limit of 5GB.

Cloud Shell is loaded with command-line tools like Docker, Kubernetes, and MySQL. You can also develop your own applications inside Cloud Shell with programming tools that are pre-installed, like Python, Go, Node.js, NET.CORE, and Ruby. Because Git is also installed in Cloud Shell, you can work on your code and commit it back to your repo.

An essential part of Cloud Shell is that it is entirely free, and there is no additional cost for using it.

## Using Cloud Shell

Now it's time to see Could Shell in action. I will show you how to create a virtual machine directly from Cloud Shell.

To start Cloud Shell, click on the Cloud Shell logo located in the GCP Management console at the top-right corner, as shown in Figure 1-23.

***Figure 1-23.*** *Start Cloud Shell*

When you use Cloud Shell for the first time, you will see the "Activate Cloud Shell" message that is shown in Figure 1-24. To active Cloud Shell, click on the Continue button.

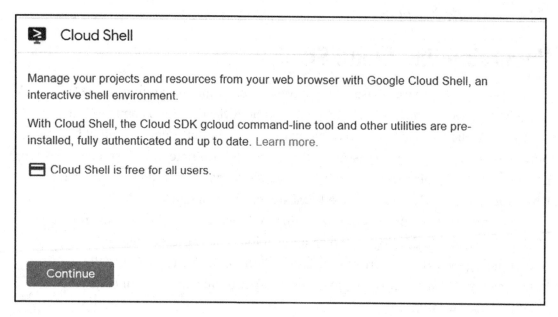

***Figure 1-24.*** *Activate Cloud Shell*

When activating Cloud Shell for the first time, it will take around two minutes for GCP to provision the instance and persistence storage for the $HOME directory.

# Deploy a VM Instance Using Cloud Shell

To deploy a VM instance to GCP using Cloud Shell, open Cloud Shell using the following URL: https://ssh.cloud.google.com. In Figure 1-25, you can see the Cloud Shell console when accessing it from the direct URL.

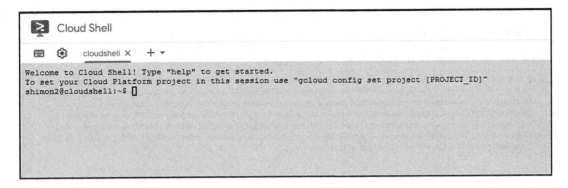

***Figure 1-25.***  *Cloud Shell console*

To create a VM instance using Cloud Shell, use the pre-configured command GCP prepared in the Create Instance wizard, as shown in Figure 1-15. You can see the gcloud command in Figure 1-26.

You can deploy the instance using gcloud with the following two options:

- Click on the "Run in Cloud Shell" link, which will open Cloud Shell and run the command.

- Copy the command and paste it into Cloud Shell.

If you use the copy option, I recommend you untick the "Line wrapping" checkbox first and copy the code.

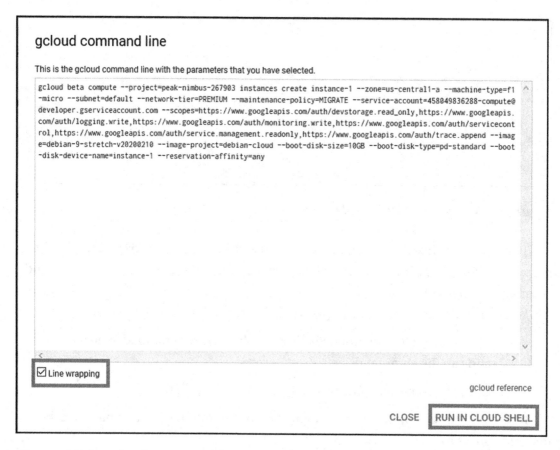

*Figure 1-26.* *gcloud command line*

# Work with Projects in Cloud Shell

When you open Cloud Shell, you will see that it has asked you to set your cloud platform project. To manage resources in Cloud Shell, you need to set the session and configure it to use the project you are working in. Do so using the following command—in my case, the project name is web-project-269903:

```
$ gcloud config set project web-project-269903
```

You can list all your projects' names by running the following command in Cloud Shell:

```
$ gcloud projects list
```

You can also use the GCP console and click on the project list menu, as shown in Figure 1-27.

When referencing a project, we need to use the project ID and not the project name, which is not unique. Figure 1-27 highlights the ID column with the project IDs.

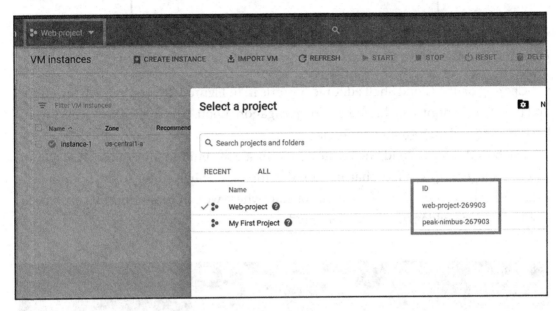

**Figure 1-27.**  *Select a project*

To view all the VM instances in a specific project, run the following command:

```
$ gcloud compute instances list --project=peak-nimbus-267903
```

# Cloud Shell Editor

Cloud Shell also comes with a code/text editor where you can write programs and run them directly from Cloud Shell. This editor also allows you to save your scripts' programs using Cloud Shell's 5GB of allocated storage and run them later. I like to keep scripts of repeated tasks and use those instead of utilizing the management portal.

## Access Cloud Shell Editor

To access the Cloud Shell editor, click on the pencil icon located next to the Cloud Shell editor, as shown in Figure 1-28.

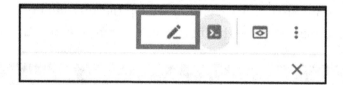

***Figure 1-28.*** *Cloud Shell editor*

Clicking on the Cloud Shell editor icon starts it. In Figure 1-29, you can see the editor and the critical options, including the top navigation menu, which gives you access to basic editing and management options.

On the left side of Cloud Shell editor, you can see the built-in file explorer that allows you to manage scripts or files that are stored in the Cloud Shell editor. At the bottom of the screen, you can see the Cloud Shell console, where we can run scripts that are stored inside the $HOME folder, or gcloud commands.

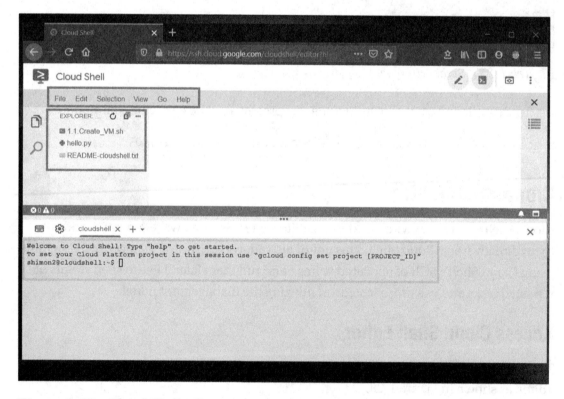

***Figure 1-29.*** *Cloud Shell editor*

## Create a Bash Script in Cloud Shell

In the following demo, I will create a Bash script inside Cloud Shell using the editor; the script contains a gcloud command that creates a VM instance. To create a Bash script, I will click on the File menu and select "New File," as shown in Figure 1-30.

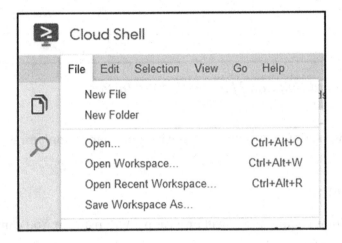

***Figure 1-30.*** *Create a new file*

In the New File menu, I will name my file with the correct file extension, as shown in Figure 1-31.

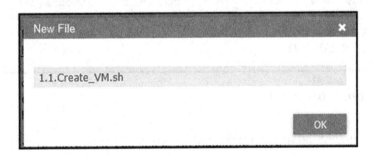

***Figure 1-31.*** *New file*

In the new file, I will paste the gcloud command for creating a new VM instance, as shown in Figure 1-32. Please note that I am using the same command I used in the "Deploy a VM Instance Using Cloud Shell" section.

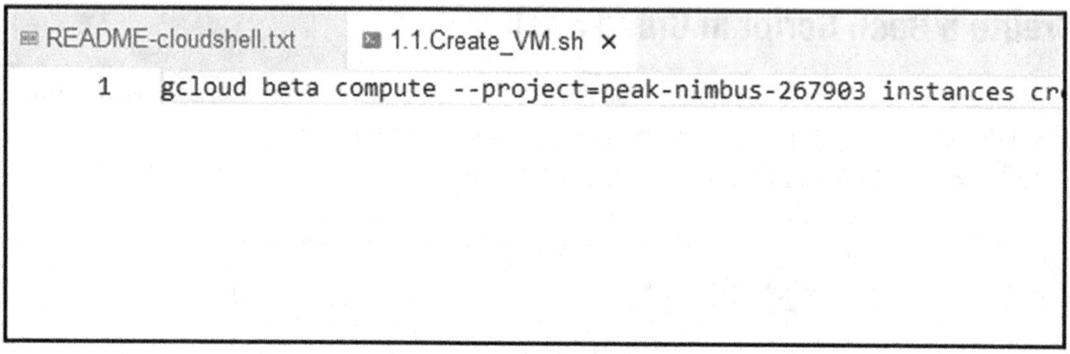

```
README-cloudshell.txt        1.1.Create_VM.sh  ×

    1    gcloud beta compute --project=peak-nimbus-267903 instances cr
```

*Figure 1-32.* *gcloud command for creating VM instance*

To run the Bash script, I will use the following command (don't forget the . before the script name):

. 1.1.Create_VM.sh

Once the script is running, GCP will provision a VM instance. You can see the output of the command in Figure 1-33.

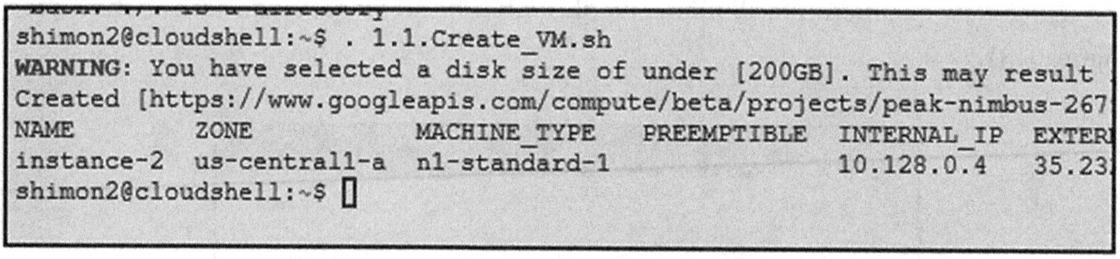

```
shimon2@cloudshell:~$ . 1.1.Create_VM.sh
WARNING: You have selected a disk size of under [200GB]. This may result
Created [https://www.googleapis.com/compute/beta/projects/peak-nimbus-267
NAME          ZONE            MACHINE_TYPE    PREEMPTIBLE   INTERNAL_IP    EXTER
instance-2  us-central1-a  n1-standard-1                 10.128.0.4     35.23
shimon2@cloudshell:~$ []
```

*Figure 1-33.* *Run Bash script*

You can also download files from the editor directly to your machine by right-clicking on a file and clicking Download, as shown in Figure 1-34.

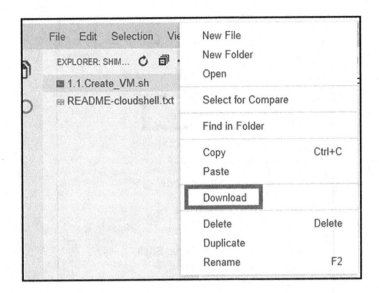

*Figure 1-34.*  *Download file*

You can also upload files to Cloud Shell using the Upload File option found in the top-right corner by clicking on the ... option and selecting Upload File, as shown in Figure 1-35.

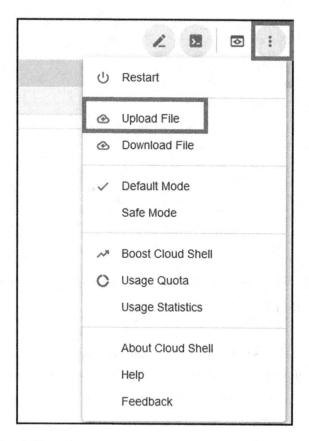

***Figure 1-35.***   *Upload file*

In the next chapters, we will explore Cloud Shell in more depth and use it to deploy workloads to GCP.

# Google Cloud SDK

It is important to note that the driving force behind gcloud and Cloud Shell is the Google Cloud SDK, which gives us the power to create GCP resources using commands and other programming languages. By default, Google Cloud SDK is installed in Cloud Shell and runs the latest version. Google also gives you the option to install the SDK on your local machine. You can download and install the SDK from the following URL:

https://cloud.google.com/sdk/docs/quickstarts

# Secure and Manage Your GCP Account

In this section, we will explore some of GCP's security best practices that are essential for keeping your tenant safe and free from malicious access.

## Multi-Factor Authentication

Enabling MFA on all your GCP user accounts can reduce the risk of someone's breaking into your GCP tenant by 80 percent. This simple best practice goes a long way in protecting your tenant, and I strongly recommend you enable it on your account and other accounts used in GCP.

You can enable MFA on your GCP account by logging in to the GCP console and going to the following URL:

```
https://myaccount.google.com/security
```

From the URL, scroll down and click on "2 step verification," and then follow the prompts.

## Create an Account with Specific Roles

GCP Identity and Access Management (IAM) has built-in roles for every role and service your administrators need. The good thing about IAM roles is that they are predefined by GCP and have all the permissions needed for every role you can think about.

To manage users and roles, you use the IAM console. However, you can also use Cloud Shell. You can access the IAM console directly using the following link:

```
https://console.cloud.google.com/iam-admin
```

When you open the IAM page, you can set permissions per project by selecting the project from the drop-down option next to the project name, as shown in Figure 1-36. To create a new user, click the Add button, shown in Figure 1-36.

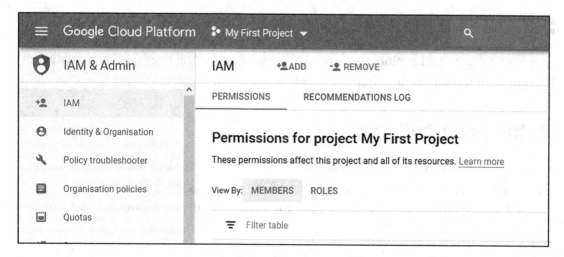

***Figure 1-36.*** *Create an account*

On the Add Member page, you need to type the email address of the new user, and, most important, you must select a role. At the time of writing, there are more than one hundred roles available to choose from; therefore, it's very important you don't give users permissions they don't need and follow the rule of assigning permissions based on least privilege.

In my case, I will select Cloud SQL, and GCP will give me four options to granulate the permissions I would like to provide my user. Figure 1-37 shows the Cloud SQL role and all the granular permissions available.

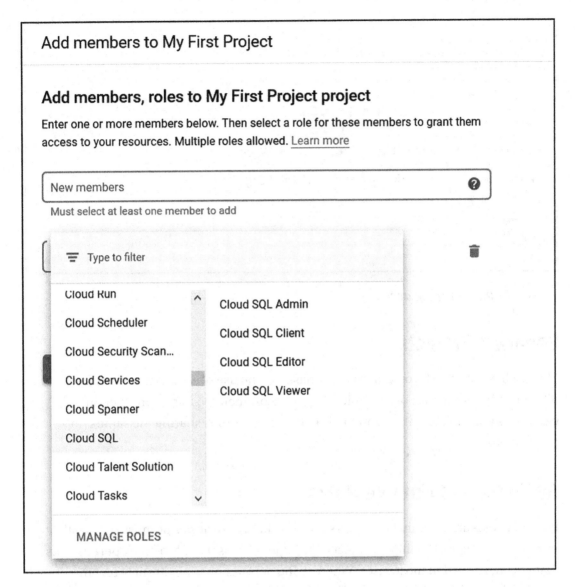

*Figure 1-37.* *IAM roles*

# Expiring Access

If you have contractors or short-term staff working on your GCP environment, it is recommended you use the "Expiring access" option, which will disable the account and its access to GCP after a specific date. This option is recommended, as many times access is given and never expires. You can set this by editing the user details from the IAM console and choosing the "Expiring access" condition, as in Figure 1-38.

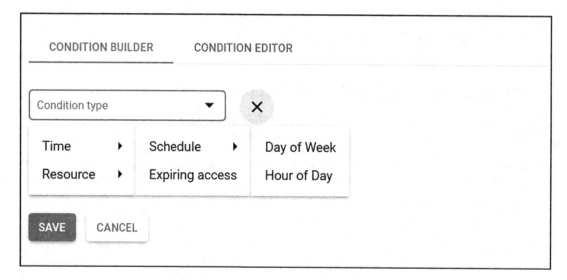

***Figure 1-38.***  *Expiring access*

# Separate Projects

The last best practice I would like to emphasize is the use of separate projects for different environments. For example, it is not recommended to run production workloads and development workloads in the same profile, sharing the same permissions.

# Avoid Using Primitive Roles

Primitive roles are roles that give users owner, editor, and viewer permissions to all resources in single or multiple projects. This option gives users too many permissions that are not needed in most cases. When giving permissions, it is strongly recommended you use the predefined IAM roles unless you must use primitive roles. If you decide to use primitive roles, make sure you enable expiring access.

# GCP Container Services Overview

I would now like to outline the core container services we will use and cover in this book. As of writing, GCP has several container services, and I have chosen the most important ones that will suit any organization.

# Google Kubernetes Service (GKE)

The Google Kubernetes Service (GKE) is GCP's flagship service for running containers and containerized applications in the cloud. GKE is based on Kubernetes, the number one container orchestration platform for running containers, batch jobs, and microservices.

Kubernetes is an open source project that was developed by Google and open sourced in 2015. GKE allows us to run Linux and Windows container workloads in an enterprise-grade world-class infrastructure.

We will discuss GKE in great detail in Chapter 4.

# Google Container Registry

Google Container Registry is a private Docker images registry that allows us to store, push, and pull Docker images to any GCP container service and external services. GCP allows us to control access to the registry using built-in security tools and features.

Google Container Registry is fully integrated with GKE and other CI\DC pipelines tools. You can easily integrate the Google Container Registry with CI\CD tools like Jenkins, Circleci, and Cloud Build, which is part of GCP.

In Chapter 2 will deep dive into Google Container Registry and learn how to use it.

# Google Cloud Run

Google Cloud Run is a stateless container runtime service that allows us to run our containerized applications in GCP. To deploy our containerized applications to Cloud Run, all we need to do is point Cloud Run to our Docker image and Cloud Run will pull the image and run it. Cloud Run can automatically scale the deployment if more resources are needed.

Cloud Run is simple and easy to use and was designed to run stateless applications that can easily be scaled as load increases. One of the most powerful features of Cloud Run is that it is serverless, which means it requires zero management effort.

In Chapter 3, we will explore Cloud Run in great detail.

# Google Compute Engine

Google Compute Engine is a GCP Compute Service offering, and we will use it to deploy a Docker container host and deploy containers. Using Google Compute Engine, we will deploy VM instances (Linux and Windows) and run containers. VM instances are great for development and testing environments, and they are also cost-effective compared to GKE and Cloud Run.

In Chapter 5, we will deploy Linux and Windows Docker container hosts and deploy containers.

# Google Cloud Platform Container Services

In Figure 1-39, you can see all four GCP container services that we will cover in great detail in this book. We will also learn about all the support services that make GCP secure and safe. Running containers in GCP without proper security, backup, and user access control is dangerous. Therefore, in this book, we will also learn and focus on the core supporting services in GCP.

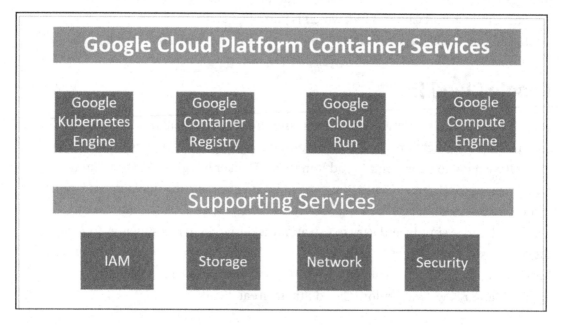

***Figure 1-39.*** *Google Container Services*

# Summary

In this chapter, we learned how to get started with GCP and Google Cloud Shell. We also learned how to secure our GCP tenant using MFA and to always use built-in security roles when creating new users. We learned how to deploy VM instances using Cloud Shell, without using the GCP management console. In the last section, we covered the core container services we will examine in this book. Next, we will take a look at the Google Container Registry service.

# CHAPTER 2

# Google Container Registry (GCR)

In this chapter, we will take a deep dive and explore the world of Google Container Registry (GCR), looking at how to take advantage of all its features. This chapter is packed with great hands-on demonstrations that will help you get going with GCR.

The topics covered in this chapter are as follows:

- Install Docker (macOS, Windows, Linux)

- Get an overview of container registries

- Set up GCR in our tenant

- Secure GCR

- Push Docker container images to GCR

- Pull Docker container images to GCR

- Examine security vulnerabilities with GCR vulnerabilities scanner

## Install Docker

Before we start working with Google Container Registry (GCR), let's take a moment and install Docker on all the major operating system platforms.

39

© Shimon Ifrah 2021
S. Ifrah, *Getting Started with Containers in Google Cloud Platform*,
https://doi.org/10.1007/978-1-4842-6470-6_2

# Install Docker on macOS

To install Docker on a macOS machine, open the following URL and download the installer:

```
https://www.docker.com/products/docker-desktop
```

After the download is complete, click on the installer, which will ask you to drag it to the Applications folder; go ahead and drag it as shown in Figure 2-1.

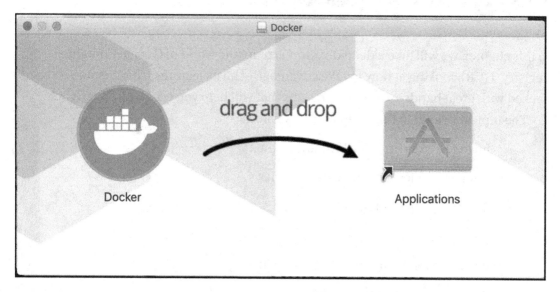

***Figure 2-1.***  *Drag and drop Docker to Applications folder*

After pulling the installer to the Applications folder, open the folder and double-click on the Docker file, as shown in Figure 2-2.

| | |
|---|---|
| 🔴 Docker | 11, |
| 🔵 ExpressVPN | 29, |
| 📹 FaceTime | 6/5 |
| 🌐 Firefox | 18, |

***Figure 2-2.***  *Select Docker icon*

After you double-click on the Docker icon, the installer will ask you to confirm whether you would like to open the Docker app, as shown in Figure 2-3. Click Open.

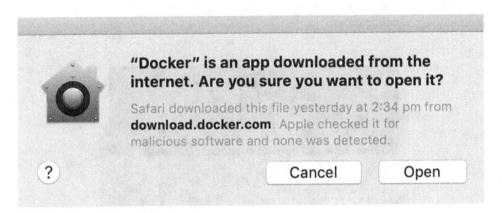

***Figure 2-3.*** *Confirm opening the file*

The final step in the installation process is giving Docker Desktop privileged access to install its networking components, as shown in Figure 2-4.

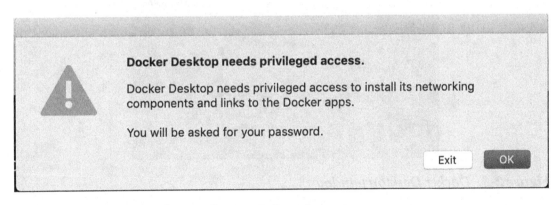

***Figure 2-4.*** *Grant Docker Desktop privileged access*

At this stage, the Docker Desktop window confirms that it is running and shows some "Get started" messages. Figure 2-5 shows the Docker Desktop window.

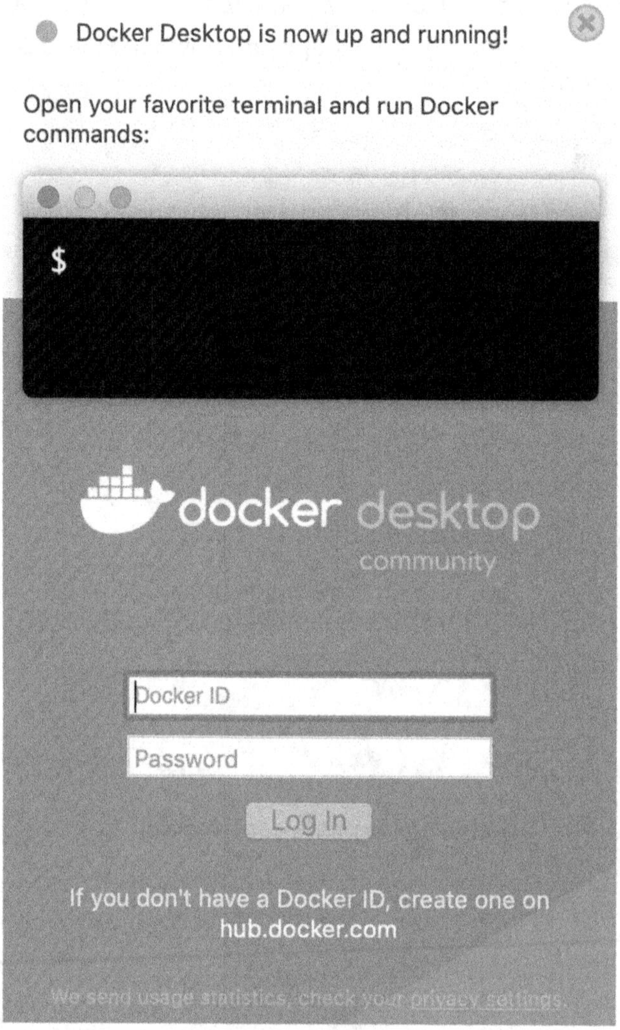

**Figure 2-5.** *Docker Desktop window*

If you would like to stop, start, or manage the Docker Desktop application, simply click on the Docker icon at the top of the navigation screen and select the appropriate option, as shown in Figure 2-6.

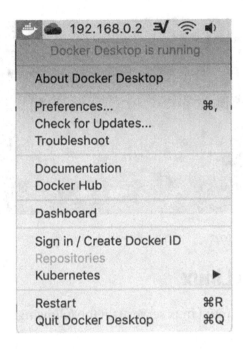

***Figure 2-6.*** *Properties menu*

Once you finish the installation, you can start using Docker from the macOS Terminal client.

# Install Docker Desktop on Windows 10

To install Docker Desktop on a Windows 10 machine, we need to download the Windows installer from the following URL:

`https://www.docker.com/products/docker-desktop`

Once the installer has been downloaded, start it and follow the prompts. When the installation process is complete, you will see the Docker icon in the Windows Taskbar, as shown in Figure 2-7. To manage it, right-click on the icon and select the appropriate option.

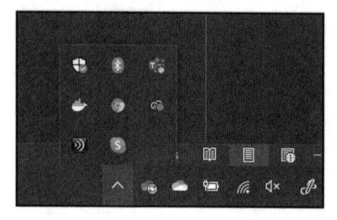

***Figure 2-7.*** *Docker Desktop*

# Install Docker on Linux

To install Docker on an Ubuntu Linux server, run the following commands. First, update the applications repository:

```
$ sudo apt-get update
```

Install the Docker engine:

```
$ sudo apt-get install docker
```

Start the service:

```
$ sudo service docker start
```

And to test if the installation was successful, run the `hello-world` container:

```
$ sudo docker run hello-world
```

# Check That Docker Is Working

To check that your Docker Desktop is working on all platforms, I recommend you run the following command, which will download then run the `hello-world` test container:

```
$ docker run hello-world
```

To check which version of Docker is installed on your machine, run the following command:

```
$ docker --version
```

# Introduction to Container Registries

A container registry is a Docker image storage/repository service hosted in the cloud or inside your actual Docker host. The registry allows you to store Docker images based on versions, names, or configuration. Using the Docker CLI command-line utility, you can either push (upload) or pull (download) images to your deployments.

Container registries are split into two kinds:

- **Public registry:** These registries are free and don't require authentication to download images; an excellent example is Docker Hub.

- **Private registry:** These are paid registries that require authentication for both push and pull requests; Google Container Registry is a great example.

## Docker Hub

The most popular public container registry service in the world is Docker Hub. You can pull images from it from any machine that is connected to the internet by using the `docker pull` command, as shown here:

```
$ docker pull ubuntu
```

## Private Registry

A private registry is a paid container repository service hosted in the cloud and requires authentication before you can push or pull images. Most private registries offer extra security features like scanning images for vulnerabilities, access control to the registry based on source IP address, and many more features.

## Create a Local Docker Registry

In this demonstration, I will show you how to create a local container registry on a Docker container host (Windows, Linux, or Mac). You first need to download a Docker image that will host the registry. Luckily, Docker has an official image for a private registry. To download the image, you need to run the following command:

```
$ docker run -d -p 5000:5000 --name myregistry myregistry:1
```

Next, download a Docker image from Docker Hub using the following command:

```
$ docker pull alpine
```

After downloading the image, tag it using the following command:

```
$ docker image tag alpine localhost:5000/myalpine
```

To check that the image was tagged successfully, run the following command:

```
$ docker images
```

To push the image to the private registry, run the following command:

```
$ docker push localhost:5000/myfalpine
```

If you run the following command, you will see the private registry image is running as a container, and that the name of the registry is myregistry.

```
$ docker ps
```

If we stop the container that runs the registry and try to push or pull, we will get an error. To test that, stop the registry container using the following command:

```
$ docker stop registry
```

Now, try to pull the image from the registry using the following command:

```
$ docker pull localhost:5000/myalpine
```

At this stage, you will get an error saying the connection refused. Restart the registry and try it again using the following command:

```
$ docker start registry
```

Try the pull operation again; this time the pull request should work.

The preceding demo shows how container registries work at a macro level on a local machine. Google Container Registry works the same way, except there is a security layer that protects the registry and prevents unauthorized access.

# Introduction to Google Container Registry (GCR)

GCR is a paid private registry that offers advanced security capabilities that allow you to secure your registry for malicious access. GCR pricing is based on the following three factors:

- **Storage:** Images stored on GCR are charged $0.26 per GB per month.

- **Same continent network access:** Pull requests in the same continent are charged at $0.01 per GB.

- **Cross-continent network access:** Pull requests between continents are charged at $0.12 to $0.19 per GB depending on the continent.

---

**Note**    Google charges only apply to egress traffic, which means traffic that is going out of GCR, like pull requests; ingress traffic (traffic entering or uploaded to GCR) is free.

---

On top of the preceding charges, you have the option to add the vulnerability scanning option, which scans all stored images for malicious code. Vulnerability scanning will cost you $0.26 per image; the charge will happen once, and then the image is pushed to the registry. Any modification and subsequent upload of an image will lead to a new charge, since the image has changed.

By default, vulnerability scanning doesn't scan existing images that are stored in the registry and will only scan newly uploaded images. To scan existing images, you will need to push again to the repository.

# Enable GCP Container Registry

To enable GCR, please use the GCP console. From the navigation menu, click on the Container Registry shortcut, as shown in Figure 2-8.

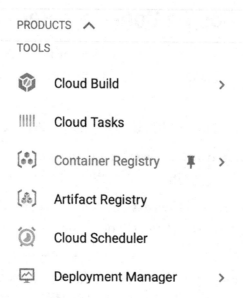

**Figure 2-8.**  *Container Registry*

From the GCR home page, click on Enable Container Registry API to enable the service, as shown in Figure 2-9.

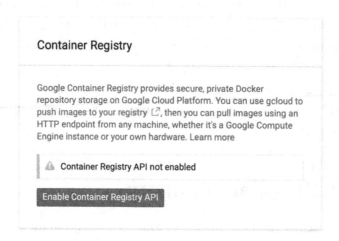

**Figure 2-9.**  *Enable Container Registry API*

Once the registry is enabled, it will take a few seconds for the service to be enabled.

To enable vulnerability scanning in GCR, click on Settings in the Container Registry navigation menu, as shown in Figure 2-10. On the Vulnerability Scanning page, click on the Enable Vulnerability Scanning button, as shown in Figure 2-10.

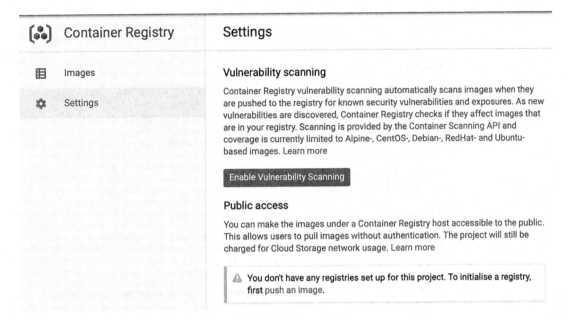

**Figure 2-10.** *Enable vulnerability scanning*

---

**Note**    Vulnerability scanning only works with the following images: Alpine, CentOS, Debian, RedHat, and Ubuntu.

---

Once vulnerability scanning is enabled, it will take five minutes for the service to start working. Figure 2-11 shows the vulnerability scanning service status I have enabled.

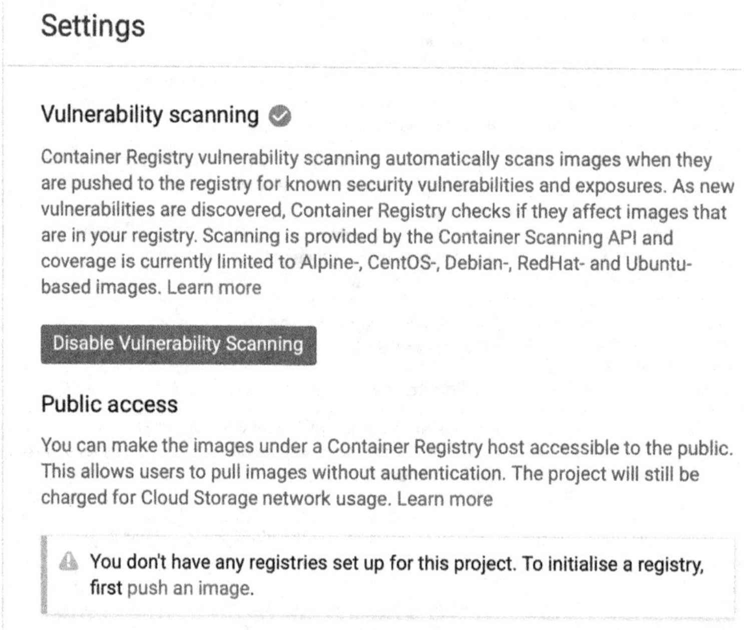

Settings

Vulnerability scanning ✓

Container Registry vulnerability scanning automatically scans images when they are pushed to the registry for known security vulnerabilities and exposures. As new vulnerabilities are discovered, Container Registry checks if they affect images that are in your registry. Scanning is provided by the Container Scanning API and coverage is currently limited to Alpine-, CentOS-, Debian-, RedHat- and Ubuntu-based images. Learn more

Disable Vulnerability Scanning

Public access

You can make the images under a Container Registry host accessible to the public. This allows users to pull images without authentication. The project will still be charged for Cloud Storage network usage. Learn more

⚠ You don't have any registries set up for this project. To initialise a registry, first push an image.

***Figure 2-11.*** *Vulnerability scanning enabled*

# Push Docker Images to Google Container Registry (GCR)

Now that we have GCR enabled and running, we will learn how to push a Docker image to the registry.

## Install Cloud SDK

To push or pull images to GCR, you will need to install the Google Cloud SDK, which is a set of command-line tools that help you connect, build, and manage resources on GCP.

**Note**    Cloud SDK on Linux and macOS requires Python 2.7.9 or higher.

# Install Cloud SDK on Linux CentOS/Red Hat

To install Cloud SDK on a Linux CentOS Docker host, run the following command, which will add the GCP repository to the repository list:

```
$ tee -a /etc/yum.repos.d/google-cloud-sdk.repo << EOM
[google-cloud-sdk]
name=Google Cloud SDK
baseurl=https://packages.cloud.google.com/yum/repos/cloud-sdk-el7-x86_64
enabled=1
gpgcheck=1
repo_gpgcheck=1
gpgkey=https://packages.cloud.google.com/yum/doc/yum-key.gpg
       https://packages.cloud.google.com/yum/doc/rpm-package-key.gpg
EOM
```

---

**Note**   Make sure you leave the line under gpgkey indented.

---

To install the package, run the following command:

```
$ yum install google-cloud-sdk
```

# Install Cloud SDK on Linux Ubuntu/Debian

To install Cloud SDK on an Ubuntu server, run the following command, which will register the GCP repository:

```
$ echo "deb [signed-by=/usr/share/keyrings/cloud.google.gpg] https://
packages.cloud.google.com/apt cloud-sdk main" | tee -a /etc/apt/sources.
list.d/google-cloud-sdk.list
```

Next, download the following packages:

```
$ apt-get install apt-transport-https ca-certificates gnupg
```

To import the GCP public security key, run the following command:

```
$ curl https://packages.cloud.google.com/apt/doc/apt-key.gpg |
  apt-key --keyring /usr/share/keyrings/cloud.google.gpg add -
```

And finally, to install the Cloud SDK package, run the following command:

```
$ apt-get update && apt-get install google-cloud-sdk
```

## Install Cloud SDK on Windows

To install Cloud SDK on a Windows machine, download the SDK installer from the following URL:

```
https://dl.google.com/dl/cloudsdk/channels/rapid/GoogleCloudSDKInstaller.exe
```

When the download is complete, start the installation by double-clicking on the installer and following the installation prompts, as shown in Figure 2-12.

***Figure 2-12.***  *Google Cloud SDK Setup*

You can also install the Cloud SDK from the Windows command line using the following one-liner command:

```
(New-Object Net.WebClient).DownloadFile("https://dl.google.com/dl/
cloudsdk/channels/rapid/GoogleCloudSDKInstaller.exe", "$env:Temp\
GoogleCloudSDKInstaller.exe")& $env:Temp\GoogleCloudSDKInstaller.exe
```

## Install Cloud SDK on macOS

To install Cloud SDK on a macOS machine, download the following package file:

https://dl.google.com/dl/cloudsdk/channels/rapid/downloads/google-cloud-sdk-290.0.0-darwin-x86_64.tar.gz

After the download is complete, extract the file to any directory on your Mac. Open a Terminal session and navigate to the SDK's location and run the following command:

```
$ ./google-cloud-sdk/bin/gcloud init
```

# Authenticate to GCP

After you complete your Cloud SDK setup, you will need to authenticate to GCR before you can push images to the service. When it comes to private registries, you will notice that the authentication part is much more complex than pushing or pulling images. To authenticate to GCR, run the following command from your command-line tool where you have the Docker Cloud SDK installed:

```
$ gcloud auth configure-docker
```

After typing the following command, you will need to copy the URL that appears on the screen and paste it into a browser, as shown in Figure 2-13:

```
$ gcloud auth login
```

The URL will ask you to authenticate to GCP.

*Figure 2-13.  Authentication URL*

After authenticating to the service, you will need to allow Google Cloud SDK access to view and manage Cloud Services, Compute Engine, and App Engine. Figure 2-14 shows the Allow Request page.

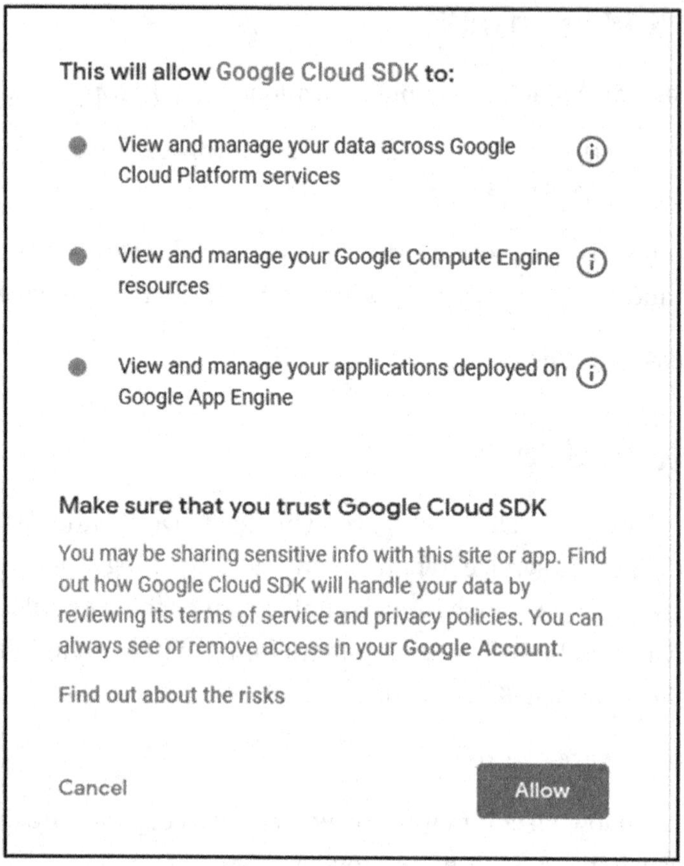

**Figure 2-14.** *Allow Request page*

After allowing the request, Google will generate an authentication code, which will act as a password, as shown in Figure 2-15.

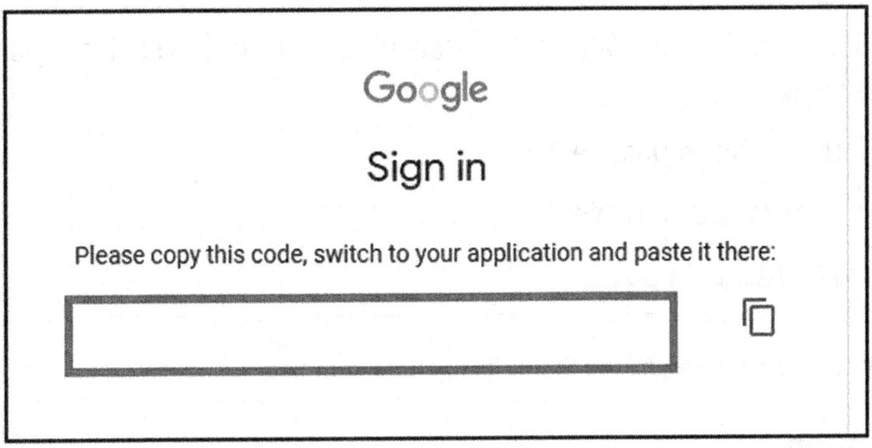

*Figure 2-15.* *Authentication code*

Go ahead and paste the authentication code into your Terminal, as shown in Figure 2-16.

## Set Project

After authenticating to GCP you will need to configure gcloud to use the project your GCR is located using the following command:

```
$ gcloud config set project web-project-269903
```

**Note**    To list all your GCP projects, run gcloud projects list.

## Tag Image

Now, it is time to tag the image you want to push to GCR using the following format:

```
Image /GCR LOCATION/PROJECTID/IMAGE
```

In my case, the code looks like the following:

```
docker tag centos gcr.io/web-project-269903/centos
```

> **Note**    To set the Registry data center location, you will need to set the registry name as follows:
>
> gcr.io — United States Data Center
>
> eu.gcr.io — Europe Data Center
>
> asia.gcr.io — Asia Data Center

In my case, I used the United States as my data center.

## Push Image

Finally, you can push the image to GCR; in my case I will use the following line:

```
docker push gcr.io/web-project-269903/centos
```

After the push is completed, the image will appear under GCR, as shown in Figure 2-16.

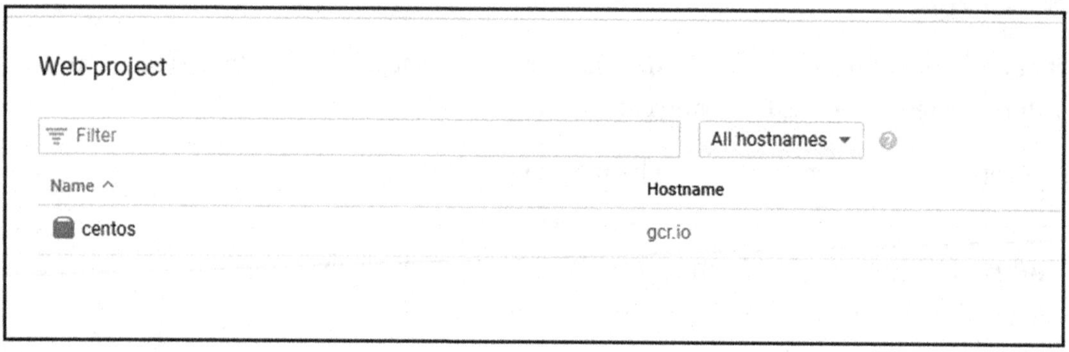

*Figure 2-16.*  *GCR image*

To view the image using the `gcloud` command line, use the following command:

```
$ gcloud container images list
```

# Pull Images from GCR Container Registry

In this section, we will learn how to pull images from GCR to our Docker host or client using Cloud SDK.

# Delete Existing Image

To fully test it and show you how it works, I will first delete the copy of the image I have on my machine, using the following command:

```
docker rmi gcr.io/web-project-269903/centos
```

---

**Note**    To delete all images on your host, run `docker image rm -f $(docker image ls)`.

---

# Pull Image

To pull the image that I pushed to GCR in the previous section, I will use the following command:

```
docker pull gcr.io/web-project-269903/centos
```

---

**Note**    If you have not authenticated to GCR, you will need to authenticate before pulling an image.

---

# Show Pull Command

If you log in to the GCR portal, you can retrieve the customized pull commands. From the portal, click on Images and then click on the extended image menu, as shown in Figure 2-17. From the extended menu, click on Show Pull Command.

***Figure 2-17.*** *Show Pull Command option*

The Pull Command menu will outline the pull commands for each image; all you need to do is copy the image and paste it into your command-line utility. Figure 2-18 shows the Pull Command screen with the pull commands for the CentOS image I pushed to GCR.

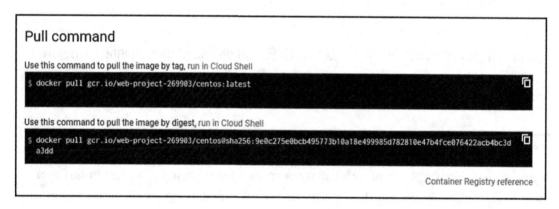

***Figure 2-18.*** *Pull command*

# Manage and Secure Images on GCR

In this section, you will learn how to secure Docker container images in GCR using Vulnerability Scanner.

# About GCR Vulnerability Scanner

GCR Vulnerability Scanner is a paid security service that allows you to discover vulnerabilities in Docker images located in GCR. It scans images when they are uploaded to GCR.

To find vulnerabilities, GCR uses publicly known Common Vulnerabilities and Exposures (CVE)—cybersecurity vulnerabilities that are known and publicly available on websites like http://cve.mitre.org/index.html.

As outlined in the previous section, every image that is scanned by GCR is charged at $ 0.26 per image.

# Review Vulnerabilities

If vulnerabilities are found in a scanned image, they will appear under the Vulnerabilities on the GCR portal header under images. In Figure 2-19, you can see that my CentOS image has three vulnerabilities and three fixes to patch them.

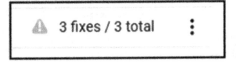

*Figure 2-19.*  *Vulnerabilities*

The reason images have vulnerabilities is because, many times, the official image is two months old, and in the meantime installed packages have had security updates that are not yet included in the image. This is the case with my CentOS image.

To review vulnerabilities, click on the "Vulnerabilities" tab and review each one. Figure 2-20 shows the three vulnerabilities that exist in the CentOS Docker image and the details of each.

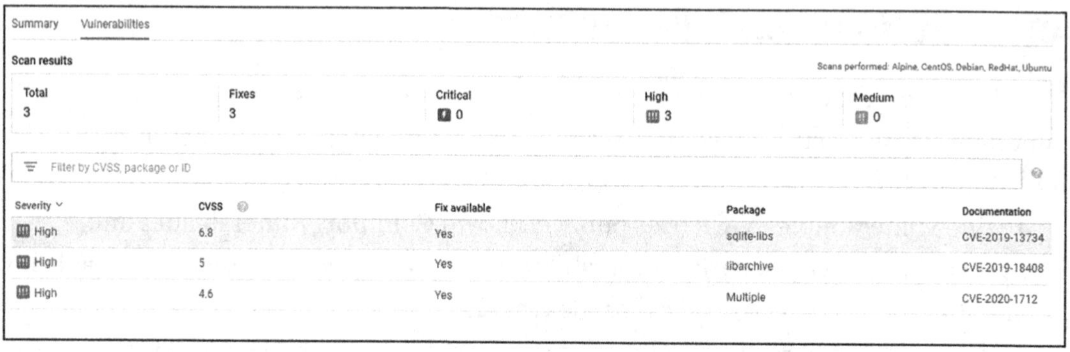

**Figure 2-20.** *Vulnerabilities*

Clicking on each vulnerability will show its details and how to fix it. As outlined in Figure 2-21, the package sqlite-lbs has a vulnerability, and it has a fix.

The scanner also outlines the version that contains the vulnerability fix.

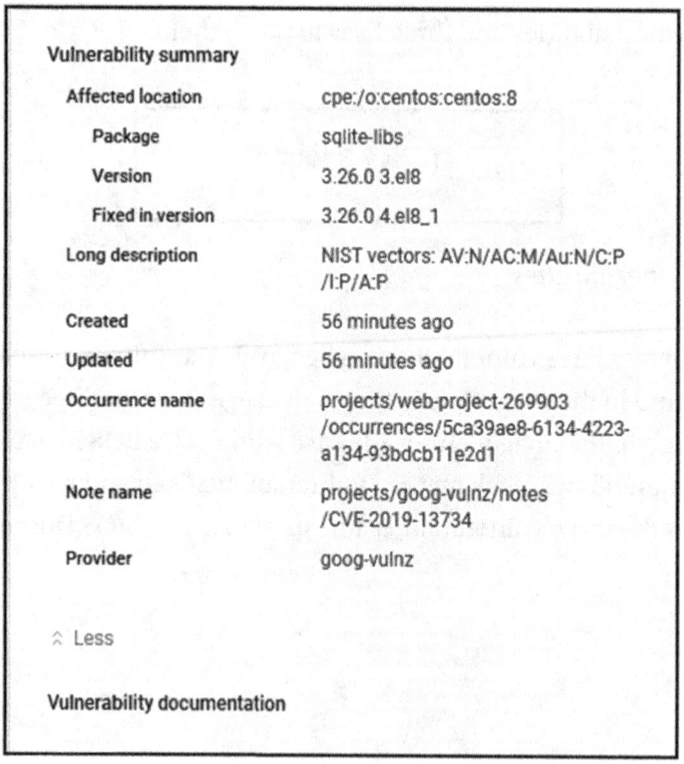

**Figure 2-21.** *Vulnerability summary*

# Fix Vulnerabilities on a Docker Image

It's great to identify an image's security vulnerabilities; however, knowing about it is only 50 percent of the solution. To fix the vulnerabilities, we need to perform the following steps:

1.  Pull the image from GCR.

2.  Patch/install vulnerabilities fix outlined in the scanner.

3.  Commit the changes to the image.

4.  Push the image back to GCR.

# Step 1: Pull the Image from GCR

Pull image using the following command:

```
$ docker pull gcr.io/web-project-269903/centos
```

# Step 2: Install Updates

To install updates on my image, I first deploy a container with the image using the following code:

```
$ docker run -it gcr.io/web-project-269903/centos
```

From the container, I install the vulnerability fixes that are needed. With the following command, I install the latest Sqlite-libs:

```
$ yum update sqlite-libs
```

# Step 3: Commit Image

Using the docker commit command, I save the image:

```
$ docker commit 332da54552f1  gcr.io/web-project-269903/centos
```

As a result of the patching, the size of the image grows to 150 MB from 83 MB before the patching.

## Step 4: Push the Image to GCR

Finally, I push the new image to GCR using the following command:

```
$ docker push  gcr.io/web-project-269903/centos
```

When the push operation is complete, I can see the updated image in GCR, as shown in Figure 2-22. You can also see in Figure 2-22 that the new image has no vulnerabilities.

| Created | Uploaded ⌄ | Vulnerabilities | |
|---------|-----------|-----------------|---|
| 1 minute ago | Just now | None found | ⋮ |
| 18 Jan 2020 | 7 minutes ago | ⚠ 3 fixes / 3 total | ⋮ |

***Figure 2-22.***  *Docker image*

# Container Registry Best Practices

Before we move to the next chapter, I would like to outline a few best practices that will help you manage your images and applications.

## Separate Environments

It is highly recommended to have separate registries for production and development workloads. Mixing development and production can cause confusion and configuration errors. When the registries are separate, there is less clutter inside the registries and fewer security vulnerabilities.

## Keep Your Registry Close to Your Applications

Make sure you deploy your registry in the same regions as your applications. Pulling images across continents can cause the following issues:

- Network latency

- Performance issues

- Extra cost

When the registry is in the same region, the pull or push requests are much faster, and performance is better.

## Security

I recommend you enable Vulnerability Scanner on your production registry if possible; the extra cost is worth it and will keep your applications secure and safe from malicious attacks.

## GCR Permissions

When it comes to permissions, GCR offers very granular options to separate the pull and push permissions, which is a bonus. In many organizations, not all developers and engineers need pull and push permissions on the registry. For example, you might want to give your tester only pull permission.

GCR breaks down the pull and push permissions into two groups:

1.  **Push:** Full access

2.  **Pull:** Read-only access

You control permissions for the registry using the storage account that the registry is attached to. If you remember from the "Introduction to Container Registries" section, registries are storage services.

## View Storage Account

To view the storage account that your registry is attached to, open the storage portal from the GCR console. From the GCR navigation menu, click on the storage icon under the Storage menu, as shown in Figure 2-23.

***Figure 2-23.*** *Storage*

The storage portal will show all the storage buckets that registries are attached to, as shown in Figure 2-24. The bucket name will include the project ID name; in my case, the bucket is called `artifacts.web-project-269903.appspot.com`. The name corresponds to the project ID.

| Storage | Storage browser | CREATE BUCKET | DELETE | REFRESH |
|---|---|---|---|---|
| Browser | Filter buckets | | | |
| Transfer | Bucket sorting and filtering are available in the Storage browser. Now you can filter your buckets by any | | | |
| Transfer for on-premises | Name ↑ | | Location type | Location |
| Transfer Appliance | artifacts.web-project-269903.appspot.co... | | Multi-region | us (multiple re... |
| Settings | | | | |

***Figure 2-24.*** *Storage buckets*

If you click on the storage bucket, you will see the bucket page and gain access to the Permissions tab. To add, remove, or edit permissions, click on the bucket name to access the Bucket Details page. From this page, click on the Permissions tab and click on the following:

**Add members:** Add users and assign permissions

**Remove:** Remove access to the registry

Figure 2-25 shows the storage bucket details in the Permissions tab.

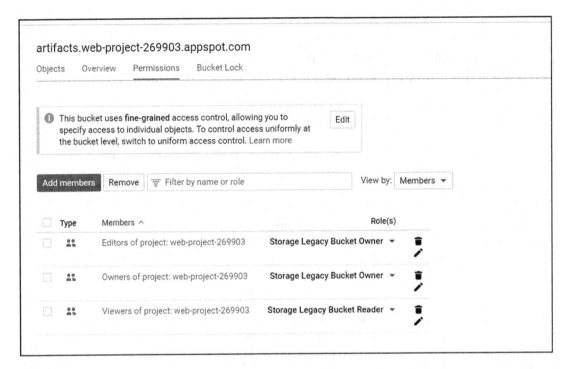

**Figure 2-25.**  *Bucket Details page*

If you click on the "Add members" link, you will have the option to add users to the registry.

## Assign Permissions to GCR

To assign permissions to GCR, click on the Add Members button. From the Add Members and Roles page, search for the user you would like to assign permissions to. Click on the "Select a role" drop-down list and scroll to Cloud Storage.

From the Cloud Storage menu, select one of the following roles:

> **Storage Admin:** Full access to the registry to push and pull images

> **Storage object viewer:** Read-only access and pull access only to the registry

Figure 2-26 shows the roles.

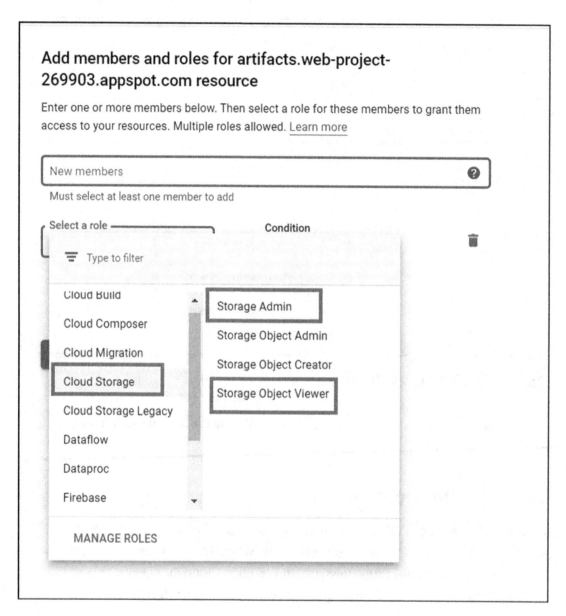

***Figure 2-26.*** *Add roles*

# Summary

In this chapter, we learned how to install Docker on all the major platforms (macOS, Windows, and Linux). We also learned about container registries and how to configure a local registry using Docker CLI. We also learned the difference between a private registry and a public registry.

We learned that before connecting to GCR we must install the Google Cloud SDK on all platforms and authenticate to GCP. We learned how to push an image and then pull an image from GCR.

In the last part, we covered the GCR Vulnerabilities Scanner, and we learned how to use it to secure our images and detect and patch vulnerabilities.

We also covered a few best practices that will help you manage the performance and security of your GCR. We also looked at how to assign push and pull permissions.

In the next chapter, we will deploy containers with Cloud Run.

# CHAPTER 3

# Deploy Containers with Cloud Run

In this chapter, we will learn how to deploy containerized applications to Google Cloud using Cloud Run. We will also take a deep dive into the following topics:

- Cloud Run

- Cloud Source

- Cloud Build

- Setting up GCP Cloud Run, etc.

- Deploying containers with Cloud Run

- Using Cloud Build and Git to deploy containers

- Source Control with GCP Cloud Source repositories

- Continuous deployment with Git and Cloud Build

## Cloud Run Introduction

Google Cloud Run is a zero infrastructure, serverless, flexible, and straightforward container as a service offering. With Cloud Run, you can deploy containerized applications directly from a Docker image stored in Google Container Registry (GCR) or from Docker Hub.

The purpose of Cloud Run is to allow you to deploy and scale containerized applications with minimum infrastructure, hosts, and servers. You pay for Cloud Run only when your containers run; there are no added or indirect costs.

© Shimon Ifrah 2021
S. Ifrah, *Getting Started with Containers in Google Cloud Platform*,
https://doi.org/10.1007/978-1-4842-6470-6_3

Cloud Run supports HTTPS and HTTP containerized applications, and it takes seconds to deploy and run an application on the platform. We can run any programming language on Cloud Run that is packaged into a Docker image.

# Get Started with Cloud Run

By default, Cloud Run is enabled with each project you deploy and doesn't cost anything extra. You can access Cloud Run using the navigation menu, by simply searching for it, or by just selecting it from the list. You will find it under the Tools section, as shown in Figure 3-1.

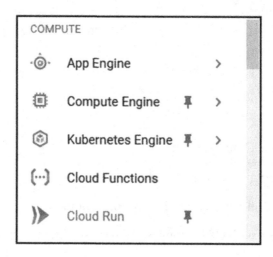

*Figure 3-1.* *Cloud Run*

# Cloud Run gcloud Commands

You can also access and manage Cloud Run using the gcloud command-line tools, which are available via Cloud Shell or by using Cloud SDK. The syntax of Cloud Shell is as follows:

```
$ gcloud run
```

To view all the available commands for Cloud Run, use the following help switch:

```
$ gcloud run --help
```

Later on in this chapter, we will use gcloud to deploy containers.

# Deploy Containers to Cloud Run

Cloud Run offers several deployment methods, the first of which uses the following steps:

**Step 1:** Package your application or deployment into a Dockerfile.

**Step 2:** Build an image from the Dockerfile on the local machine.

**Step 3:** Push the image to GCR.

**Step 4:** Deploy the application from GCR into Cloud Run.

As you can see, GCR plays a critical role in the deployment process.

## Step 1: Package Application

For our first application to deploy to Cloud Run, I have a very basic app that generates a random number and runs it on Python and Flask. Let's look at the code of the application, which is called randomapp.py.

---

**Note**   This code is available in the book code section under CH03.

---

```
#randomapp.py
import random
import string
from flask import Flask
app = Flask(__name__)

@app.route('/')
def rannum():
    x = random.randint(5000770880,9008800000)
    y = str(x)
    return y

if __name__ == '__main__':
  app.run(debug=True, host='0.0.0.0',port=80)
```

The app uses Flask and prints a random number to the screen using port 80. To deploy the app, I have created the following Dockerfile:

```
FROM    python
RUN     apt-get update
```

```
RUN     apt-get install -y python python-pip wget
RUN     pip install Flask
RUN      mkdir /app
COPY    . /app/
WORKDIR app
ENTRYPOINT ["python"]
CMD ["randomapp.py"]
```

The Dockerfile does the following:

Uses the latest Python Docker image

Installs Flask

Copies the randomapp.py file to the container and runs it using port 80.

The result of the deployment should look like Figure 3-2.

***Figure 3-2.***  *Random app*

## Step 2: Build an Image

To build the image using the two files from Step 1, I run the following Docker `build` command:

```
$ docker build -t random:latest .
```

To test the application after the build, I deploy a container using the following command before pushing the image to GCR:

```
$ docker run -it -p 80:80 random
```

# Step 3: Push the Image to GCR

In this step, I need to push the image to GCR so it is available from Cloud Run. Following what we learned in Chapter 2 about GCR, I push the image using the following commands.

## Connect to gcloud

Using Cloud SDK, I connect to GCP as follows:

```
$ gcloud auth login
```

## Set Project

I set the project using the following command:

```
$ gcloud config set project web-project-269903
```

## Tag Image

Before pushing the image, I tag it using the following command:

```
$ docker tag random gcr.io/web-project-269903/random
```

## Push Image

The final step and command push the image to GCR:

```
$ docker push gcr.io/web-project-269903/random
```

## View Images

After I push the image to GCR, I verify that the image was uploaded successfully with the following command:

```
$ gcloud container images list
```

All together, the first three steps are the most important to get the application deployed to Cloud Run.

# Step 4: Deploy the Application from GCR into Cloud Run

After completing the first three steps of the deployment, we will move to run the app on Cloud Run. To run the app, I open the Cloud Run console from the GCP console. You can see the Cloud Run console in Figure 3-3.

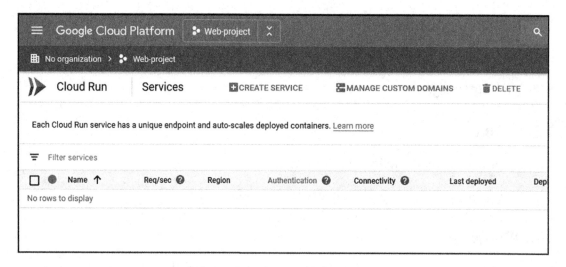

***Figure 3-3.***  *Cloud Run console*

---

**Note**    Make sure you select the same project you pushed the image to.

---

From the Cloud Run console, I click on Create Service to create a deployment. On the Create Service page, I fill in the mandatory details, which include the following:

- Region
- Service name
- Authentication

After filling in the details, I continue to the second configuration step. You can see the Create Service page in Figure 3-4.

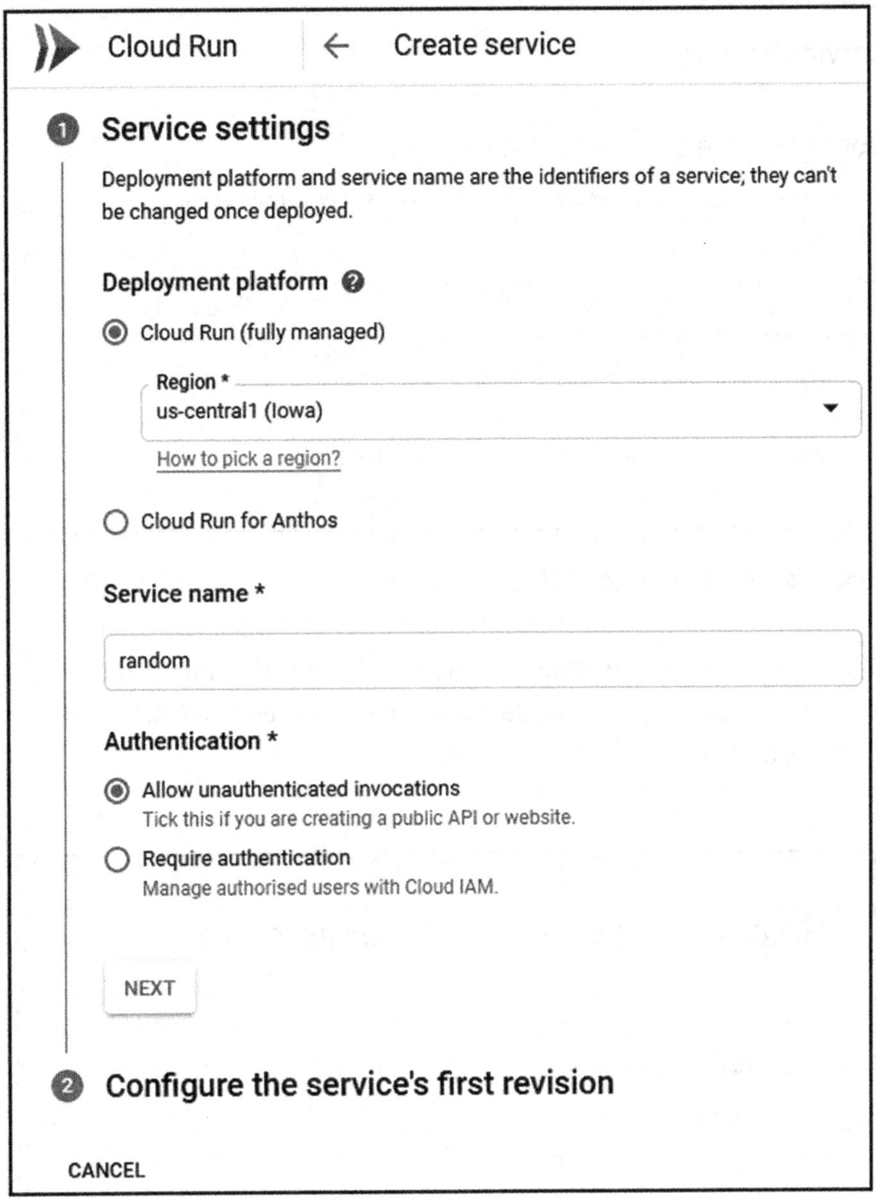

**Figure 3-4.** *Create Service*

In the second configuration step, I select the image I pushed to GCR. You can see the Select button on the right side of the "Container image URL" search box, shown in Figure 3-5.

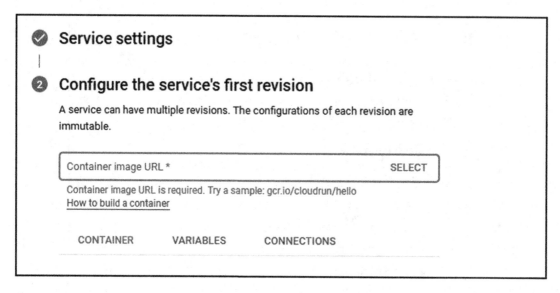

*Figure 3-5.* *Container image URL*

The Select Google Container Registry image page will show all the images that you have in GCR. In my case, you can see the image that I pushed to GCR. The name of my image is random, as you can see in Figure 3-6.

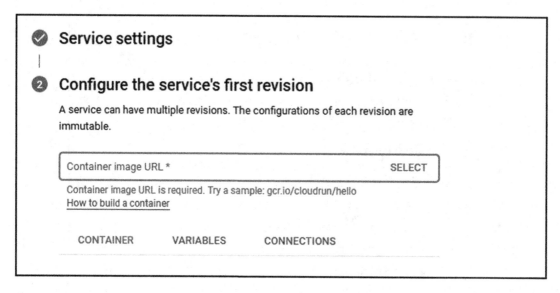

*Figure 3-6.* *Select image*

In the General section of the configuration, you can select the port you would like your application to be accessible on. I am using port 80. In Figure 3-7, you can see the General section.

You can also set variables you would like the container to use during runtime.

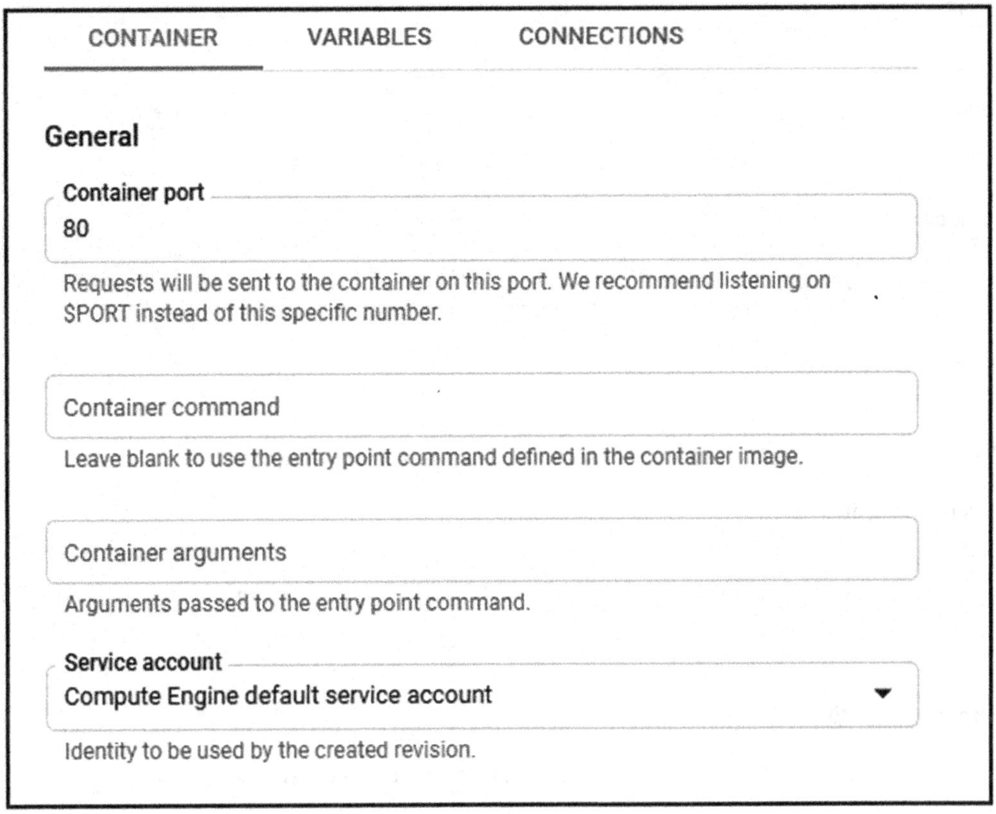

| CONTAINER | VARIABLES | CONNECTIONS |

**General**

**Container port**

80

Requests will be sent to the container on this port. We recommend listening on $PORT instead of this specific number.

Container command

Leave blank to use the entry point command defined in the container image.

Container arguments

Arguments passed to the entry point command.

**Service account**

Compute Engine default service account ▼

Identity to be used by the created revision.

***Figure 3-7.*** *Select port number*

The final step in the configuration process allows you to set the capacity of the container, which means how much RAM and CPU we would like to allocate to it. The minimum amount of RAM is 128 MB and 1 VCPC. You can see the capacity screen in Figure 3-8.

To start the deployment, I click Create.

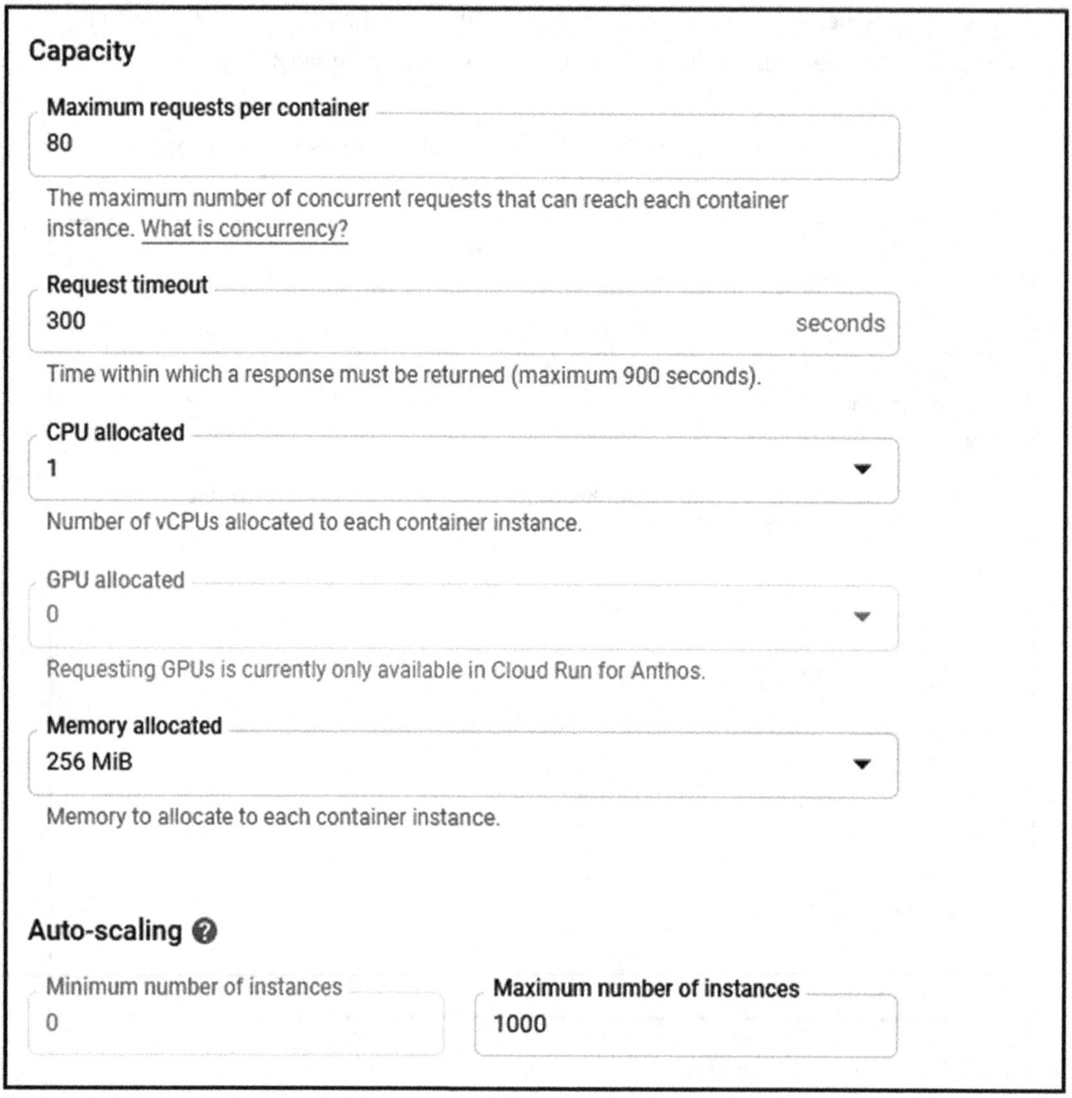

**Capacity**

Maximum requests per container

80

The maximum number of concurrent requests that can reach each container instance. What is concurrency?

Request timeout

300                                                                                                    seconds

Time within which a response must be returned (maximum 900 seconds).

CPU allocated

1                                                                                                             ▼

Number of vCPUs allocated to each container instance.

GPU allocated

0                                                                                                             ▼

Requesting GPUs is currently only available in Cloud Run for Anthos.

Memory allocated

256 MiB                                                                                              ▼

Memory to allocate to each container instance.

**Auto-scaling** ❓

Minimum number of instances                    Maximum number of instances

0                                                                    1000

***Figure 3-8.*** *Set capacity*

After the Create button has been clicked, Cloud Run will pull the image from GCR and allocate the compute resource the deployment needs. You can monitor the deployment from the Service Details page.

When Cloud Run has completed the deployment, all the details will show up in the Service Details page. Figure 3-9 shows the details of the deployment. You can see the public-facing URL where I can access the application and the status of the container running the application.

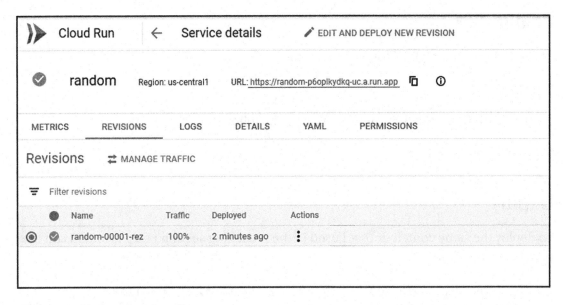

*Figure 3-9.*  *Service details*

You can see the final result in Figure 3-10.

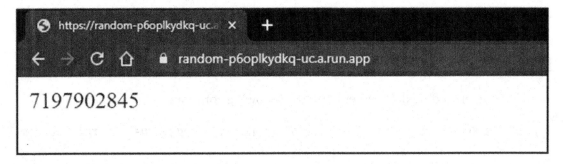

*Figure 3-10.*  *Final result*

# Deploy Containers to Cloud Run Using gcloud

Now that we have used the Cloud Run management console to deploy our Docker image, it is time to explore gcloud. Using gcloud and Cloud SDK, we can automate the entire process and use just a one-line command. This process is pretty solid and can prevent deployment errors that can happen when using the console. We can also shorten the process by using gcloud.

## gcloud run

The gcloud command for Cloud Run is as follows:

```
$ gcloud run
```

To view all the available commands, type the following:

```
$ gcloud run --help
```

## Deploy

To deploy the same container that I used in the preceding section using gcloud, I run the following command:

```
$ gcloud run deploy random --port 80 --platform=managed -allow-
unauthenticated --region=us-central1 -image=gcr.io/web-project-269903/
random@sha256:15baf8ffa7c4f53200f56899b082a6bd4ed8c3cc25884a76181a4970cdc6899c
```

The deployment is the same; it uses the same region, image, and port.

Once you invoke the command from Cloud SDK or Cloud Shell, it takes a minute or two for the container to be up and running.

## Delete

To delete the preceding deployment, use the following command:

```
$ gcloud run services delete --platform=managed --region=us-central1 random
```

---

**Note**    To delete, use the gcloud run services.

---

I believe you will find that sometimes it is just more convenient and efficient to use Cloud SDK because it offers an automated process to deploy workloads.

# Use Cloud Build and Git to Deploy Containers to Cloud Run

Up until now, we have used the Cloud Run management console and Cloud SDK using gcloud to deploy containers. Google Cloud Platform gives another excellent method by which to utilize Cloud Run for deployment—using an automated build pipeline using Git. This process is also called continuous deployment (CD/CI) using Git.

## The Process

This process works as follow:

- Create a Git in GitHub or GCP Cloud Source.

- Add Dockerfile, application files, and cloudbuild.yaml.

- Configure trigger in Cloud Build.

- Push repository.

- The application is deployed automatically to Cloud Run.

- During the Cloud Build process, we will do three things:

  - Build a Docker image (in my case, I will use my random app).

  - Push the image to Google Container Registry (GCR).

  - Deploy the image from GCR to Cloud Run.

This is an end-to-end process that is fully automated and takes most of the manual steps we have covered up to now, and in Chapter 2, and automates them.

## Set Up Cloud Source Repositories

Before we can deploy applications to Cloud Run using Git, Cloud Build, and Cloud Source, we must review the setup process for Cloud Source repositories. In my case, I am using Cloud Source; however, you can use GitHub if you like. It is important to note that Cloud Source is a paid service; however, it is free for the first five users and up to 500 GB of data storage. Once you reach five users, you must pay $1 per user per month.

# Create Repository

To set up your first repository, open Cloud Source from the Navigation menu. You will find the link under the Products section, as shown in Figure 3-11.

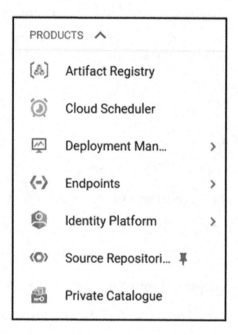

*Figure 3-11.* *Cloud Source*

To create your first repository, click on the Get Started button. From the Getting Started page, click on Create Repository to start the wizard. Figure 3-12 shows the Cloud Repository console.

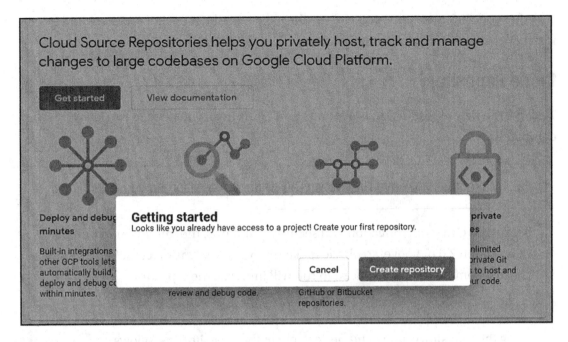

*Figure 3-12.* *Create repository*

The Create New Repository page is very straightforward. To create a repository, you need to give it a name and select the project that it will be associated with. Figure 3-13 shows the Create New Repository page.

**Create new repository**

Repository name *
web-project

Project *
web-project-269903                          OR    Create project    ⑦

ℹ  Your repository is billed based on Cloud Source Repositories pricing  ☒.

Cancel    Create

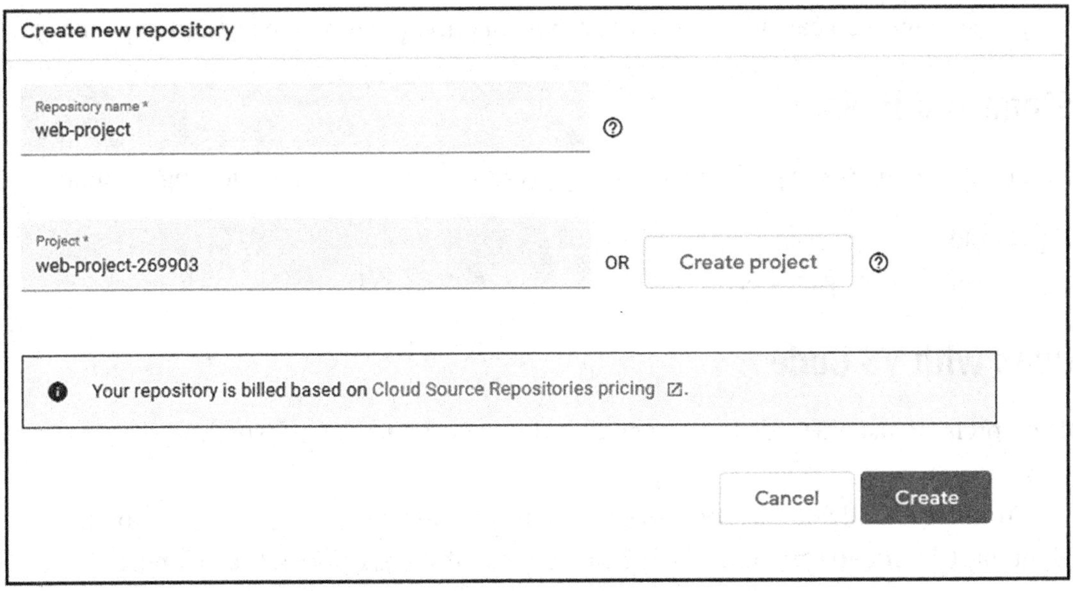

*Figure 3-13.* *Create repository*

After you click on Create, you will see the page with the repository address and instructions for how to clone the repository.

## Clone Repository

To clone the new repository on a Windows or a Linux host, you need to run a few commands.

---

**Note**    Make sure you have Git version 2.0 or above installed on your machine.

---

Because of GCP authentication and security standards, the minimum requirement for Git is version 2.0 or above, so please make sure your systems meet the requirements.

The first command that you need to run will initialize the repository

```
$ gcloud init
```

Using the repository name and project, clone the repository as follows:

```
$ gcloud source repos clone web-project --project=web-project-269903
```

After the clone is completed, open the repository using the following command:

```
$ cd web-project
```

At this stage, you can add files to the repository and push it to the Cloud Repository.

## Stage and Push

To stage the changes and push the repository to Cloud Source, run the following commands:

```
$ git add .
$ git push -u origin master
```

## Open with VS Code

If you prefer to use VS Code to manage Cloud Source, you can perform the following steps.

From the Cloud Source repository details page, shown in Figure 3-14, click on the Manually Generated Credentials tab. From the list of steps, click on the link next to number one, "Generate and store your Git credentials."

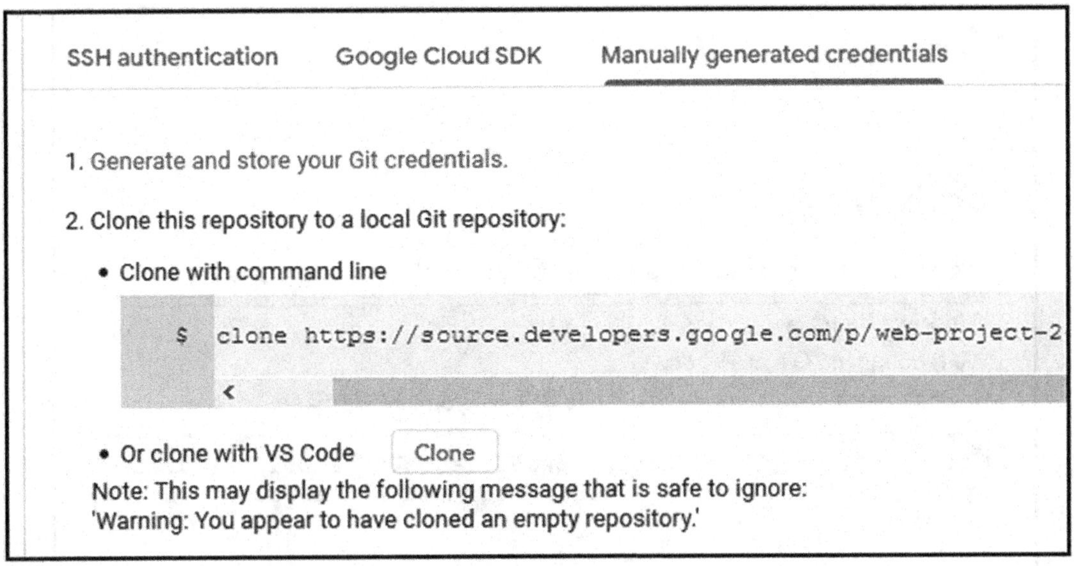

SSH authentication        Google Cloud SDK        Manually generated credentials

1. Generate and store your Git credentials.

2. Clone this repository to a local Git repository:

   • Clone with command line

   ```
   $  clone https://source.developers.google.com/p/web-project-2
   <
   ```

   • Or clone with VS Code      Clone
   Note: This may display the following message that is safe to ignore:
   'Warning: You appear to have cloned an empty repository.'

*Figure 3-14.*  *Generate and store your Git credentials*

The link will redirect to a GCP authentication page, where you will see a few commands that you will need to run on your machine. The commands will create trust between your machine and Cloud Source and will control the authentication to the repository. Figures 3-15 and 3-16 show the commands you need to run. The commands need to run from a Git Bash client.

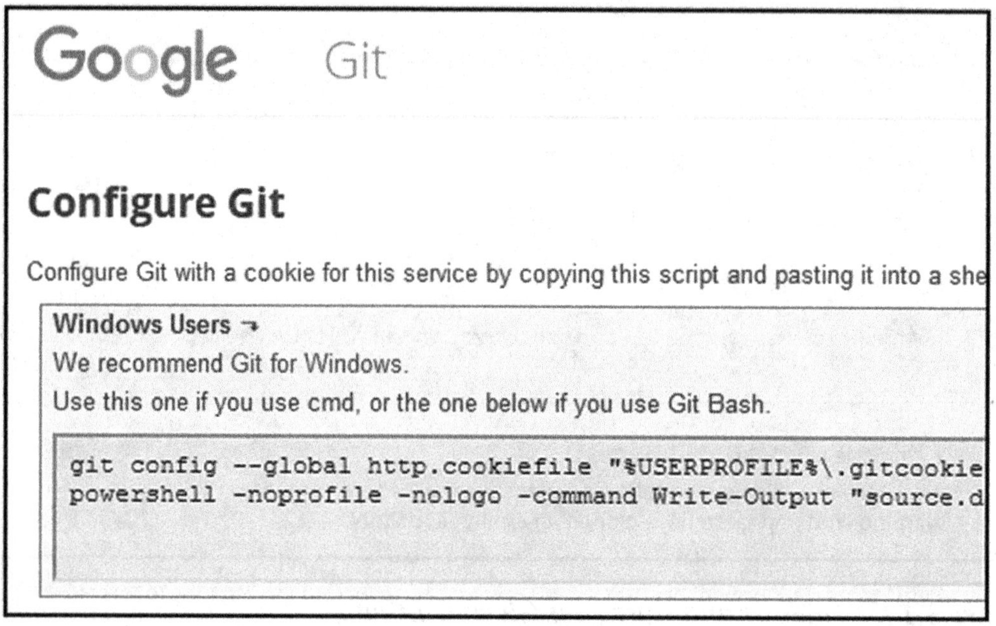

**Google**   Git

## Configure Git

Configure Git with a cookie for this service by copying this script and pasting it into a she

Windows Users →
We recommend Git for Windows.
Use this one if you use cmd, or the one below if you use Git Bash.

```
git config --global http.cookiefile "%USERPROFILE%\.gitcookie
powershell -noprofile -nologo -command Write-Output "source.d
```

*Figure 3-15.*

The commands in Figure 3-15 are for Windows users. If you are a macOS user, please run the commands shown in Figure 3-16.

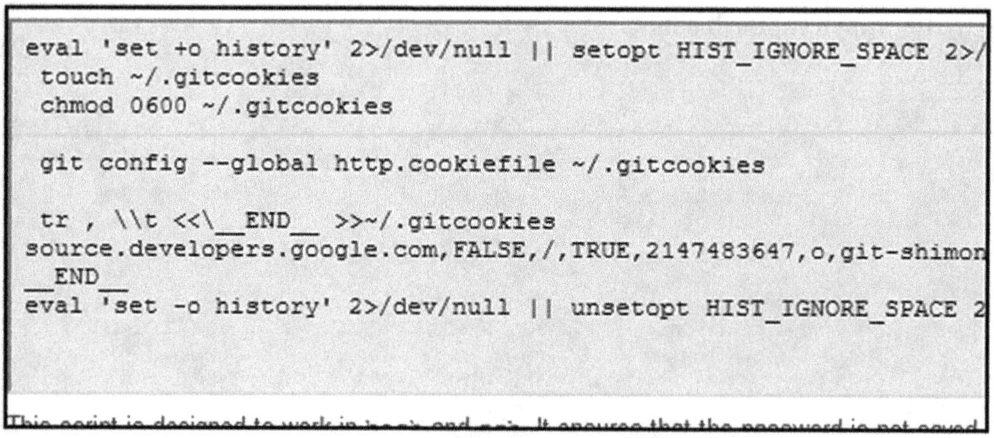

```
eval 'set +o history' 2>/dev/null || setopt HIST_IGNORE_SPACE 2>/
touch ~/.gitcookies
chmod 0600 ~/.gitcookies

git config --global http.cookiefile ~/.gitcookies

tr , \\t <<\__END__ >>~/.gitcookies
source.developers.google.com,FALSE,/,TRUE,2147483647,o,git-shimon
__END__
eval 'set -o history' 2>/dev/null || unsetopt HIST_IGNORE_SPACE 2
```

*Figure 3-16.*

To run the commands on a Windows machine, search for Git Bash, as shown in Figure 3-17.

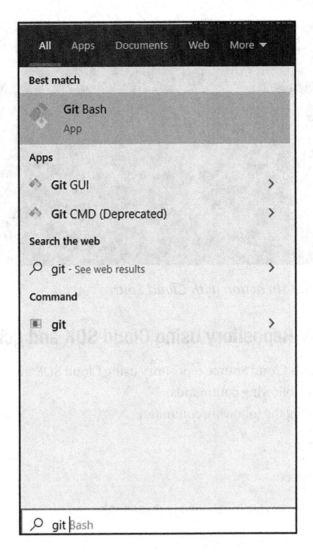

***Figure 3-17.***  *Git Bash*

After you finish running the commands, click the Clone button shown in Figure 3-14. VS Code will open the repository and make it ready to use. Figure 3-18 shows the VS Code console and Web-Project Cloud Source repository.

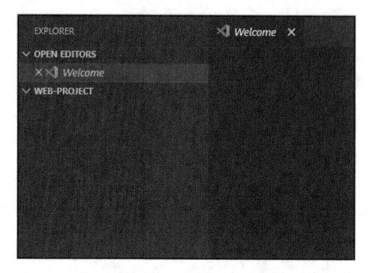

***Figure 3-18.*** *VS Code in action with Cloud Source*

## Create a Source Repository Using Cloud SDK and gcloud

If you prefer to create a Cloud Source repository using Cloud SDK and gcloud, you can easily do so using the following commands.

Log in to GCP using the following command:

```
$ gcloud auth login
```

Set your GCP project:

```
$ gcloud config set project web-project-269903
```

Create a Cloud Source repository:

```
$ gcloud source repos create web-project-269903 project web-project
```

# Enable Cloud Build

At this stage, you should have your Cloud Repository enabled and available on your machine. We will next enable Cloud Build and set up the needed permissions for the service to run and automatically deploy containers to Cloud Run.

# Enable Cloud Build and Grant Deploy Permissions

To enable Cloud Build from the GCP management console, open the left navigation menu and locate the Cloud Build icon; click on it. From the Cloud Build console, click Enable. Figure 3-19 shows the Enable button.

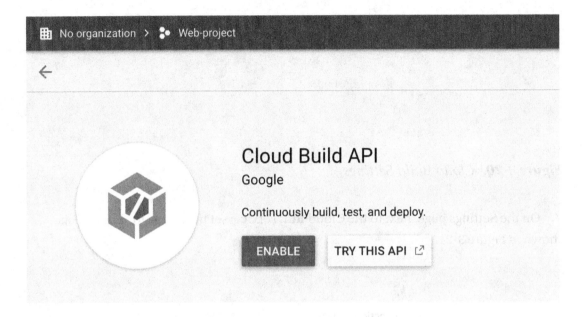

*Figure 3-19.*  *Enable Cloud Build*

# Grant Cloud Build Permission to Deploy

After you have enabled Cloud Build, you need to set up the permissions that will allow the Cloud Build service to deploy containers to Cloud Run. To grant Cloud Build permissions, click on the Settings button on the left-hand side of the Cloud Build console, as shown in Figure 3-20.

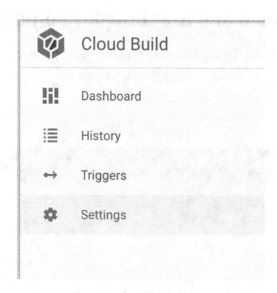

***Figure 3-20.***   *Cloud Build Settings*

On the Settings page, next to the Cloud Run service, set the Status to "Enable," as shown in Figure 3-21.

| GCP service | Role ❓ | Status |
|---|---|---|
| Cloud Functions | Cloud Functions Developer | DISABLED ▾ |
| Cloud Run | Cloud Run Admin | DISABLED ▾ |
| App Engine | App Engine Admin | Enable |
| Kubernetes Engine | Kubernetes Engine Developer | Disable |
| Compute Engine | Compute Instance Admin (v1) | |
| Firebase | Firebase Admin | DISABLED ▾ |
| Cloud KMS | Cloud KMS CryptoKey Decrypter | DISABLED ▾ |
| Service Accounts | Service Account User | DISABLED ▾ |

***Figure 3-21.***   *Cloud Run permissions*

If you receive the "Additional steps may be required" message that is shown in Figure 3-22, select "Grant Access to All Service Accounts."

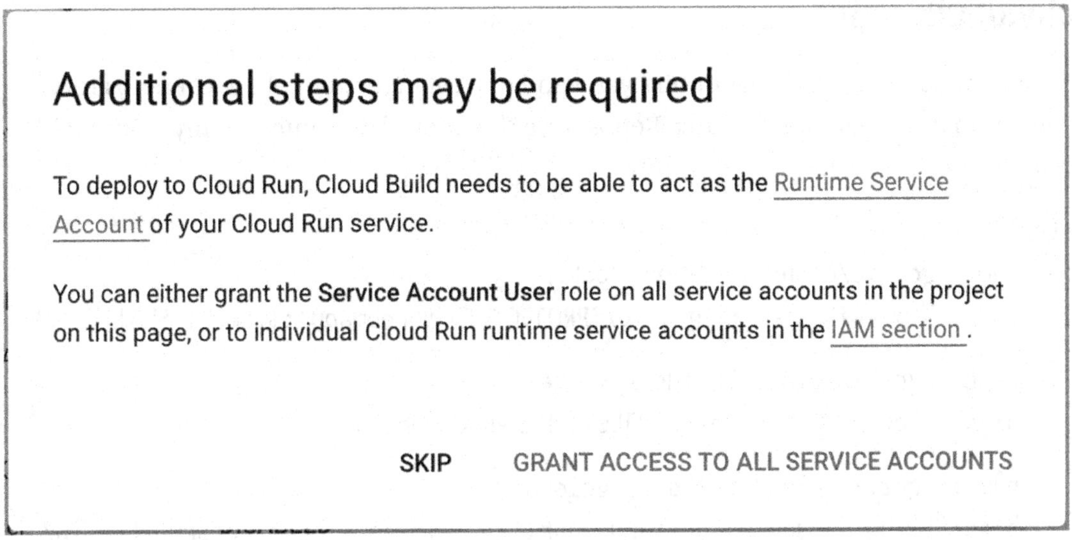

## Additional steps may be required

To deploy to Cloud Run, Cloud Build needs to be able to act as the Runtime Service Account of your Cloud Run service.

You can either grant the **Service Account User** role on all service accounts in the project on this page, or to individual Cloud Run runtime service accounts in the IAM section .

SKIP          GRANT ACCESS TO ALL SERVICE ACCOUNTS

***Figure 3-22.*** *Grant access*

# Cloudbuild.yaml File Configuration

We will now work on the configuration files that we need to add and push to the repository in order for the build to work.

---

**Note**   The files for this demonstration are located on CH03\Randomapp.

---

In my case, I have the following files:

> **Cloudbuild.yaml:** A necessary file that we need to create for Cloud Build with build, push, and run instructions for the Cloud Build service to build the image, push it to GCR, and deploy it to Cloud Run.

> **Dockerfile:** This is my Dockerfile that builds the randomapp Python app.

> **randomapp.py:** This is the actual randomapp application.

## cloudbuild.yaml

Please create a file called cloudbuild.yaml and place it in the root of the Git repository you set up in "Setup Cloud Source Repositories" section. The content of my cloudbuild.yaml file looks as follows:

```
steps:
  - name: gcr.io/cloud-builders/docker
    args: ['build', '-t', 'gcr.io/$PROJECT_ID/randomapp1:${SHORT_SHA}', '.']

  - name: 'gcr.io/cloud-builders/docker'
    args: ["push", "gcr.io/$PROJECT_ID/randomapp1"]

  - name: 'gcr.io/cloud-builders/gcloud'
    args: ['run', 'deploy', 'randomapp1', '--image', 'gcr.io/$PROJECT_ID/
    randomapp1:${SHORT_SHA}', '--region', 'us-central1', '--platform',
    'managed', --port, '80', '--allow-unauthenticated'    ]
```

If you look closely, you will see that the file has three steps:

1. Build

2. Push

3. Run

The final steps are made up of the same gcloud commands used in the "Deploy Containers to Cloud Run Using gcloud" section. Each command can be modified and customized according to your code.

## Dockerfile

The content of the Dockerfile looks as follows:

```
FROM    python
RUN     apt-get update
RUN     apt-get install -y python python-pip wget
RUN     pip install Flask
RUN     mkdir /app
COPY    . /app/
WORKDIR app
```

```
ENTRYPOINT ["python"]
CMD ["randomapp.py"]
```

This is the same Dockerfile I used previously in the book to deploy my random app image.

## Randomapp.py

And finally, randomapp.py contains my random number application. The code looks as follows:

```
import random
import string
from flask import Flask
app = Flask(__name__)

@app.route('/')
def rannum():
    x = random.randint(500077088099,900880000099)
    y = str(x)
    return y

if __name__ == '__main__':
  app.run(debug=True, host='0.0.0.0',port=80)
```

Again, this is the same app I deployed previously without any automation.

## Deployment Notes

In this deployment, Cloud Build will create a Docker image called randomapp and a Cloud Run service called randomapp. You can change the names, though you have to make them the same; however, I think it is a good idea to keep the names the same. My Cloud Source repository is called Web-project.

## Repository File Structure

In Figure 3-23, you can see the structure of my Git repository with the three files mentioned previously.

**Figure 3-23.** *Git repository*

# Cloud Build Trigger Event

A Cloud Build trigger is what starts the deployment process that runs all the build steps we would like to automate. We set the trigger by configuring an event that will initiate the Cloud Build tasks.

In our case, the trigger event will include a Push command to the Git repository we created. Every time we do a Git push to the repository, a build event will read the cloudbuild.yaml file and activate the commands inside.

## Create a Trigger

Go ahead and create your first Trigger event. From the Cloud Build console, click on Triggers, as shown in Figure 3-24.

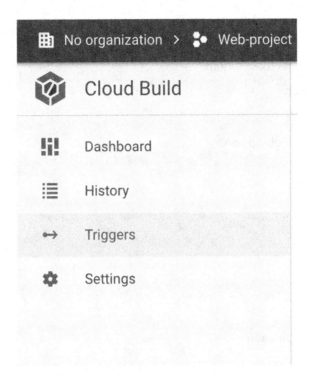

***Figure 3-24.*** *Triggers*

From the Triggers page, click the Create Trigger button, shown in Figure 3-25.

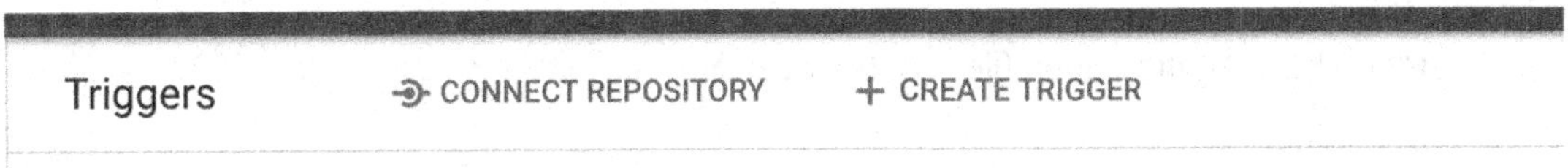

Triggers          ⊸ CONNECT REPOSITORY          + CREATE TRIGGER

***Figure 3-25.*** *Create a trigger*

On the Create Event page, fill in the following details:

> **Name:** Name the trigger event.
>
> **Event:** Use "Push to a branch" and select the master branch option for the source section.
>
> **Build configuration:** In the file type, select "Cloud Build configuration file" and use cloudbuild.yaml.

Click Save to save the trigger. Figure 3-26 shows the Create Event page and settings needed.

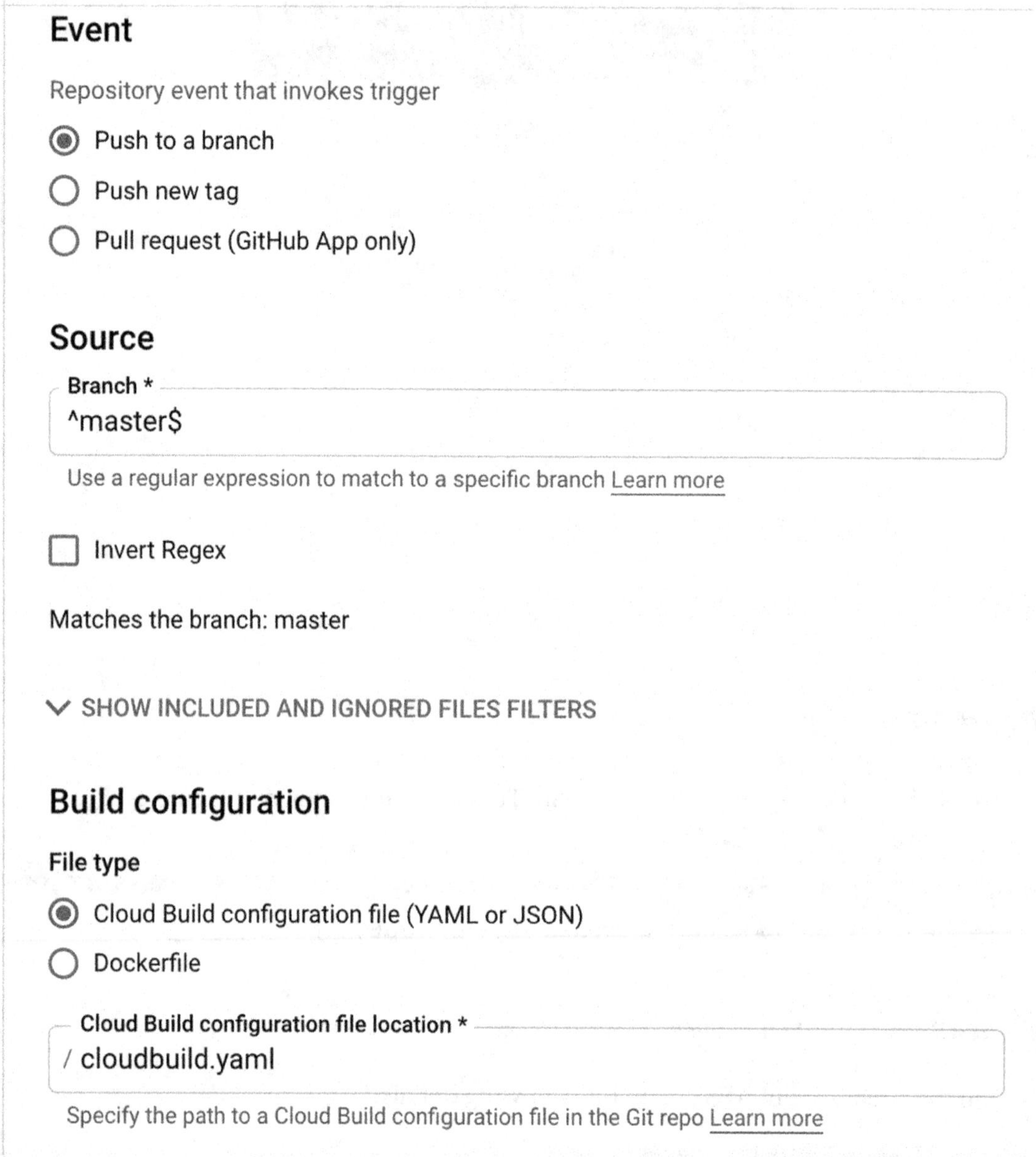

## Event

Repository event that invokes trigger

- ◉ Push to a branch
- ○ Push new tag
- ○ Pull request (GitHub App only)

## Source

Branch *

^master$

Use a regular expression to match to a specific branch Learn more

☐ Invert Regex

Matches the branch: master

∨ SHOW INCLUDED AND IGNORED FILES FILTERS

## Build configuration

**File type**

- ◉ Cloud Build configuration file (YAML or JSON)
- ○ Dockerfile

Cloud Build configuration file location *

/ cloudbuild.yaml

Specify the path to a Cloud Build configuration file in the Git repo Learn more

***Figure 3-26.*** *Create a trigger*

Once the trigger has been created, we are ready to deploy the build and see Cloud Build in action. I will go ahead and initiate a Git push event from my repository. In my case, I am just adding a comment to the code. To stage the change from VS Code, I click on the plus button below the Changes section, as shown in Figure 3-27.

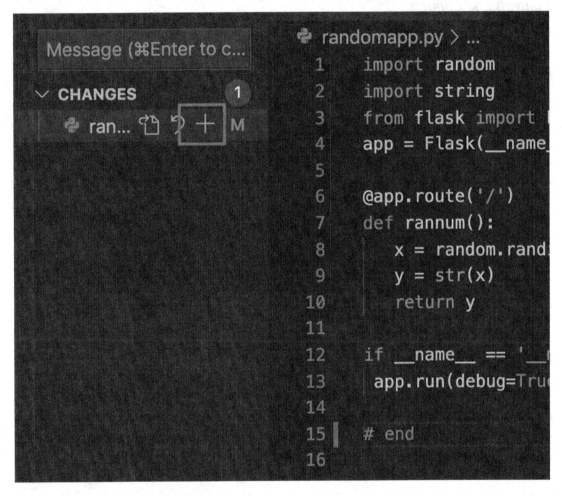

*Figure 3-27.* *Stage changes*

Next, I commit the changes using the Commit button in VS Code, as shown in Figure 3-28.

97

***Figure 3-28.*** *Commit*

The final step will be pushing the repository to the master branch using the Push command in VS code, as shown in Figure 3-29.

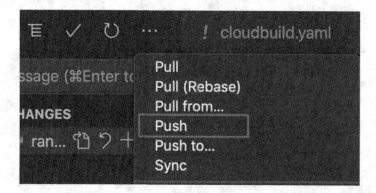

***Figure 3-29.*** *Git Push command using VS Code*

## Review Cloud Build

After the push process is started from VS Code, Cloud Build will begin the process and deploy the application. You can monitor the deployment process from the Cloud Build console's History section. Figure 3-30 shows the History button in the navigation bar. Go ahead and click on it to review the deployment status.

**Figure 3-30.** *Cloud Run History*

As shown in Figure 3-31, you can see the active deployment we just started using the Git push, marked by the blue spinning circle. You can also see a previous successful deployment, marked with a green circle and checkmark.

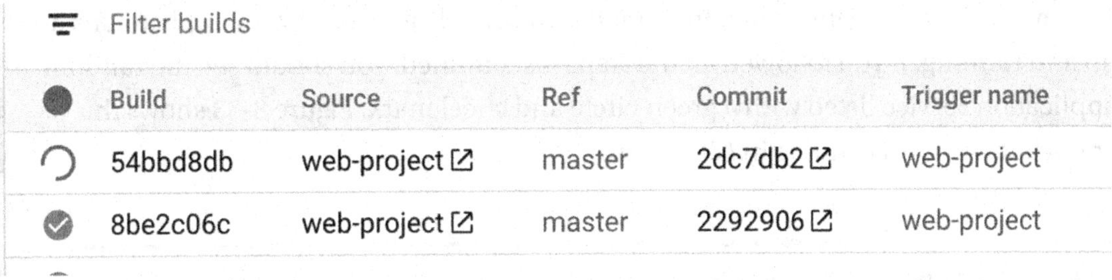

| | Build | Source | Ref | Commit | Trigger name |
|---|---|---|---|---|---|
| ◗ | 54bbd8db | web-project ☑ | master | 2dc7db2 ☑ | web-project |
| ✔ | 8be2c06c | web-project ☑ | master | 2292906 ☑ | web-project |

**Figure 3-31.** *Build history*

If you click on the active deployment, you will see all the steps the Cloud Build runs and executes in real-time. If you click on each step, you will see a detailed log of what is happening. Figure 3-32 shows the deployment steps in action.

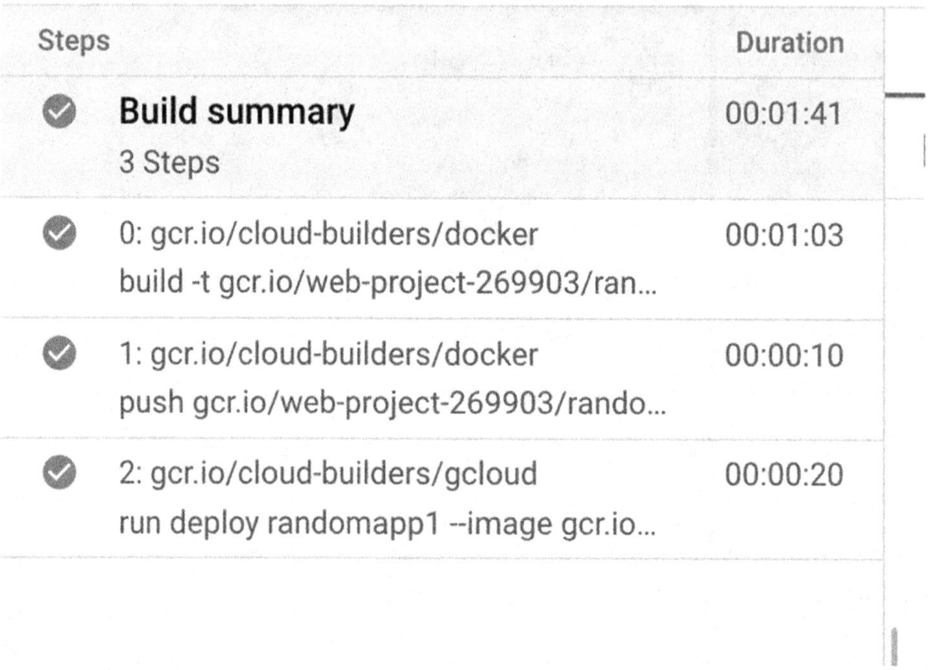

| Steps | Duration |
|---|---|
| ✅ **Build summary**<br>3 Steps | 00:01:41 |
| ✅ 0: gcr.io/cloud-builders/docker<br>build -t gcr.io/web-project-269903/ran... | 00:01:03 |
| ✅ 1: gcr.io/cloud-builders/docker<br>push gcr.io/web-project-269903/rando... | 00:00:10 |
| ✅ 2: gcr.io/cloud-builders/gcloud<br>run deploy randomapp1 --image gcr.io... | 00:00:20 |

*Figure 3-32.* *Build summary*

## Review Cloud Run Console

To view the final outcome, open the Cloud Run console and see if your applications are up and running. If you followed all the steps just outlined, you should see the random application service listed with a green circle and checkmark. Figure 3-33 shows the application up and running in Cloud Run.

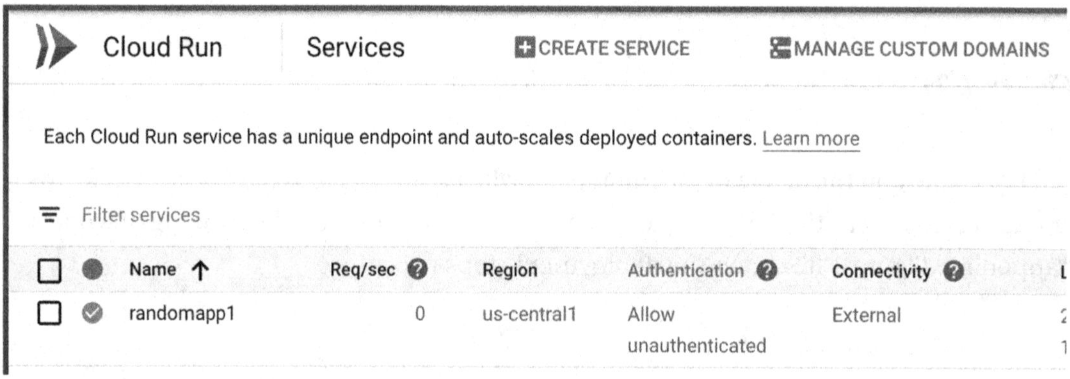

| | | Cloud Run | Services | ➕CREATE SERVICE | 🔧MANAGE CUSTOM DOMAINS |
|---|---|---|---|---|---|

Each Cloud Run service has a unique endpoint and auto-scales deployed containers. Learn more

⬇ Filter services

| | | Name ↑ | Req/sec ❓ | Region | Authentication ❓ | Connectivity ❓ | L |
|---|---|---|---|---|---|---|---|
| ☐ | ✅ | randomapp1 | 0 | us-central1 | Allow<br>unauthenticated | External | 2<br>1 |

*Figure 3-33.* *Random app*

Click on the service and view all the details. On the Service Details page, you can see the application's public URL; Figure 3-34 shows it in the top section.

In the marked bottom section, you can see all the revisions of the application. The revisions are Git commit versions of the application. In my case, I made a few changes to the app, and every time I pushed it, Cloud Build redeployed the new commit to Cloud Run.

This is true end-to-end automation with a lot of smarts built into it.

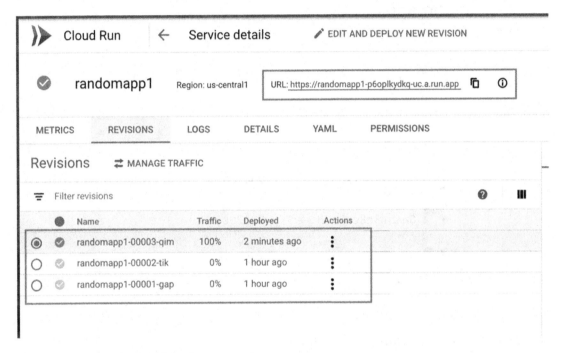

***Figure 3-34.*** *Service details*

If you click on the URL, you will see the random app in action, as shown in Figure 3-35.

809417077826

***Figure 3-35.*** *Random app*

## GCR Image

If you open your GCR console, you should see the Docker container image that Cloud Build has built and pushed to GCR. Figure 3-36 shows the `randomapp1` Docker image that Cloud Build deployed.

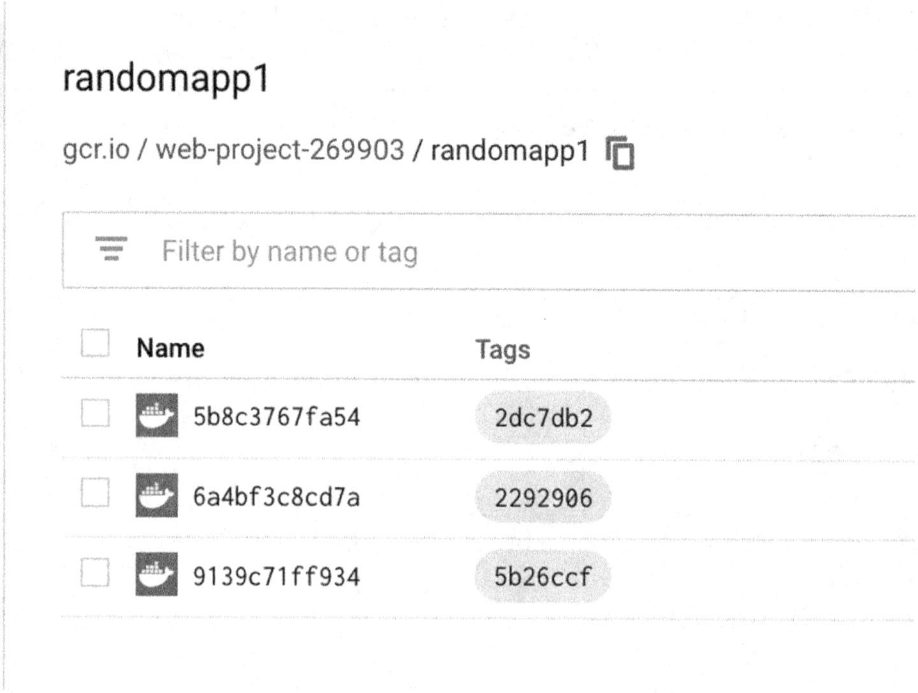
randomapp1
gcr.io / web-project-269903 / randomapp1
Filter by name or tag
Name
Tags
5b8c3767fa54
2dc7db2
6a4bf3c8cd7a
2292906
9139c71ff934
5b26ccf

*Figure 3-36. Random app Docker image*

## Conclusions for Cloud Build

I recommend you go over this section and make sure you understand the actual workflow of Cloud Build and Cloud Run. This process is also used on Google Kubernetes Engine (GKE) with a minor code change, which means if you master this section, you will be able to automate your deployments to GKE as well.

# Summary

This chapter is packed with in-depth technical knowledge about Cloud Run and the various options to deploy services. Cloud Run is a serverless solution that takes the hard work of setting up servers, hosts, and networking and gives you a deployment platform that can deploy applications in seconds.

Cloud Run deployments can be optimized by using Cloud SDK and gcloud rather than using the GUI. You can copy your gcloud commands to a shell script and run them or simply copy and paste them to the Terminal.

To get the most out of Cloud Run, you can also use continuous deployment, using Git to not only use serverless infrastructure but also use Cloud Build to build Docker images, push them to GCR, and deploy them to Cloud Run.

With so many deployment options, I am sure you will find an option that works well for you and your application.

To get your source code under control, GCP offers the Cloud Source Repositories service for source control. In this section, we used it to automate our build; however, Cloud Build can work with other services if needed.

In the next section, we will take a deep dive into the world of Kubernetes and Google Kubernetes Engine (GKE). Building on the knowledge we have gained so far in this book, we will take the random app and deploy it to Google Kubernetes Engine (GKE).

# CHAPTER 4

# Deploy Containerized Applications with Google Kubernetes Engine (GKE)

In this chapter, we are going to explore the world of Google Kubernetes Engine (GKE) service and see how we can benefit from using it in our infrastructure. This chapter is packed with great content that will get you going with deploying stateless, stateful, and job applications to GKE. We will also cover the new Anthos for GKE Cloud Run experience.

The following topics will be covered in this chapter:

- Getting a Kubernetes overview

- Getting started with GKE

- Deploying our first GKE cluster

- Deploying stateless apps to GKE

- Deploying stateful apps to GKE (storage)

- Running jobs on Kubernetes

- Deploying apps with Anthos for GKE and Cloud Run

## Kubernetes Overview

Before we head over to the GKE and the actual deployment and configuration of our first cluster, I would like to start with a short overview of Kubernetes. Kubernetes is an open source container orchestration system that was developed by Google many years ago. The first version (1.0) of Kubernetes was released on July 10, 2015; the latest version is 1.18.

© Shimon Ifrah 2021
S. Ifrah, *Getting Started with Containers in Google Cloud Platform*,
https://doi.org/10.1007/978-1-4842-6470-6_4

Kubernetes is considered the gold standard tool for containerized application orchestration and holds a market share of 70 percent and is growing fast. All major public cloud providers offer Kubernetes as a managed service, and only a small number of companies deploy it in their datacenter.

Kubernetes was designed as cloud service by Google to run its workloads, and rumors say Google runs over one billion containers to power its web assets worldwide.

# Core Components

Let's explore the core components of Kubernetes by covering them from the top level and moving down. At the heart of each Kubernetes deployment there is a cluster that forms the Kubernetes system and has the following components.

## Control Plane

Also known as the master node, the control plane is the brain behind the Kubernetes system and is responsible for the deployment of containers, schedulers, worker nodes, and everything that runs in the cluster. The control plane manages the cluster using several components that handle various specific tasks. Because specific components manage each task, the operation of the cluster is smooth, and there is no double handling of processes by the same component.

The main components of the control plane are as follows:

> **API Server:** This is the component that sends and receives requests and instructions to all nodes and clients that connect and interact with the cluster.

> **Scheduler:** This is responsible for deploying containers (also known as pods) on worker nodes that have the Docker runtime installed.

> **Etcd:** This holds the database with the cluster configuration.

> **Controller manager:** This manages all running components and objects in the cluster, like nodes, pods, and services.

# Worker Nodes

Worker nodes are the server hosts that the containers (pods) run on. Each node has the Docker runtime installed and running the actual containers. The nodes are controlled and managed by the master nodes, and all communication to them and from them goes through the API server.

Each worker node has the following components installed:

> **Kubelet:** This manages, starts, stops, and checks the health of all containers on the host; in other words, it is responsible for the lifecycle of each container on the node.

> **Kube-proxy:** This manages all networking operations on the node that include load-balancer and network proxy.

> **Container runtime:** This includes all the runtime libraries that require the Docker engine to run containers.

# Add-ons

Add-ons are components that are not considered core, but are essential to the operation of our cluster.

## DNS

All running pods and services are allowed to access a DNS service on a cluster level without reaching external services that are located outside of the cluster. By using the DNS service inside the Kubernetes service, applications running inside the pods are more responsive to requests and are faster.

## Resource Monitor

Resource Monitor allows us to monitor all running pods and applications that run inside the Kubernetes cluster and get real-time information about the health and performance of our applications.

## Cluster Logging

The cluster logging add-on gives us the ability to use third-party solutions and tap into the logs of our nodes, pods, and services.

## Objects

The last components that make a Kubernetes cluster are as follows:

**Pods:** In the world of Kubernetes, pods are logical grouping of containers; a pod can be single or multiple containers that make what we call a deployment.

**Volumes:** For our pods to access persistent storage and dynamic configuration files, we need a storage volume that is available across the deployment and cluster regardless of the state of the cluster.

**Services:** A service is a group of containers that form a deployment of back-end and front-end servers (pods). For example, a WordPress deployment will have a front-end container for the actual WordPress application and a back-end container running MySQL database that is mapped to a persistent storage volume.

**Namespaces:** Kubernetes namespaces help us break down our cluster into a logical environment that does not cross-reference another **cluster** or share the same resources.

# Getting Started with GKE

Before we deploy our first cluster, nodes, and containers on GKE, let's explore the main features of GKE. GKE is a managed Kubernetes service in the GCP cloud infrastructure. It provides a running, enterprise-ready, world-class Kubernetes infrastructure as a service (IaaS) and does the difficult task of configuring the actual underlining services.

GCP manages the master nodes in the cluster and gives us access to the management layer and the freedom to deploy our application without worrying about infrastructure.

# Single- or Multi-Zone Deployment

When it comes to deploying our cluster, GCP gives us a choice to implement it in a single region or in multiple regions for higher availability, more redundancy, and zero downtime. Whichever option you go with, your cluster will be hosted in a state-of-the-art data center and will be managed by GCP. For development purposes, I recommend you go with a single-zone deployment with one master server.

If your infrastructure is large or growing fast, it is a good idea to consider deploying your cluster in a multi-zone deployment where GCP will use three master servers.

# Auto-scaling

Any deployed GKE cluster can use cluster auto-scaling, which will increase the number of nodes in the cluster automatically based on resource demand. Cluster auto-scaling scales the number of nodes up and down, so when demand declines the number of nodes will be reduced. The process is fully automated and doesn't need a human touch.

If we are trying to deploy workloads and the current number of nodes cannot handle the load, auto-scaling will kick in and add new nodes to the cluster to serve the demand.

# Vertical Pod Auto-scaling (VPA)

Vertical pod auto-scaling (VPA) takes the guesswork out of sizing pods. VPA is smart enough to recommend and adjust running pods' resources on the fly without redeploying new pods. With VPA, we no longer need to plan and calculate how much memory each node needs and how many pods can run on each node.

# Private Cluster

If your organization's security policy prohibits internet traffic to your pods and nodes, GKE can be deployed as a private cluster without any internet access coming in or out. GKE will deploy the private cluster inside a private network that has no internet traffic.

# Updates

By default, GCP will update all the nodes and clusters automatically for us without our needing to do anything or worry about it; however, we have the option to change this behavior and opt for a manual update.

On a single-zone cluster, we cannot deploy any pods/applications while the update is in progress. In a multi-zone configuration, we can deploy new pods on the nodes and clusters that are being updated.

# Deploy Our First GKE Cluster

In this section, you will deploy your first GKE cluster in the single-zone configuration using the GCP management console and as well as Cloud Shell and gcloud.

To start, open the GCP console, go to the left-hand navigation menu, and click on the Kubernetes Engine icon. After clicking on the icon, you will see the GKE console, as shown in Figure 4-1.

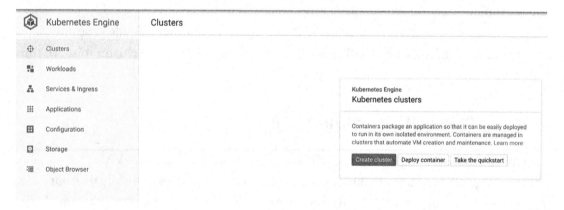

***Figure 4-1.*** *GKE console*

To create your first GKE cluster, go ahead and click on the Create Cluster button in the middle of the screen.

# Express or Standard Setup Option

On the Create Cluster screen, you can see that Google gives you two options to create a GKE cluster, as in Figure 4-2.

**Express setup:** Shown on the right side of Figure 4-2 where GCP has selected all the settings for you.

**Standard setup:** Shown on the left side of Figure 4-2, where you have the option to configure every single option of your GKE cluster.

***Figure 4-2.*** *GKE setup options*

# Express Setup

If you click on the "My first cluster" option that appears on the right side of the console, you will see all the settings the GCP set for you. Figure 4-3 shows the "My first cluster" link.

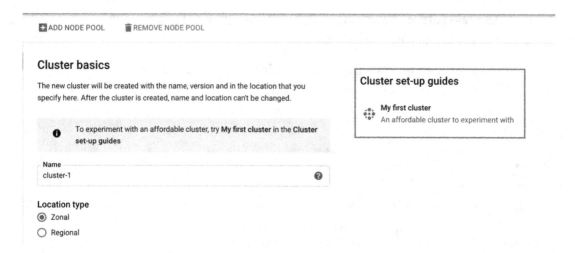

*Figure 4-3.*  *My first cluster*

Because GCP assumes that you will use this cluster for testing purposes, the selected machines are set to small instances with auto-scaling disabled, and it sets you up with Kubernetes 1.17. Figure 4-4 shows the specific experience page. To deploy the cluster, all you need to do is click Create Now.

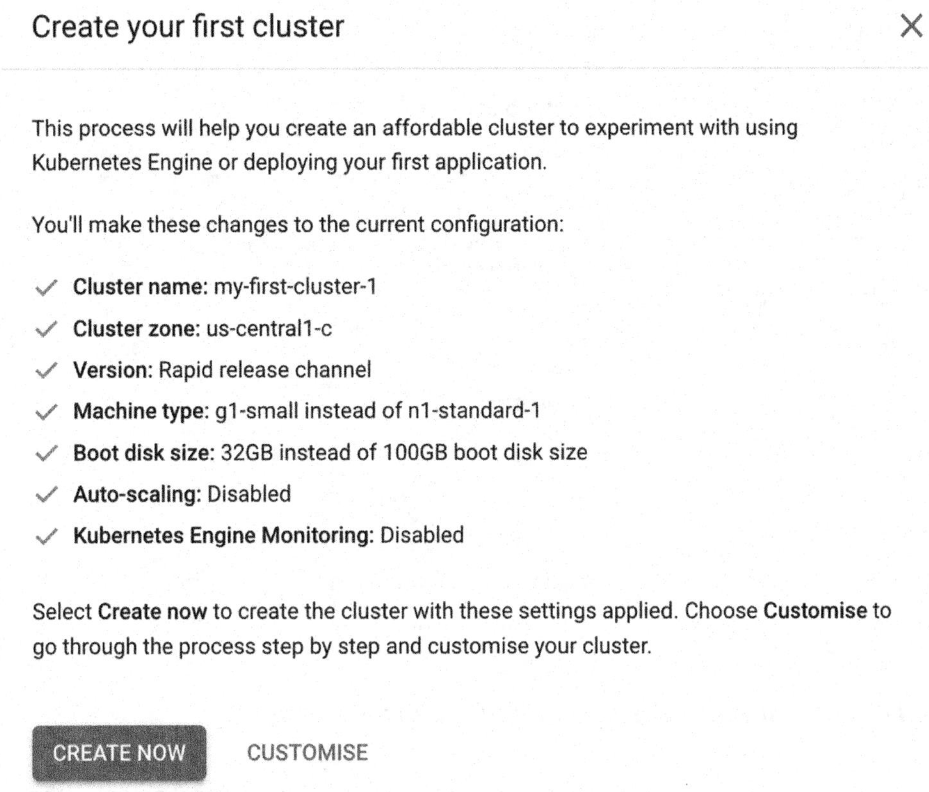

Create your first cluster                                                    ✕

This process will help you create an affordable cluster to experiment with using
Kubernetes Engine or deploying your first application.

You'll make these changes to the current configuration:

✓ **Cluster name:** my-first-cluster-1

✓ **Cluster zone:** us-central1-c

✓ **Version:** Rapid release channel

✓ **Machine type:** g1-small instead of n1-standard-1

✓ **Boot disk size:** 32GB instead of 100GB boot disk size

✓ **Auto-scaling:** Disabled

✓ **Kubernetes Engine Monitoring:** Disabled

Select **Create now** to create the cluster with these settings applied. Choose **Customise** to
go through the process step by step and customise your cluster.

     CREATE NOW        CUSTOMISE

*Figure 4-4.  Express setup*

At this stage, the cluster will get deployed, and you can check the Clusters section to
see when it is ready.

# Standard Setup

To set up your cluster for production or to get a better understanding of all the options,
it is recommended you use the standard setup method. As shown in Figure 4-5 and
highlighted in red, you have control over almost every possible option in setting up your
GKE cluster.

On the left-hand navigation bar, you can see the settings for the node pools and
cluster. GCP goes deep on each option, as we will explore very shortly.

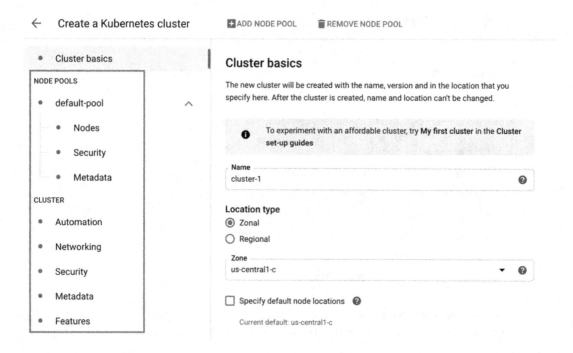

**Figure 4-5.** *GKE standard setup navigation bar options*

To set up your first cluster, start by giving the cluster a name and select either single zone or multi-zone (regional). You can also select the zone the cluster will get deployed to and which master version you will deploy. Figure 4-6 shows the main GKE setup page.

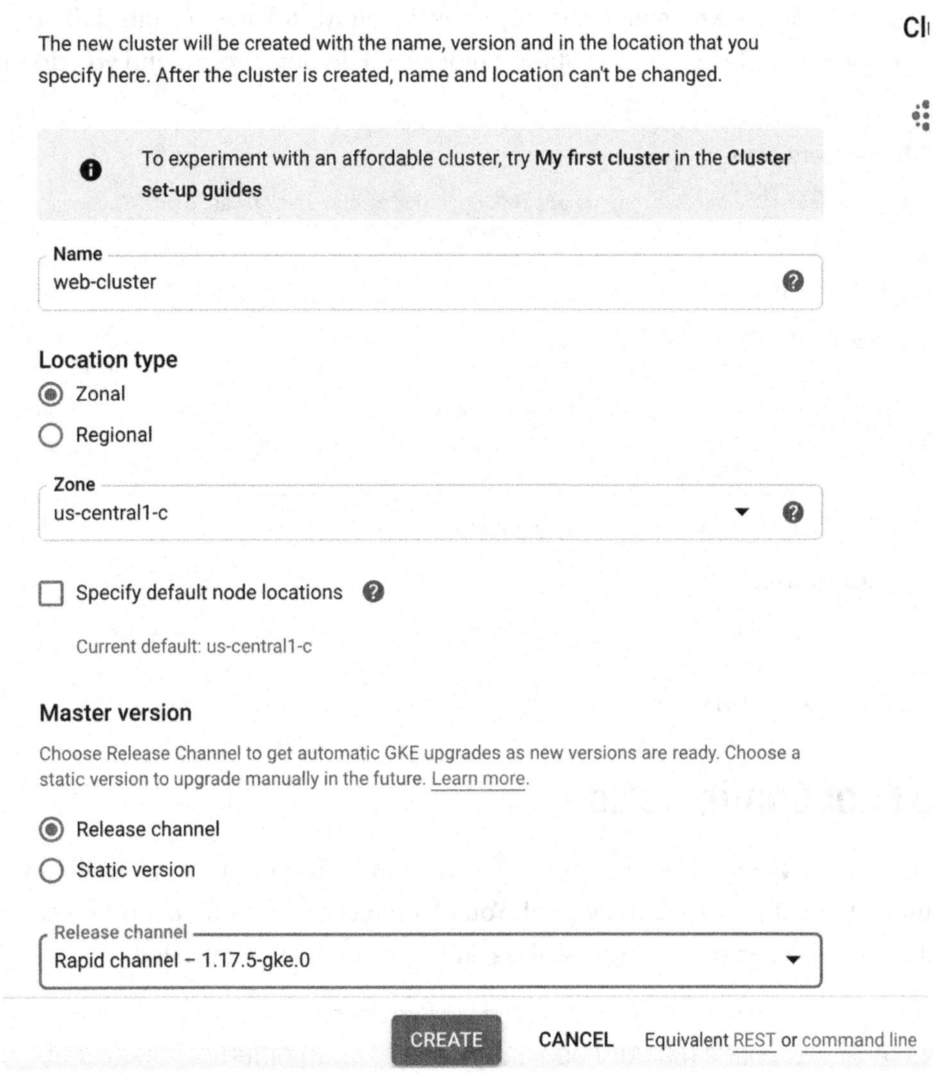

The new cluster will be created with the name, version and in the location that you
specify here. After the cluster is created, name and location can't be changed.

> ⓘ   To experiment with an affordable cluster, try **My first cluster** in the **Cluster set-up guides**

Name
web-cluster                                                                    ❷

**Location type**

◉ Zonal

◯ Regional

Zone
us-central1-c                                                        ▾    ❷

☐ Specify default node locations  ❷

Current default: us-central1-c

**Master version**

Choose Release Channel to get automatic GKE upgrades as new versions are ready. Choose a
static version to upgrade manually in the future. Learn more.

◉ Release channel

◯ Static version

Release channel
Rapid channel – 1.17.5-gke.0                                           ▾

CREATE    **CANCEL**    Equivalent REST or command line

***Figure 4-6.*** *GKE main setup page*

# Master Version

When selecting the master version of your control plane, you have three options:

> **Rapid channel:** Latest version of Kubernetes (or closer to latest)

> **Regular channel:** This is the default option and is one version
> below the latest version.

> **Stable channel:** This version is considered stable because it is a bit old.

Figure 4-7 shows the master version options. If you would like to control the update process of your GKE cluster, select "Static"; however, I do not recommend you do that.

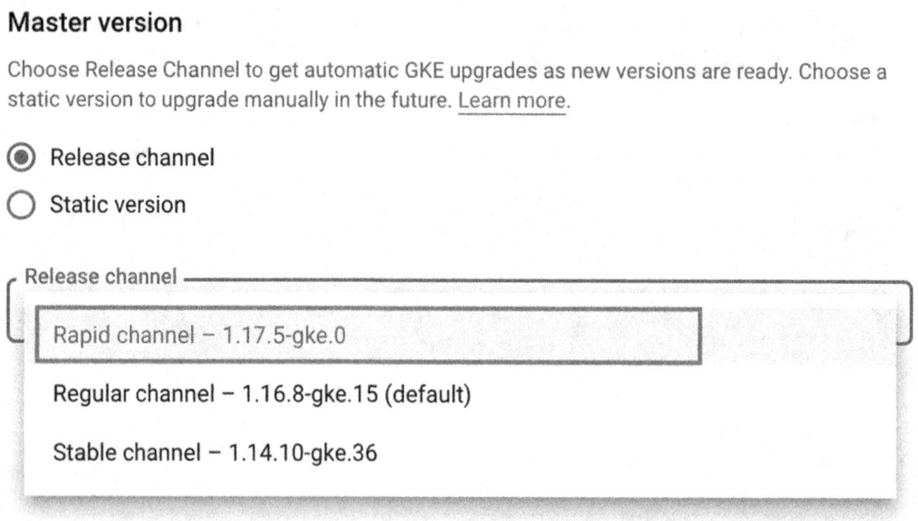

**Master version**

Choose Release Channel to get automatic GKE upgrades as new versions are ready. Choose a static version to upgrade manually in the future. Learn more.

◉ Release channel

◯ Static version

Release channel

Rapid channel – 1.17.5-gke.0

Regular channel – 1.16.8-gke.15 (default)

Stable channel – 1.14.10-gke.36

***Figure 4-7.*** *Master version*

# Node Pool Configuration

If you click on the default-pool option on the left-hand navigation bar, you will have the opportunity to configure your node pool. You can select the number of nodes that you will have in the cluster, enable auto-scaling, and choose the node version.

---

**Node**    A GKE cluster's master node and nodes can run different versions of Kubernetes.

---

Figure 4-8 shows the default-pool options.

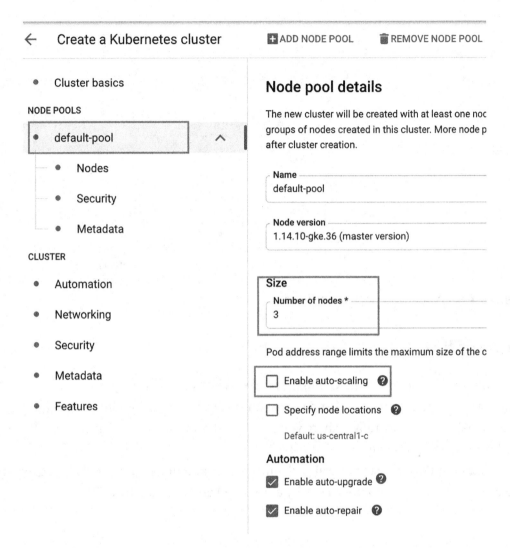

*Figure 4-8.* *Default pool configuration*

Continuing with the default-pool configuration, you have the option to select which operating system the nodes will run. GCP has developed its own Linux image for Kubernetes nodes, called Container-Optimized OS (cos), and it is set as the default option. You also have the option to select Ubuntu Linux as your node OS.

Figure 4-9 shows the node image type options.

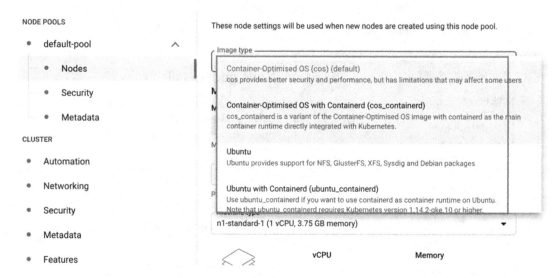

*Figure 4-9.* *Node image type options*

# Automation

The Automation section in the Configuration wizard gives you the option to set a schedule to allow GCP to install and update the GKE cluster. You control this setting using a maintenance window, where you specify a day or days on which you are OK with GCP patching the GKE cluster (Figure 4-10).

Another option is to set vertical pod auto-scaling and node auto-provisioning, where the task of sizing pods and nodes is fully automated and handled by GCP.

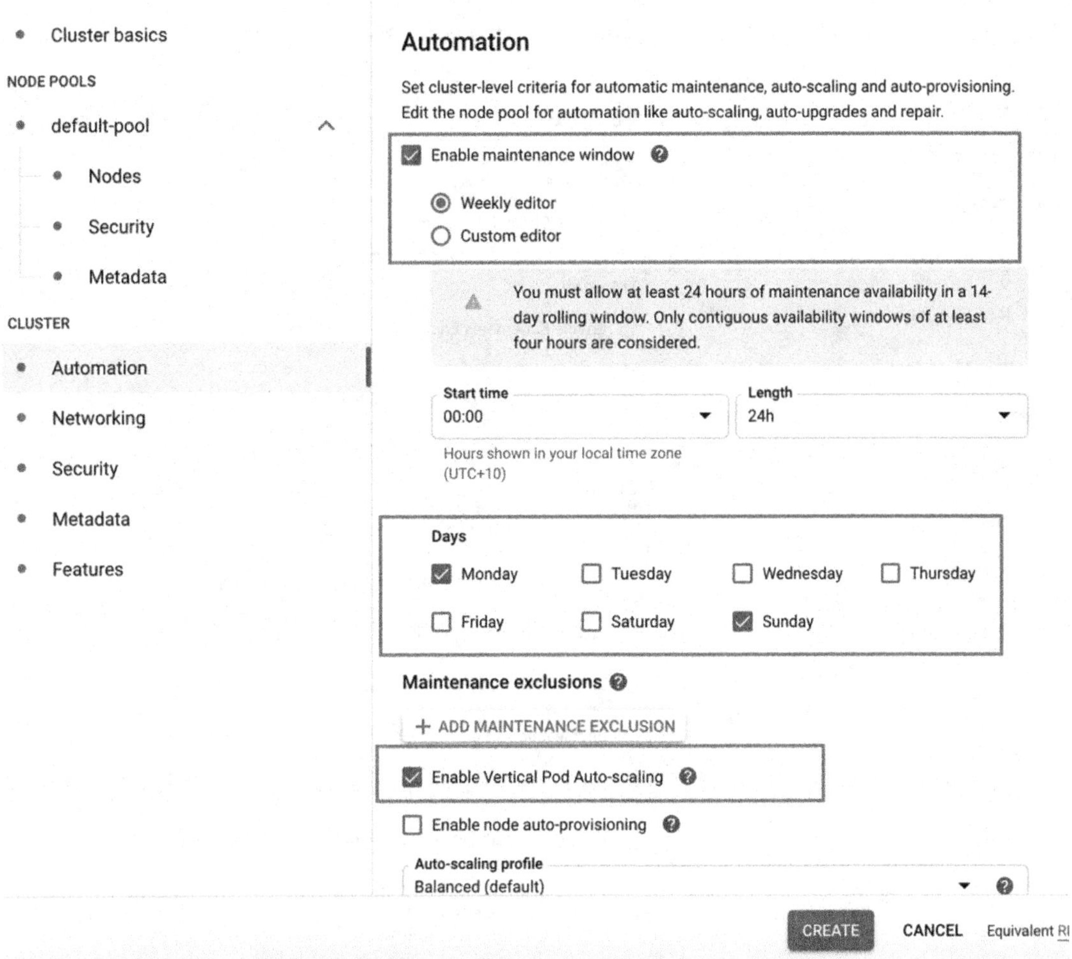

*Figure 4-10.*  *GKE automation*

# Features

The Features section of the wizard allows you to enable Anthos, which connects the
Cloud Run deployment experience with your GKE cluster. You can also enable advanced
monitoring of the GKE cluster and other settings, like Kubernetes Dashboard, which is
deprecated. You can see the Features page in Figure 4-11.

**Figure 4-11.**  *GKE features*

Now that you understand how to set up your first GKE cluster, go ahead and change the default values or deploy the group using the default settings. When you are ready, click Create. When the cluster is available, you will see the green tick box next to its name on the Clusters screen, as shown in Figure 4-12.

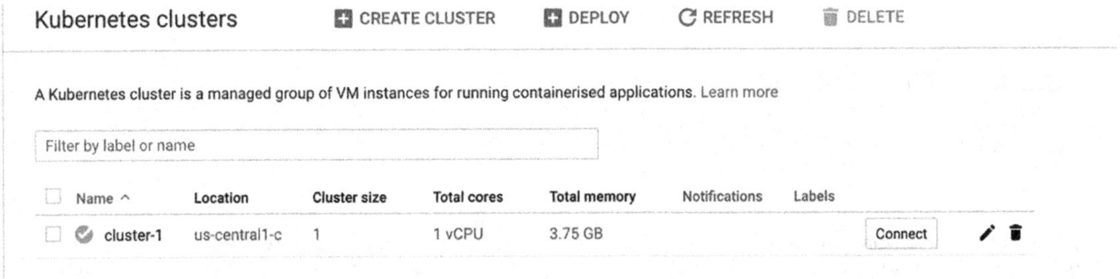

Kubernetes clusters        ➕ CREATE CLUSTER        ➕ DEPLOY        ↻ REFRESH        🗑 DELETE

A Kubernetes cluster is a managed group of VM instances for running containerised applications. Learn more

Filter by label or name

| Name ^ | Location | Cluster size | Total cores | Total memory | Notifications | Labels | | |
|---|---|---|---|---|---|---|---|---|
| ✔ cluster-1 | us-central1-c | 1 | 1 vCPU | 3.75 GB | | | Connect | ✏ 🗑 |

***Figure 4-12.*** *Clusters*

# Deploy a GKE Cluster Using Cloud SDK and gcloud

Up until now, we have explored the deployment method and options of GKE using the management console; however, there is another way to deploy GKE. We can use Cloud SDK and gcloud to deploy a cluster and save time—and get the same results every time.

If you followed the preceding steps on how to use the console to deploy GKE, you probably noticed that next to the Create button shown in Figure 4-13 you have the option to use a command line.

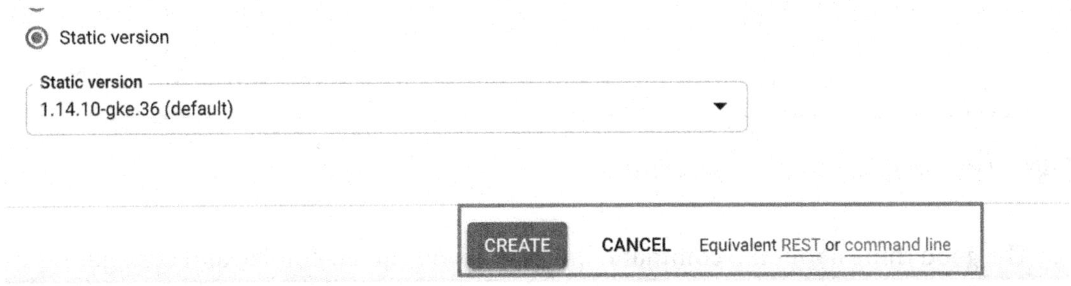

⊙ Static version

Static version
1.14.10-gke.36 (default)                                          ▾

CREATE    CANCEL    Equivalent REST or command line

***Figure 4-13.*** *Command-line option*

If you click on the command-line option, you will see a very long gcloud command that does everything that the console does. Figure 4-14 shows the gcloud command line with my GKE configuration.

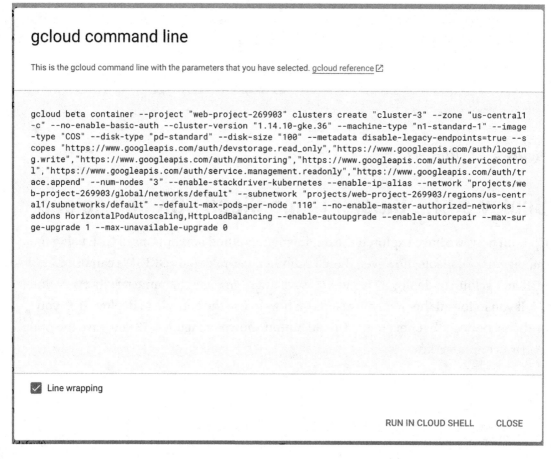

*Figure 4-14.  gcloud command line*

The good thing about the command line is that you can customize and configure your cluster the way you like it and copy changes to the code without using the console to deploy the cluster.

```
$ gcloud beta container --project "web-project-269903" clusters create
"cluster-2" --zone "us-central1-c" --no-enable-basic-auth --release-channel
"rapid" --machine-type "n1-standard-1" --image-type "COS" --disk-type
"pd-standard" --disk-size "100" --metadata disable-legacy-endpoints=
true --scopes "https://www.googleapis.com/auth/devstorage.read_only","https://
www.googleapis.com/auth/logging.write","https://www.googleapis.com/auth/
monitoring","https://www.googleapis.com/auth/servicecontrol","https://www.
googleapis.com/auth/service.management.readonly","https://www.googleapis.
```

com/auth/trace.append" --num-nodes "1" --enable-stackdriver-kubernetes --
enable-ip-alias --network "projects/web-project-269903/global/networks/
default" --subnetwork "projects/web-project-269903/regions/us-central1/
subnetworks/default" --default-max-pods-per-node "110" --no-enable-master-
authorized-networks --addons HorizontalPodAutoscaling,HttpLoadBalancing --
enable-autoupgrade --enable-autorepair --max-surge-upgrade 1 --max-
unavailable-upgrade 0

# Create a Bash Script for GKE Deployment

I like to save the deployment command inside a Bash script and run it over and over
again for testing and redeployment. To create a Bash script on a Linux host, use the
following command, which will open the script with the nano text editor:

```
$ nano 4.1.create_gke.sh
```

After the file opens, paste the gcloud command-line code and save. Give the script
run permissions using the following command:

```
$ chmod +x 4.1.create_gke.sh
```

To deploy the GKE cluster, run the script:

```
$ ./4.1.create_gke.sh
```

After a few seconds, you will see a new GKE cluster in the "Clusters" section, as
shown in Figure 4-15.

| | Name ^ | Location | Cluster size | Total cores | Total memory | Notifications | Labels | | |
|---|---|---|---|---|---|---|---|---|---|
| ☐ | cluster-1 | us-central1-c | 1 | 1 vCPU | 3.75 GB | | | Connect | ✎ 🗑 |
| ☐ | cluster-2 | us-central1-c | 1 | 1 vCPU | 3.75 GB | | | Connect | ✎ 🗑 |

*Figure 4-15.* GKE clusters

At this stage, we have finished with the cluster deployment part; in the next section,
we will start deploying apps and containers to GKE.

# Deploy Apps to GKE

In this section, we will learn how to deploy stateless and stateful applications to our GKE cluster. GCP's definition of a stateless application is an application that doesn't store any configuration or data.

A stateful application is the opposite of a stateless application—persistent storage attached to the application is used to store configuration and data.

The most basic deployment type is of a stateless application, where a Docker container image is deployed to GKE; in our case, we will use GCR to do so.

# Deploy a Stateless Application to GKE Using kubectl

We will start by deploying a basic app to GKE; in my case, I will use my random-app, which is available in the repository of the book.

Before we go ahead, we will need to install the Kubernetes command-line utility on our system. In my case, I am using a Linux CentOS VM as my deployment and management machine. To install the tool on a CentOS machine, I will use the yum package manager.

## Install Kubectl

To install the kubectl command-line utility, run the following command:

```
$ yum install kubectl
```

I also recommend you install the kubectl command auto-complete, which can save you a lot of time. Use the following command to install the kubectl auto-complete:

```
$ kubectl completion bash >/etc/bash_completion.d/kubectl
$ source /usr/share/bash-completion/bash_completion
```

## Deploy YAML File

When deploying an application to GKE, Kubernetes, or any managed Kubernetes cluster, you need to use a YAML file. Below is a YAML file that will deploy the random-app application. The application will deploy the Docker container image from GCR.

I am also enabling port 80, which I will use later to make the application available over the internet.

```
#Deploy.yaml
apiVersion: apps/v1
kind: Deployment
metadata:
  name: random-app
spec:
  replicas: 2
  selector:
    matchLabels:
      run: random-app
  template:
    metadata:
      labels:
        run: random-app
    spec:
      containers:
      - name: random-app
        image: gcr.io/web-project-269903/random
        ports:
          - containerPort: 80
```

## Deploy App

To deploy, I copy it to my Linux management server, where I have the Cloud SDK and kubectl installed.

---

**Note**    I am using Cloud Repository to copy the files to my Linux machine.

---

To deploy my app, I run the following command with my deploy.yaml file:

```
$ kubectl apply -f deploy.yaml
```

To check the deployment status, I can use the following two commands:

```
$ kubectl get pods
```

The first command shows the deployed containers (pods), which I set to two in the YAML file.

To check the entire deployment, I run the following command:

```
$ kubectl get deployment random-app
```

You can also use the GKE "Workloads" section in the GKE management console to view all active deployments, as shown in Figure 4-16.

| | Name ↑ | Status | Type | Pods | Namespace | Cluster |
|---|---|---|---|---|---|---|
| ☐ | random-app | ✓ OK | Deployment | 2/2 | default | cluster-2 |

*Figure 4-16.  GKE workloads*

## Expose Port

By default, applications that are deployed to GKE or Kubernetes are not exposed or available externally. This is a good design that stops you from making a mistake and exposing your application to the internet without knowing.

To allow external access to your app, you need to explicitly expose it. You do so on GKE using the kubectl expose command, as you can see in the following code:

```
$ kubectl expose deployment random-app --type=LoadBalancer --name=random-app
```

After the code is run, you can check the external IP of your app and open your browser to test it.

## Get External IP Address

To get the external IP of my application, I run the following command:

```
Kubectl get service random-app
```

I go ahead and open my browser to do the final step and check if it works. As shown in Figure 4-17, my random application is up and running, and accessible from the internet.

6817587605

*Figure 4-17. Random-app available over the internet*

## Deploy a Stateful Application to GKE

By GCP's definition, a stateful application is an application that has access to persistent storage. In GKE, you do that by attaching a storage volume to your deployment and mounting the storage.

## YAML Deployment File

In this following example, I am going to deploy my random app to GKE, but this time I'm adding a piece of code that will mount a storage volume to my deployment. The volume name is random, and the location is /usr/random.

By adding a volume to my deployment, anything that is saved to /usr/random will exist long after the pods are deleted. If needed, I can deploy the existing pods to create new ones, and the data will remain.

---

**Note**   You can find the following code in the code library of this book under the name deploy_storage.yaml.

---

```
9    apiVersion: v1
10   kind: Service
11   metadata:
12     name: random-app-storage
13     labels:
14       app: random-app-storage
15   spec:
16     ports:
17     - port: 80
18       name: web
19     clusterIP: None
```

```
20    selector:
21      app: random-app-storage
22    ---
23    apiVersion: apps/v1
24    kind: StatefulSet
25    metadata:
26      name: web
27    spec:
28      selector:
29        matchLabels:
30          app: random-app-storage
31      serviceName: "random-app-storage"
32      replicas: 2
33      template:
34        metadata:
35          labels:
36            app: random-app-storage
37        spec:
38          terminationGracePeriodSeconds: 10
39          containers:
40          - name: random-app-storage
41            image: gcr.io/web-project-269903/random
42            ports:
43            - containerPort: 80
44            name: web
45            - volumeMounts:
46            - name: random
47              mountPath: /usr/random
48      volumeClaimTemplates:
49      - metadata:
50          name: random
51        spec:
52          accessModes: [ "ReadWriteOnce" ]
53          resources:
54            requests:
55              storage: 1Gi
```

# Deploy a Stateful Application

To deploy my stateful application to GKE, I use the kubectl command line with the YAML file, as follows:

```
$ kubectl apply -f deploy_storage.yaml
```

To view the storage volumes that were created by my deployment, I open the GKE console and click on Storage, as shown in Figure 4-18. Since I deployed two pods, each received its own volume.

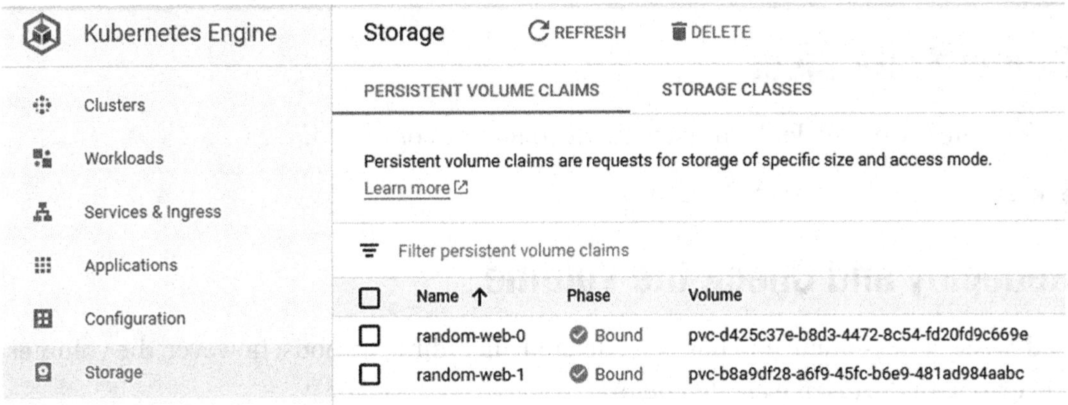

*Figure 4-18.*  *Storage volume*

Let's go ahead and see what a stateful pod looks like from the inside by SSH-ing into it and examining the mounted volume.

# SSH into a Running Pod

Using the kubectl command-line utility, we are going to SSH into a pod and check the file system structure. To list all the running pods in GKE, run the following command:

```
$ kubectl get pods
```

In our case, I use pod web-0 and run the following command:

```
$ kubectl exec -it web-0 -- /bin/bash
```

## Create File

Inside the pod, I browse to the /usr/random directory, which we mapped to a storage volume. I create a file inside the directory, which I use to test that the storage is persistent.

First, I browse to the directory using the following code:

```
$ cd /usr/random
```

To create a file (called a file), I use the following command:

```
$ touch file
```

## Delete Statefulset

Let's delete the entire deployment with the following command:

```
$ kubectl delete statefulset web
```

## Redeploy and Check the Volume

At this stage, the stateful app has been deleted, including the pods; however, the volumes still exist with the test file created before.

I redeploy using the following command:

```
$ kubectl apply -f deploy_storage.yaml
```

SSH into the pod with the following command:

```
$ kubectl exec -it web-0 -- /bin/bash
```

I open the mapped volume using the following command to check if the test file exists:

```
$ cd /usr/random/
```

As shown in Figure 4-19, the file is there.

```
[root@centos GKE]# kubectl exec -it web-0 -- /bin/bash
root@web-0:/app# cd ..
root@web-0:/# cd usr/random/
root@web-0:/usr/random# ls
file   lost+found
```

***Figure 4-19.***  *Check mapped volume*

To summarize stateful applications and volumes, we learned that data stored inside pods that have volumes attached are kept long after the pods are deleted. When recreating the deployment, the pods have the same access to the data as they had before they were deleted.

# Run Jobs on GKE

GKE gives us another deployment type to use—jobs. Jobs are applications that we need to run once, and we don't care what happens after. For that reason, GKE gives us the option to deploy our application as a job using the same YAML file format but with a different type.

# Deploy a Job on GKE

The following code for the random app used in the stateless deployment can be easily transformed into a job by changing the deployment kind to job, as shown in the following code:

```
56   apiVersion: batch/v1
57   kind: Job
58   metadata:
59
60     name: random-app-job
61   spec:
62     template:
63       metadata:
64         name: random-app-job
65       spec:
66         containers:
67         - name: random
68           image: gcr.io/web-project-269903/random
69           command: ["perl"]
70         restartPolicy: Never
71     backoffLimit: 2
```

To deploy a job, use the same method as for any app, as shown in the following code:

```
$ kubectl apply -f deploy_job.yaml
```

## Check Workloads

To check our deployments, we can use the GKE console's "Workloads" section. In Figure 4-20, we can see the GKE job we deployed, but more interesting is that under the "Type" section, we can see all the deployment types we used in this chapter. This is very helpful and handy for monitoring, and GCP has done a great job in putting such a great GUI together.

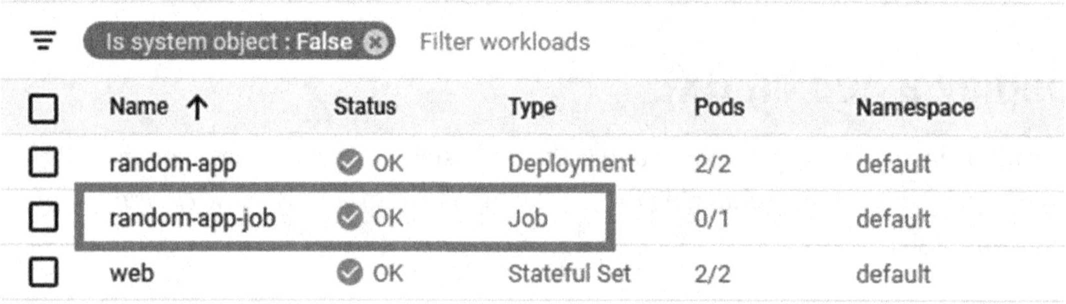

| | Name ↑ | Status | Type | Pods | Namespace |
|---|---|---|---|---|---|
| ☐ | random-app | ✓ OK | Deployment | 2/2 | default |
| ☐ | random-app-job | ✓ OK | Job | 0/1 | default |
| ☐ | web | ✓ OK | Stateful Set | 2/2 | default |

*Figure 4-20.* *GKE workloads*

# Deploy Workloads to GKE Using Cloud Run for Anthos

Before we finish this chapter, I would like to take another deep dive into GKE and show you how GCP allows you to use the same Cloud Run user experience and tools to deploy workloads to GKE.

Anthos allows you to turn your GKE cluster to Cloud Run–enabled infrastructure, which means that you can deploy your workload to GKE with the Cloud Run tools. You can also use Cloud Build to automate pipelines, as we did in Chapter 3, and deploy directly to GKE.

# Enable Anthos

Anthos is not enabled on the GKE cluster by default, because it requires worker nodes that are a bit more powerful for the cluster. To enable Anthos on a new GKE cluster, we can use the "Features" section of the GKE Create Cluster wizard, as shown in Figure 4-21.

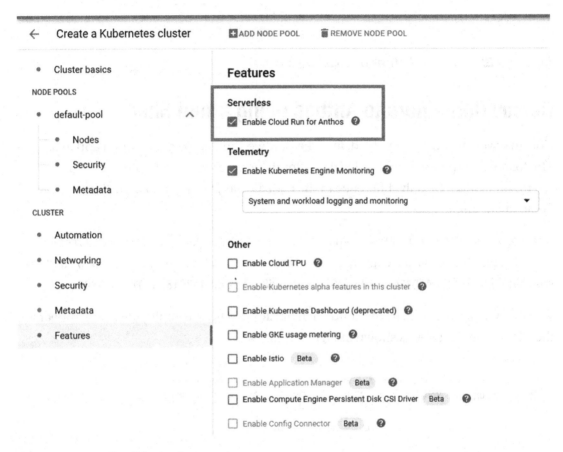

***Figure 4-21.*** *Enable Anthos*

To enable Anthos on an existing GKE cluster, we use the "Edit Cluster" option and set the Cloud Run for Anthos value to "enabled," as shown in Figure 4-22.

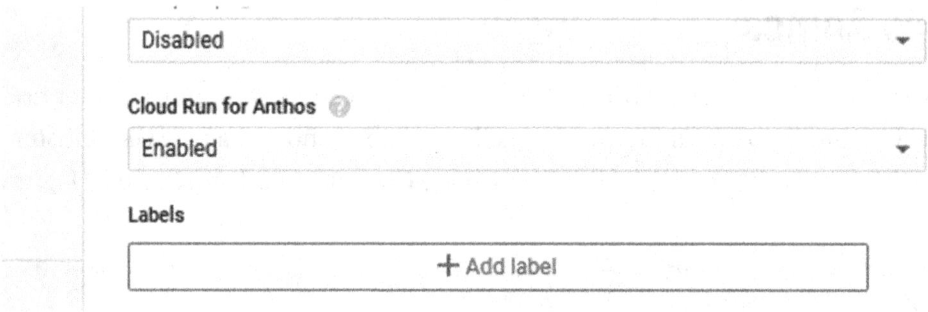

Disabled                                                              ▼

Cloud Run for Anthos  ?

Enabled                                                               ▼

Labels

+ Add label

***Figure 4-22.***  *Enable Anthos on existing cluster*

# Deploy Containers to Anthos Using Cloud Shell

Now that we have Anthos enabled, let's see how we can deploy our random app to it. The following is part of the Cloud SDK's gcloud code we used in Chapter 3 to deploy the random app. The only difference in the code is that we tell it to use GKE for the deployment platform.

```
$ gcloud run deploy random  --port 80 --platform=gke --cluster=cluster-
3 --cluster-location=us-central1-c  --image=gcr.io/web-project-269903/random@
sha256:15baf8ffa7c4f53200f56899b082a6bd4ed8c3cc25884a76181a4970cdc6899c
```

After we run the code from Cloud Shell or Cloud SDK, the deployment will appear in the Cloud Run console, as shown in Figure 4-23.

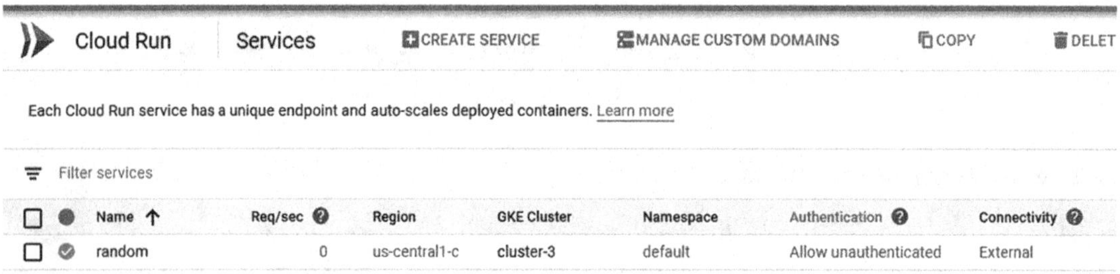

| | | Name ↑ | Req/sec ? | Region | GKE Cluster | Namespace | Authentication ? | Connectivity ? |
|---|---|---|---|---|---|---|---|---|
| ☐ | ⊘ | random | 0 | us-central1-c | cluster-3 | default | Allow unauthenticated | External |

▶▶ Cloud Run    Services    ⊞ CREATE SERVICE    ⊟ MANAGE CUSTOM DOMAINS    ⊡ COPY    🗑 DELET

Each Cloud Run service has a unique endpoint and auto-scales deployed containers. Learn more

▽ Filter services

***Figure 4-23.***  *Cloud Run console*

## Deploy Containers to Anthos Using Cloud Run Console

If we want to use the Cloud Run GUI for deployment, we can use the same console; however, under "Deployment platform," we will need to select "Cloud Run for Anthos." Figure 4-24 shows this option.

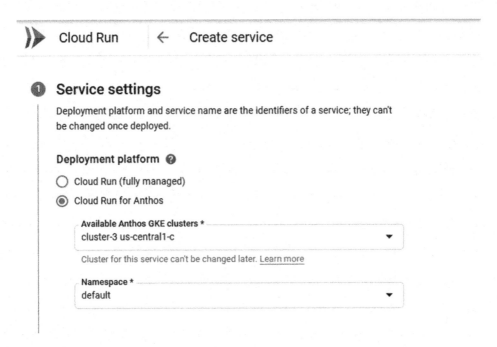

***Figure 4-24.*** *Cloud Run for Anthos*

# Summary

In this chapter, we have learned so much about GKE and its various deployment options. We used the Cloud SDK and glcoud to deploy our cluster, but also used the GUI.

During the configuration steps of the GKE cluster, we explored all the deployment options of the cluster.

When we moved to the apps deployment section, we learned how to deploy applications that don't store any data, and also deployed applications that require persistent storage in the form of volumes.

In the final section of this chapter, we learned about GKE jobs and Anthos.

From here, we will progress to deploying Docker container hosts on GCP.

# CHAPTER 5

# Deploy Docker Containers on GCP Compute Engine

In this chapter, we are going to explore Google Compute Engine and its key features, which allow us to run containers on GCP. The Google Compute Engine service sits under the GCP Compute Service offering, which includes services like App Engine, Cloud Run, Cloud Function, and more. The purpose of the compute services is to give us processing power to run applications, services, containers, and any other services that require access to CPU power. In essence, Compute Engine allows us to create and run virtual machines inside the GCP infrastructure, similar to AWS EC2 instances and Microsoft Azure virtual machines.

GCP has a highly optimized, secure, and reliable infrastructure that allows us to create Windows or Linux virtual machines that run Docker engine and deploy containers inside. A virtual machine running Docker is called a Docker host, and in this chapter, I will use the term "Docker host" a lot.

We will learn about the following topics in this chapter:

- Compute Engine overview

- Container-optimized OS from Google

- Installing Docker container host on Ubuntu Linux VM

- Installing Docker container host on Windows Server 2019 VM

- Deploying and managing containers on Azure VM (Linux and Windows)

- Deploying containers on GCP Compute Engine using GCP container-optimized OS

© Shimon Ifrah 2021
S. Ifrah, *Getting Started with Containers in Google Cloud Platform*,
https://doi.org/10.1007/978-1-4842-6470-6_5

# Compute Engine Overview

We will start by using GCP Compute Engine to deploy a Docker container host on a virtual machine. First, we will deploy a Linux host, and later we will deploy a Windows Server 2019 host since Docker runs on both platforms and the Docker client commands are the same.

Compute Engine is a very knowledgeable service and therefore offers advanced features, such as the following:

- **Custom size instance:** Besides the standard predefined VM sizes, we can create custom-size VMs on which to put our apps.

- **OS patch management:** This is a paid service, but it allows us to review and apply security features and updates to virtual machines.

- **Preemptible VMs, also known as spot instance VMs:** These VMs are suitable for defined batch jobs that need to run without worrying about uptime or user access where cost is 80 percent less than standard-size VMs.

GCP pricing is based on computing seconds, meaning you are paying per second of use; however, network and SSD storage pricing is not included in this price.

# Container-Optimized OS from Google

Before we get into the deployment of our instance, I would like to review the Google container-optimized OS; it is similar to AWS Linux 2, which I covered in the first book of this series. This OS is based on Linux; however, it is optimized to do two things:

- Run GCP infrastructure in an optimized and secure manner.

- Run Docker containers very efficiently.

Google manages the OS; however, it is part of the open source project called Chromium OS.

The main advantages of the container-optimized OS are as follows:

- **Docker:** Docker is pre-loaded and configured in an optimal state.

- **Less attachment surface:** As a result of a small package count, and since the image is optimized for the container, unnecessary packages are left out, resulting in a more secure instance.

- **Updates:** By default, the image is configured to download updates every week, keeping it secure and optimized all the time.

It is also important to note that the GKE cluster we deployed in Chapter 4 and the Cloud Run container we deployed in Chapter 3 were running the container-optimized OS image.

---

**Note**   You can't install packages on the instance since there is no package manager installed on the image.

---

# Deploy Linux Docker Container Host

Let's deploy your first Docker host using Cloud SDK and gcloud, as we did in the past few chapters.

## Use Cloud Shell to Create a VM

Building on your previous knowledge and learning, you will create a Docker host running the Google container-optimized OS image. Remember that you can run the gcloud command directly and paste it into the shell terminal on your MacOS, Linux, or Windows machine. I prefer to save the command to a Bash shell script and reuse it, which allows me to set and forget the process.

## Create a Script or Run Command

The first step will be creating the Bash script using the following command:

```
touch 5.1.Create_Linux_Host.sh
```

You can find the script in the code library of this book.

## Give Script Permission to Run

Before copying the command to the script, give it permission to run using the following command:

```
chmod u+x 5.1.Create_Linux_host.sh
```

Copy the following gcloud command, which will create a virtual machine based on the Google container-optimized OS:

```
gcloud beta compute --project=web-project-269903 instances create
linuxdockerhost --zone=us-central1-a --machine-type=n1-standard-2 --subnet=
default --network-tier=PREMIUM --maintenance-policy=MIGRATE --service-
account=359956861522-compute@developer.gserviceaccount.com --scopes=
https://www.googleapis.com/auth/devstorage.read_only,https://www.
googleapis.com/auth/logging.write,https://www.googleapis.com/auth/
monitoring.write,https://www.googleapis.com/auth/servicecontrol,https://
www.googleapis.com/auth/service.management.readonly,https://www.googleapis.
com/auth/trace.append --image=cos-69-10895-385-0 --image-project=cos-
cloud --boot-disk-size=10GB --boot-disk-type=pd-standard --boot-disk-
device-name=linuxdockerhost --reservation-affinity=any
```

After pasting the code to the shell script, go ahead and run it. It will take a minute or two for the VM to be ready for use.

# Connect to VM Using SSH

It is excellent that you deployed your Docker host, but now you need to connect to it and pull a Docker image to it. This part is essential and cannot be skipped.

When it comes to connecting to your VM in GCP, Google made sure security was not compromised, and a good process is in place. GCP gives you a few SSH methods with which to connect to your VM, and we will look at two of them that I think are good.

## Use Cloud Shell SSH Command

The most secure method is using Cloud Shell and gcloud command to connect to your host. This method is built on the core fundamentals of gcloud, and because we already have Cloud SDK installed and authenticated to GCP, we can use it.

To connect to your new host from Cloud SDK, use the following command. Since we used Cloud SDK to deploy the VM two minutes ago, the effort and time to connect to the VM are minimal.

```
gcloud beta compute ssh --zone "us-central1-a" "linuxdockerhost" --project
"web-project-269903"
```

---

**Note**   You can get the custom command to connect to your host from the SSH details button, as shown in Figure 5-1.

---

## Use SSH Using the Browser

Another excellent method with which to connect to the VM is via web browser directly from the GCP Compute Engine console. This option is useful if you are not connected to Cloud Shell and just want to connect to the VM without using a terminal.

As shown in Figure 5-1, the SSH button presents a few SSH options; just select the first option, "Open in browse window."

*Figure 5-1.*  *SSH options*

After you click the browser option, a new page will open that will let you access the VM shell.

## Connect to GCR and Pull Docker Image

After connecting to your VM, you now need to authenticate to GCR and pull your image from the registry. Without images, your Docker host is useless. Since the image has some GCP tools built into it, the authentication process is straightforward. Because your login details were passed to the VM from the GCP console or Cloud Shell, to connect to GCR you need to run the following command:

```
$ docker-credential-gcr configure-docker
```

After running the command, all you need to do is pull the image you need using docker run or pull, as you will see soon.

## Deploy Container

To deploy your first container, use Docker and specify the Docker image from your GCR registry. In my case, I pull my random app from GCR using the following code:

```
$ docker run --rm -p 80:80 gcr.io/web-project-269903/web-service@sha256:af4
b91c8a18f3d7aa33a21b429ebd4e1091a0dfbac640f30f063e61cca3c44f9
```

## Open Port

To test that the app is working, open port 80 on the VM because this is the port the app is using. Use the Compute Engine console to do so. From the console, click on the VM and, from the top menu, click on Edit, as shown in Figure 5-2.

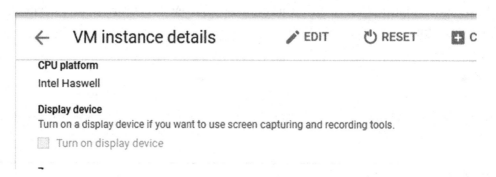

***Figure 5-2.***  *VM Instance Details page*

Scroll down to the Firewalls settings and select "Allow HTTP," as shown in Figure 5-3.

**Firewalls**
☑ Allow HTTP traffic
☑ Allow HTTPS traffic

**Network tags**

http-server ⊗    https-server ⊗

***Figure 5-3.***  *Firewall settings*

## Final Test

The final result can be seen in Figure 5-4, where the random app generated a random number in the browser. To find the external IP of your VM, check the VM Details page.

537513659390

*Figure 5-4.* *Random app in action*

# Create Linux Docker Host Using the Console

In this section, you will use the Cloud Platform management console to create a Docker host, and will also use a built-in feature that allows you to deploy a container image with the VM directly from the setup wizard.

To create a VM using the console, open the Compute Engine management console from the navigation menu. Click on Create to start the VM wizard. Figure 5-5 shows the console.

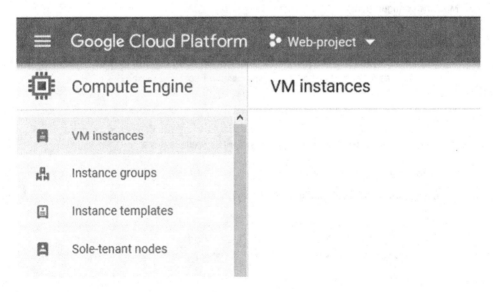

*Figure 5-5.* *Compute Engine console*

When you click on the Create button to create a new VM, you will see the Create an Instance page. The setup process flows very well, and it is similar to setting up a GKE cluster—but much shorter.

The first section allows you to name the instance and add labels for billing and auditing purposes. You can also set the region and zone.

Under the Machine Configuration section, you can select the size of the VM (this can be changed later on). Using the three tabs, you can select your instance size based on workload type. Figure 5-6 shows the first section of the wizard.

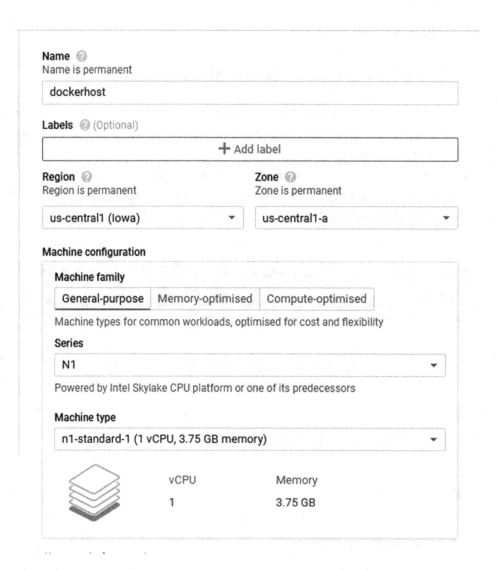

***Figure 5-6.*** *Machine configuration*

## Deploy Container

The main feature that I wanted to show you in this wizard is the Container part. Using the Container feature, you can specify a GCR container image that you would like to run on the VM without needing to run a single command like docker run. This feature is great if you need to run a single container image on your VM directly from GCR. In my case, I will select my random app Docker image, which is stored in GCR. When the VM starts, the image will deploy immediately and will continue to run.

We can also specify the restart policy for the container.

In the Firewall section, you can also open the port so the app is available from the internet.

The Container features are shown in Figure 5-7.

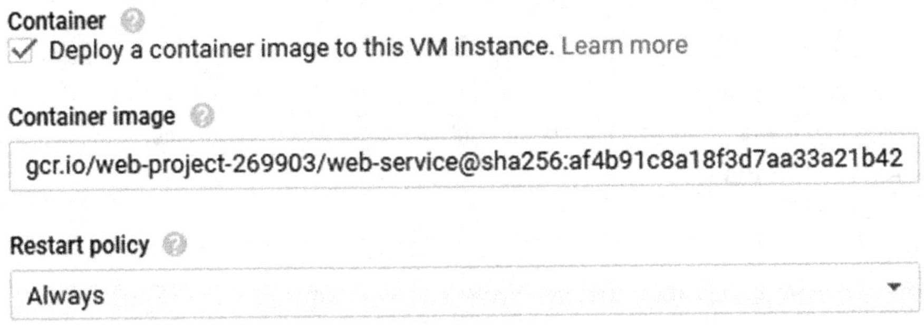

Container
✓ Deploy a container image to this VM instance. Learn more

Container image
gcr.io/web-project-269903/web-service@sha256:af4b91c8a18f3d7aa33a21b42

Restart policy
Always                                                              ▼

***Figure 5-7.*** *Container image*

On the Boot Disk configuration screen, you can select which OS you would like the instance to run. You can use Linux and select your favorite distribution, or use Windows server.

In the Firewall section, you can allow external traffic to the VM, and in my case I will allow port 80.

The boot configuration and firewall settings are shown in Figure 5-8.

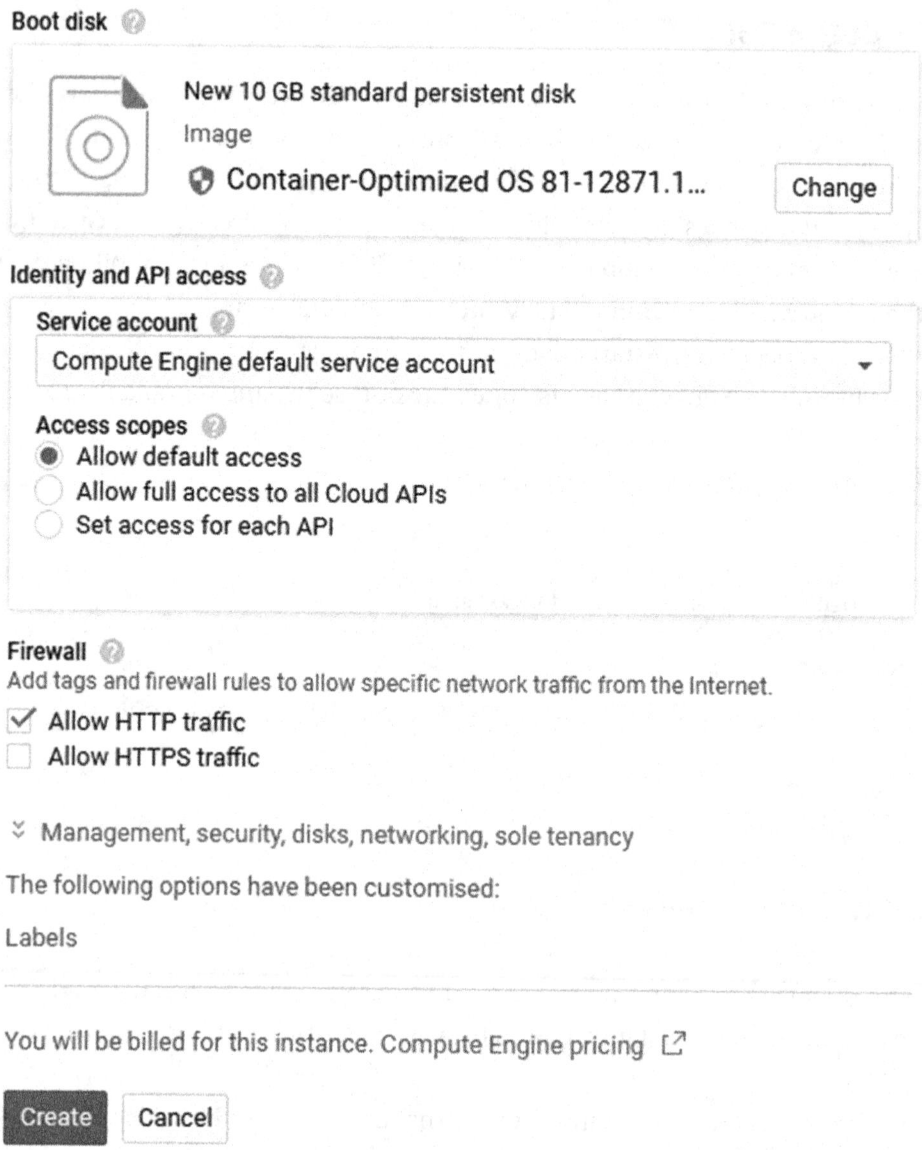

**Boot disk** ⓘ

New 10 GB standard persistent disk

Image

🛡 Container-Optimized OS 81-12871.1...        Change

**Identity and API access** ⓘ

Service account ⓘ

Compute Engine default service account                    ▾

Access scopes ⓘ
⦿ Allow default access
◯ Allow full access to all Cloud APIs
◯ Set access for each API

**Firewall** ⓘ
Add tags and firewall rules to allow specific network traffic from the Internet.

☑ Allow HTTP traffic
☐ Allow HTTPS traffic

⌄ Management, security, disks, networking, sole tenancy

The following options have been customised:

Labels

You will be billed for this instance. Compute Engine pricing ⬈

Create     Cancel

***Figure 5-8.*** *Boot disk and firewall configuration*

After finishing the wizard, wait for the VM to come online and check the external IP address. The internal and external IP addresses will appear in the VM Instances page next to the VM, as shown in Figure 5-9. Go ahead and copy the external IP address and paste it into your browser.

| Name ^ | Zone | Recommendation | In use by | Internal IP | External IP |
|---|---|---|---|---|---|
| ☐ ✅ dockerhost | us-central1-a | | | 10.128.0.13 (nic0) | 104.197.90.35 ↗ |

***Figure 5-9.*** *VM instance*

Before you check the result, if you SSH into the VM using the browser and run the docker ps command, you will see that your container is running, as shown in Figure 5-10.

```
shimon2@dockerhost ~ $ docker ps
CONTAINER ID        IMAGE
                    STATUS          PORTS                   NAMES
442b74deb62d            gcr.io/web-project-269903/web-service
nds ago        Up 35 seconds                       klt-dockerhost-vewx
6f3f856d3ea4            gcr.io/stackdriver-agents/stackdriver-logging-agent:0.2-1.5.33-1-1
 minute ago    Up 58 seconds                       stackdriver-logging-agent
shimon2@dockerhost ~ $ []
```

***Figure 5-10.*** *Running containers*

The final result is shown in Figure 5-11, where my random app is running and available from the internet.

642948484864

***Figure 5-11.*** *Random app*

My recommendation is to use the container feature when you know that your VM will run a single image. By using this feature, your container image will run smoothly, without any moving parts or manual interaction with the Docker client on the VM.

# Deploy Windows Server 2019 Docker Host

If you prefer to use Windows for your application or if your applications run on Windows containers, you can deploy a Windows Server Docker host. The Windows version of Docker has come a long way in Windows Server 2019, and it is production-ready, which means that Microsoft fully supports it.

To get started with deploying a Windows host, you can use the Cloud Engine console or Cloud SDK. The process to deploy a Windows Server host is the same as doing so on a Linux machine, except that you need to select the Windows Server image, as you will learn soon.

To create a Windows host, use the same wizard you used for the Linux host; however, when you select "Windows Server" from the operating system drop-down menu, as shown in Figure 5-12, you can select the Windows Server version with support for containers.

## Boot disk

Select an image or snapshot to create a boot disk; or attach an existing disk. Can't find what you'r

| Public images | Custom images | Snapshots | Existing disks |

**Operating system**

Windows Server ▼

**Version**

Windows Server version 1809 Datacenter Core for Containers ▼

Server Core, x64 built on 20200609, supports Shielded VM features ⌃

**Windows Server 2012 R2 Datacenter Core**
Server Core, x64 built on 20200609, supports Shielded VM features

**Windows Server 2012 R2 Datacenter**
Server with Desktop Experience, x64 built on 20200609, supports Shield

**Windows Server 2016 Datacenter Core**
Server Core, x64 built on 20200609, supports Shielded VM features

**Windows Server 2016 Datacenter**
Server with Desktop Experience, x64 built on 20200609, supports Shield

**Windows Server 2019 Datacenter Core for Containers**
Server Core, x64 built on 20200609, supports Shielded VM features

**Windows Server 2019 Datacenter Core**
Server Core, x64 built on 20200609, supports Shielded VM features

**Windows Server 2019 Datacenter for Containers**
x64 built on 20200609, supports Shielded VM features

**Windows Server 2019 Datacenter**
Server with Desktop Experience, x64 built on 20200609, supports Shield ⌄

*Figure 5-12.* *Windows Server 2019 Datacenter for Containers*

**Note**    You have to select the version with containers to run Docker.

After you select the operating system and version, you can also select the boot disk type, as shown in Figure 5-13.

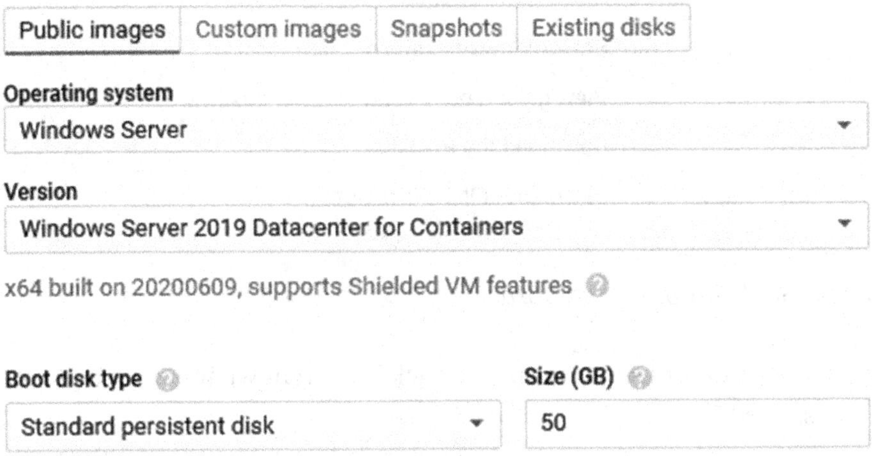

| Public images | Custom images | Snapshots | Existing disks |

**Operating system**

Windows Server

**Version**

Windows Server 2019 Datacenter for Containers

x64 built on 20200609, supports Shielded VM features

**Boot disk type**

Standard persistent disk

**Size (GB)**

50

**Figure 5-13.** *Boot disk*

As discussed in the previous section, you can also use the Container option and select a GCR or public image during the setup wizard, as shown in Figure 5-14.

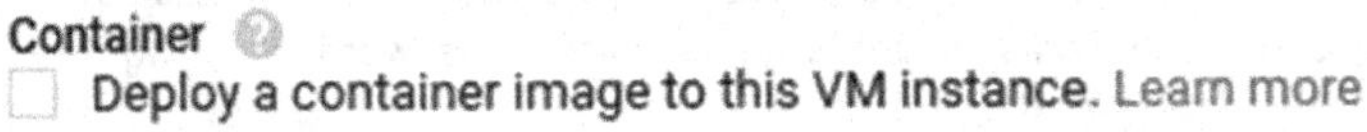

**Container**
Deploy a container image to this VM instance. Learn more

**Figure 5-14.** *Container option*

Once the VM is ready, it will appear under VM instances, as shown in Figure 5-15. Before you can connect to it, you need to set up a login password for your user account. Do that by clicking on the RDP button on the right side of the instance, under Connect.

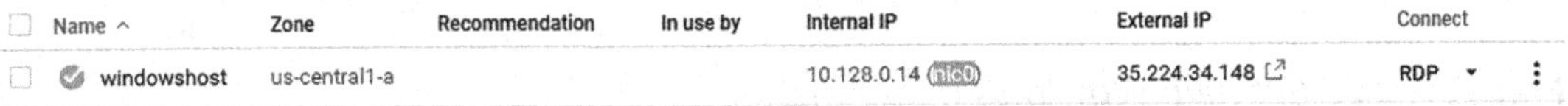

| Name ^ | Zone | Recommendation | In use by | Internal IP | External IP | Connect |
|---|---|---|---|---|---|---|
| windowshost | us-central1-a | | | 10.128.0.14 (nic0) | 35.224.34.148 | RDP ▾ |

**Figure 5-15.** *VM instance*

When you click on the RDP button, you will be presented with a few options to help you connect to the VM. The first thing you need is to select the first option, "Set Windows password," as shown in Figure 5-16.

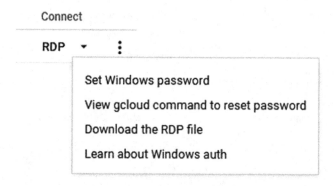

**Figure 5-16.**  *Set Windows password*

When the Set Password screen pops up, click Set, as shown in Figure 5-17, to generate a password.

## Set new Windows password

If a Windows account with the following username does not exist, it will be created and a new password assigned. If the account exists, its password will be reset.

> ⚠ If the account already exists, resetting the password can cause the loss of encrypted data secured with the current password, including files and stored passwords. Learn more

Username ⓘ

shimon2

CANCEL    SET

**Figure 5-17.**  *Set new Windows password*

To complete the new password setup, copy the password from the Password screen, as shown in Figure 5-18.

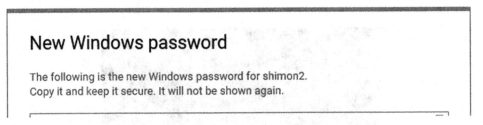

**New Windows password**

The following is the new Windows password for shimon2.
Copy it and keep it secure. It will not be shown again.

***Figure 5-18.*** *New password*

---

**Note**    Make sure you note the password down as you will not be able to retrieve it.

---

To connect, click on the Download the RDP file from the RDP button menu and open it. At the prompt, enter the RDP username and password and connect. The RDP screen is shown in Figure 5-19.

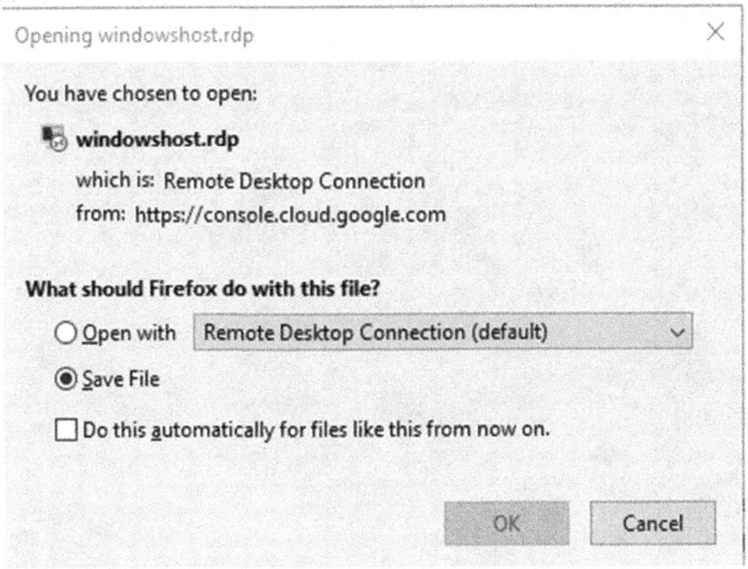

Opening windowshost.rdp                                                 ✕

You have chosen to open:

🗔 **windowshost.rdp**

    which is:  Remote Desktop Connection

    from:  https://console.cloud.google.com

**What should Firefox do with this file?**

◯ <u>O</u>pen with    | Remote Desktop Connection (default)              ⌄ |

◉ <u>S</u>ave File

☐ Do this <u>a</u>utomatically for files like this from now on.

                                                      OK        |    Cancel

***Figure 5-19.*** *RDP screen*

Once you log in, you will see that the Windows image comes equipped with Google Cloud SDK tools and gcloud. Figure 5-20 shows the Google Cloud SDK icon on the desktop.

***Figure 5-20.***  *Google Cloud SDK*

To run Docker commands, you can right-click on the Google Cloud SDK icon and click on Run as Administrator. Running Docker as administrator will allow Windows to use elevated permissions to run containers. You can see the Run as Administrator option in Figure 5-21.

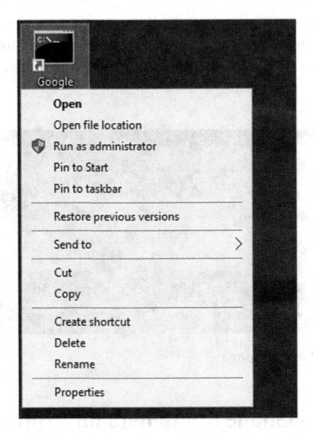

***Figure 5-21.*** *Run as administrator*

To check the installed Docker version, run the following command:

```
$ docker --version
```

# Deploy Windows Containers

Let's go ahead and have you deploy a Windows Server IIS Web Server using the public image that is available from Docker Hub. Start by pulling the IIS image using the following command:

```
$ docker pull mcr.microsoft.com/windows/servercore/iis
```

Once the image is downloaded, deploy your first image and make it available on port 80. Use the following command to run it:

```
$ docker run -it -p 80:80 mcr.microsoft.com/windows/servercore/iis
```

Once the container is deployed, open a web browser and test it by going to the VM's public IP address, which you can find on the Instance Details page. Also enable port 80 (HTTP) during the setup wizard. The end result appears in Figure 5-22, and as you can see, the IIS Welcome page is live.

***Figure 5-22.***  *IIS Welcome page*

# Deploy and Manage Containers on Azure VM (Linux and Windows)

In the last section of this chapter, we will go over some handy Docker management commands and strategies that will help you manage your container host. When you use Cloud Run and GKE, many administrative tasks are taken away from you because you don't have access to the underlying compute level, which is represented by the Docker host.

Let's start with some basic administrative tasks. To check your Docker engine version, run the following command:

```
$ docker version
```

# Update Docker on Linux

To update Docker on a Linux host, which in my case is CentOS, use the following process.

First, check for updates and list all the packages you are using with the following command:

```
yum check-update
```

In my case, I have the following Docker packages:

```
Docker-ce    - This is the Docker Engine community edition
Docker-ce-cli - This the Docker command engine
```

I can go ahead and update them individually by running the following commands:

```
yum update docker-ce
yum update docker-ce-cli
```

Or I can run the following command, which will update both of them in one go:

```
yum update docker*
```

# Update Docker on Windows

On Windows machines, run the following one-line PowerShell command, which will update Docker immediately:

```
$ Install-Package -Name Docker -ProviderName DockerMSFTProvider -Update -Force
```

---

**Note**   Please note that updating Docker will cause the Docker service to restart, and, as a result, all running containers will be restarted.

---

# Create and Map Volumes

To view all the volumes on your Docker host, use the following command:

```
$ docker volume ls
```

To create a new volume, use the following command:

```
$ docker volume create my-volume
```

Once the volume has been created, you can create a Docker container and map it using the following command:

```
$ docker container run -it -v my-volume:/app centos /bin/bash
```

In the preceding command, you are creating a container and mounting the my-volume volume to a directory called app. After creating the container, any data saved to the app directory will be available after the container is deleted. If a new container is created, you can map it to the same volume and use the data.

## Map Container Host Volume

You can also map a directory on the Docker container host to a container. In the following example, I mount the Docker host /home/admin/web directory to the directory called app inside the container. So any file saved into the app directory will actually be saved to the host.

```
$ docker container run -it -v /home/admin/web:/app centos /bin/sh
```

## Start a Docker Container in Bash

To start a Docker container with Bash Shell, run the following command:

```
$ docker container run -it  centos /bin/sh
```

## Expose Port

To export a port from a container to the outside world, you need to use the port command, which has a shortcut of -p. In the following example, I deploy an Apache web server with port 80 (HTTP) exposed to the outside world:

```
$ docker run -d --name apache-web -p 80:80 httpd:latest
```

# Create Image

There are times when you will need to create a custom Docker image and are installing or configuring an application before pushing Image to a Docker registry (public or private). After creating a container and installing all the necessary applications, you need to commit the image using a commit command. The following command will commit the image:

```
$ docker container commit webserver webserver-v1
```

The image in this example is called webserver, and here it is called webserver-v1. After the image has been committed, you can deploy a container using the following command:

```
$ docker container run -it --name server webserver-v1
```

You can also push it to a registry using the steps learned in Chapter 2.

# Install Docker Compose

To deploy an application using Docker Compose, you need to install Docker Compose first. By default, it is not installed with Docker CE or Enterprise.

In case you are not familiar with Docker Compose, it is used to deploy applications as a solution. For example, you can install a Docker application that has frontend and backend components that communicate with each other.

With Compose, you use a YAML file to deploy the application, and it is deployed as a stack with a single command. You run Compose from the directory of the YAML file.

To install Docker Compose, use the following commands:

```
$ curl -L "https://github.com/docker/compose/releases/download/1.25.5/
docker-compose-$(uname -s)-$(uname -m)" -o /usr/local/bin/docker-compose
$ chmod +x /usr/local/bin/docker-compose
$ ln -s /usr/local/bin/docker-compose /usr/bin/docker-compose
```

To check which version of Docker Compose it is, run the following command:

```
$ docker-compose --version
```

# Deploy a Docker Compose Application

In the following example, you will deploy WordPress with Docker Compose using the following YAML file.

---

**Note**    You can find this file in the code library of this book under the name 5.2.Wordpress.yaml.

---

5.2.Wordpress.yaml

```
version: '3.3'
services:
  db:
    image: mysql:5.7
    volumes:
      - db_data:/var/lib/mysql
    restart: always
    environment:
      MYSQL_ROOT_PASSWORD: enterpassword
      MYSQL_DATABASE: wp01
      MYSQL_USER: wordpress
      MYSQL_PASSWORD: wordpress

  wordpress:
    depends_on:
      - db
    image: wordpress:latest
    volumes:
      - wp_data:/var/www/html
    ports:
      - "80:80"
    restart: always
    environment:
      WORDPRESS_DB_HOST: db:3306
      WORDPRESS_DB_USER: wordpress
```

```
      WORDPRESS_DB_PASSWORD: wordpress
      WORDPRESS_DB_NAME: wp01
volumes:
   db_data: {}
   wp_data: {}
```

This will deploy a WordPress container and a MySQL container for the database. To start the deployment, create a folder for the app and name it any name you feel like. Copy the YAML file into the folder and run the following command:

```
$ docker-compose up -d
```

The command will start the deployment and create volumes for the application and database. To clean up the deployment and delete the containers, run the following command:

```
$ docker-compose down
```

To delete the containers and volumes, run the following command:

```
$ docker-compose down --volume
```

# Patch a Docker Image

If you need to maintain a custom image, you probably will also need to make sure the image is patched with the latest security updates. You patch a Docker image by running the image, installing the latest patches, and committing it.

The following commands will help you patch a Linux image. Let's start with first deploying an image:

```
$ docker run -it --name myserver centos
```

Before you use the -it switch, the image will log you into the container shell. From the shell, run the following command to check for updates:

```
yum check-update
```

From here, you can review which packages need updating and run the following command to update all packages:

```
yum update
```

To update a single package, you can use the following command:

```
yum install package
```

When the update is complete, you can commit the image using the following command:

```
$ docker commit webserver webservercore
```

## One-Line to Delete All Running and Non-running Containers

I don't know about you, but many times I find my container host running out of space because I have too many undeleted images. This is a common issue on development hosts. For that reason, you have the option to delete all the running and non-running containers using a one-line single image.

The following command will delete all the containers that you have on your host:

```
$ docker container rm -f $(docker container ls -aq)
```

## Delete Container on Exit

Another handy command is to delete the container on exit. This option is great if you need to test something quickly and get rid of the container.

The following command will delete the container on exit:

```
$ docker container run --rm -it centos /bin/sh
```

## Delete Unused Docker Images

Continuing with tidying up, you can use the following command to delete unused Docker images on your host:

```
Docker images prune -f
```

## Delete All Docker Volumes

To delete all the Docker volumes on your container host using a one-line command, you can use the following:

```
$ docker volume rm -f $(docker volume ls)
```

I recommend you use the delete commands on your development environment just to keep things tidy.

## View Changes in Docker Image

If you have a custom image and need to view all the changes that were made to it, Docker provides a great option. Using the following command, you can check all the changes that were made to a custom image called webserver:

```
$ docker container diff webserver
```

## Check Docker Image Build History

To view the build history of an image, use the history command, which will show you the change history of the build.

```
$ docker history webserver:latest
```

## Run Multiple Websites on Docker Using HTTP and HTTPS

The most common question people who run Docker and are planning to move it to production ask is, How do you host multiple websites that are using port HTTP or HTTPS on a single Docker host?

The short answer is that you must use a reverse proxy that will handle all the requests that come to the host and route each one to the correct container/website. At the beginning of this chapter, you deployed a container and opened port 80 on the container and host, which worked well but only helped you deploy one container and make it available externally. This will not work in an environment where you need to host more than one website, which is the case in most deployments.

The most common reverse proxy solution is Nginx, which we usually deploy as a container and use as an entry point for all HTTP or HTTPS requests using custom configuration; we route the traffic to the appropriate container/website.

In the following example, I am going to deploy two WordPress websites on a Docker host where both use port HTTP and HTTPS.

# Create Network

I will start with creating a Docker network for the reverse proxy using the following command:

```
$ docker network create wordpress
```

The following command will deploy the reverse proxy container using Nginx:

```
$ docker run --name nginx-proxy --net wordpress -p 80:80 -p 443:443 -v ~/
certs:/etc/nginx/certs -v /etc/nginx/vhost.d -v /usr/share/nginx/html -v
/var/run/docker.sock:/tmp/docker.sock:ro --label com.github.jrcs.
letsencrypt_nginx_proxy_companion.nginx_proxy -d --restart always jwilder/
nginx-proxy
```

# Deploy Letsencrypt

Because I am going to use port HTTPS for my deployment, I will use Letsencrypt as my certificate authority and create SSL certificates, as follows:

```
$ docker run --name letsencrypt-nginx-proxy-companion --net wordpress -v ~/
certs:/etc/nginx/certs:rw -v /var/run/docker.sock:/var/run/docker.sock:
ro --volumes-from nginx-proxy -d --restart always jrcs/letsencrypt-nginx-
proxy-companion
```

Next, I will deploy MySQL for my two WordPress applications.

# Create MySQL Database

```
$ docker run --name mysqlserver --net wordpress -v mysqldb01:/var/lib/mysql -e
MYSQL_ROOT_PASSWORD=SETROOTPASSWORD -e MYSQL_DATABASE=db1 -e MYSQL_
USER=db1user -e MYSQL_PASSWORD=MYQLPASSWORD -d --restart always mysql:5.7
```

# Deploy WordPress

Finally, I will deploy my website using the following command.

---

**Note**    I am using `www.website.local` as the URL, but in the real world you will use .COM or a public DNS domain.

---

```
$ docker run --name website01 --net wordpress -v website01:/var/www/
html -v ~/uploads.ini:/usr/local/etc/php/conf.d/uploads.ini -e WORDPRESS_
DB_HOST=mysqlserver:3306 -e WORDPRESS_DB_NAME=db1 -e WORDPRESS_DB_
USER=db1user -e WORDPRESS_DB_PASSWORD=MYQLPASSWORD -e VIRTUAL_HOST=www.
website01.local -e LETSENCRYPT_HOST=www.website01.local -e LETSENCRYPT_
EMAIL=emailaddress@yourdomain.local  -d --restart always wordpress
```

From here, I could use the same code to deploy another WordPress application, but using a different URL. The app can use the same MySQL server, or you can create another MySQL server.

# Summary

In this chapter, we covered a lot and learned how to deploy a Docker container host on Linux and Windows Server 2019. The main feature that we covered in Compute Engine was the container feature, which allows us to deploy a Docker image directly from the setup wizard, bypassing the need to deploy a container from inside the VM.

This is handy in case we have the need for a one-on-one deployment where one VM is used for a single container, which is not very common or cost-effective.

For the preceding reason, I have shown you in the last section how to run multiple websites that are using the same port (HTTP or HTTPS) on a single host.

We achieved that by using a reverse proxy container that handles all incoming requests and forwards them to the appropriate website based on the hostname of the website. These practices are well known on web servers without the use of Docker; however, doing the same thing on Docker requires a different configuration and tools.

We also covered many administrative tasks for keeping our Docker host healthy and tidy from unused images, volumes, and containers.

In the next chapter, we will secure your GCP environment and containers.

# CHAPTER 6

# Secure Your GCP Environment and Containers

In this chapter, we will focus on GCP security and, more specifically, how to secure your GCP environment.

GCP has a built-in security layer that, by default, is designed to give you a good base level of security without extra cost. The default protection helps by doing two things: first, giving a starting point and basic measurements that help protect you from external security risks like DoS attacks; and second, preventing you from making mistakes that can compromise your environment.

In this chapter, we will cover some best practices and various defense mechanisms, such as the following:

- Introduction to GCP identify infrastructure

- Audit logs

- Admin best practices

- Secret Manager API

- Firewalls

- Shielded VMs

## Introduction to GCP Identify Infrastructure

In this section, we will go over the core components of the GCP security layer, services, and offers.

© Shimon Ifrah 2021
S. Ifrah, *Getting Started with Containers in Google Cloud Platform*,
https://doi.org/10.1007/978-1-4842-6470-6_6

# Audit Logs

The most fundamental component of any security layer is the audit logs. Audit logs give you the power to monitor, capture, and analyze changes in your environment. Without audit logs, it is impossible to get insight into your cloud environments and changes that occurred. The logs can tell you when a change was made and who made the change. They can be archived and kept for many years. In some countries and sectors, by law enterprises must keep audit logs for many years in case of a data breach.

## GCP Cloud Audit Logs

When it comes to GCP, Google has an innovative approach to handling logs. GCP logs are divided into three main logs:

- Data access
- Admin activities and access
- System events

Using these three logs, you can get insight into what was accessed, who accessed it, and where. Logs are maintained for each project, folder, and GCP organization. Currently, 90 percent of GCP services offer audit logs, and I believe that very soon every service will offer the option for audit logs.

## Default Configuration

By default, admin activity and system events logs are enabled on the organization, folder, and project levels without any admin configuration. The only audit log that is not enabled by default is the data access log. These logs can be large in size and cost extra because of the storage usage involved.

## View Logs

Let's explore how to access audit logs. From the GCP management console, click on the Logging icon on the left navigation menu. You can see the Logging icon in Figure 6-1.

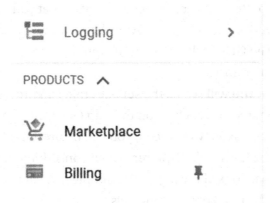

***Figure 6-1.*** *Logging icon*

# Use Query Builder

When it comes to viewing logs, first you need to build a query and be specific with the data you are trying to get. To be more specific about which data you are trying to view, use the Query Builder menu, as shown in Figure 6-2.

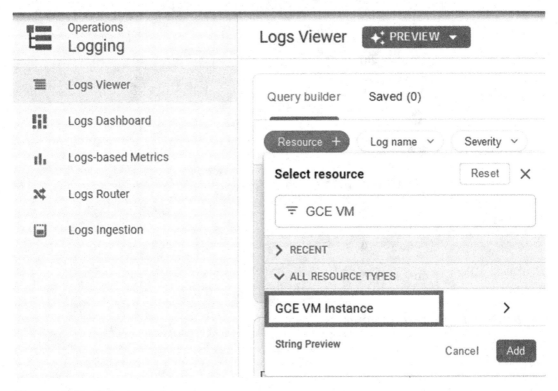

***Figure 6-2.*** *Select service*

Using the Resource button, you can select the service that you would like to view logs for. In my case, I am going to select the GCE VM Instance, which stands for Google Compute Engine. We used GCE in the previous chapter, where we created Linux and Windows Docker container hosts.

If you expand the list, you will see all the services that can provide audit logs.

After adding the resource and clicking on the Run Query button that is located at the top-right corner of the Log Viewer screen, you will be presented with the logs. In Figure 6-3 you can see the Logs Field Explorer, which consolidates all the logs' details and groups the various sections of the logs. For example, you can see that GCE generated 1,171 entries, as well as the breakdown of the logs.

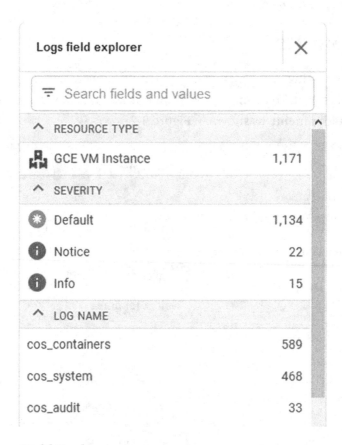

***Figure 6-3.*** *Logs Field Explorer*

The main screen. and what we are really after, shows the actual log entries for the audit log. The entries are action-by-action detailed results of what, when, and who accessed, created, and modified objects on GCE. Figure 6-4 shows the Query Results screen.

| Query results | | | Jump to Now |
|---|---|---|---|
| SEVERITY | TIMESTAMP | AEST ▾ | SUMMARY |
| > ⚙ | 2020-06-18 19:48:21.673 AEST | | "{"status":"Extracting","progressDetail":{"current":79659008,"total":192210881},"progress":"[= |
| > ⚙ | 2020-06-18 19:48:21.673 AEST | | "{"status":"Extracting","progressDetail":{"current":82444288,"total":192210881},"progress":"[= |
| > ⚙ | 2020-06-18 19:48:21.673 AEST | | "{"status":"Extracting","progressDetail":{"current":85229568,"total":192210881},"progress":"[= |
| > ⚙ | 2020-06-18 19:48:21.673 AEST | | "{"status":"Extracting","progressDetail":{"current":88014848,"total":192210881},"progress":"[= |
| > ⚙ | 2020-06-18 19:48:21.673 AEST | | "{"status":"Extracting","progressDetail":{"current":90800128,"total":192210881},"progress":"[= |
| > ⚙ | 2020-06-18 19:48:21.673 AEST | | "{"status":"Extracting","progressDetail":{"current":93585408,"total":192210881},"progress":"[= |
| > ⚙ | 2020-06-18 19:48:21.673 AEST | | "{"status":"Extracting","progressDetail":{"current":97484800,"total":192210881},"progress":"[= |
| > ⚙ | 2020-06-18 19:48:21.673 AEST | | "{"status":"Extracting","progressDetail":{"current":101384192,"total":192210881},"progress":"[ |

***Figure 6-4.*** *Query results*

Another interesting detail of information logging gives us is the histogram graph, which shows the time the logs were generated and how many entries there are. Figure 6-5 shows the histogram graph.

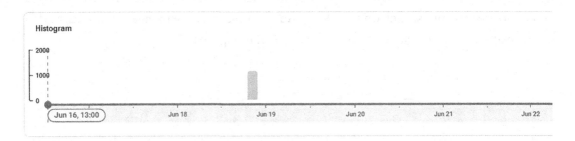

***Figure 6-5.*** *Histogram*

In Figure 6-6, you can see the entire screen of the Logs Viewer console, which is in preview and probably will go live by the time this book gets published.

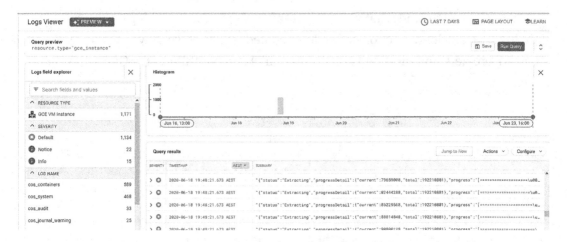

**Figure 6-6.**  *Logs Viewer console*

I believe it takes time to perfect the console and get around all the options it gives us, and I know that in the beginning, it can be a bit overwhelming to get used to it, but it is best to start small with simple output before trying to cross-check logs from different services.

# Change Default Logging

As I mentioned earlier in this chapter, GCP has default logging settings that apply on the tenant level. However, you can change these settings and add new ones. To change the default logging settings, click on the IAM & Admin link from the navigation menu, and on the expanded menu, select "Audit logs," shown in Figure 6-7.

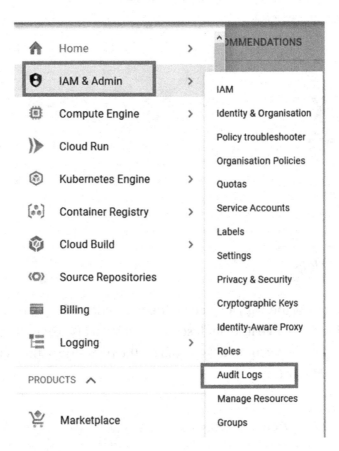

***Figure 6-7.***  *Audit logs*

From the Audit Logs page, you can scroll down and view all the available services that offer audit log options. If you look at the list, there are fifty-nine pages of GCP services and APIs that allow you to tap into their logs. Figure 6-8 shows the Audit Logs page.

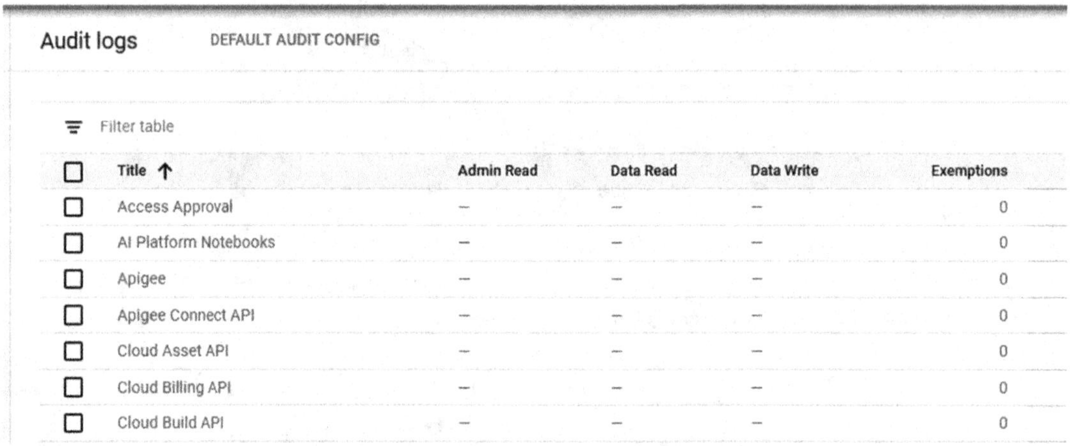

| Audit logs | DEFAULT AUDIT CONFIG | | | | |
| --- | --- | --- | --- | --- | --- |

| Title ↑ | Admin Read | Data Read | Data Write | Exemptions |
| --- | --- | --- | --- | --- |
| Access Approval | – | – | – | 0 |
| AI Platform Notebooks | – | – | – | 0 |
| Apigee | – | – | – | 0 |
| Apigee Connect API | – | – | – | 0 |
| Cloud Asset API | – | – | – | 0 |
| Cloud Billing API | – | – | – | 0 |
| Cloud Build API | – | – | – | 0 |

*Figure 6-8.*  *Audit logs*

If you click on one of the logs, located on the right side of the page, you will see that you have the option to change its default settings. You can also exempt users from being audited by clicking on the Exempted Users tab on the right side of the Access Approval menu, as shown in Figure 6-9.

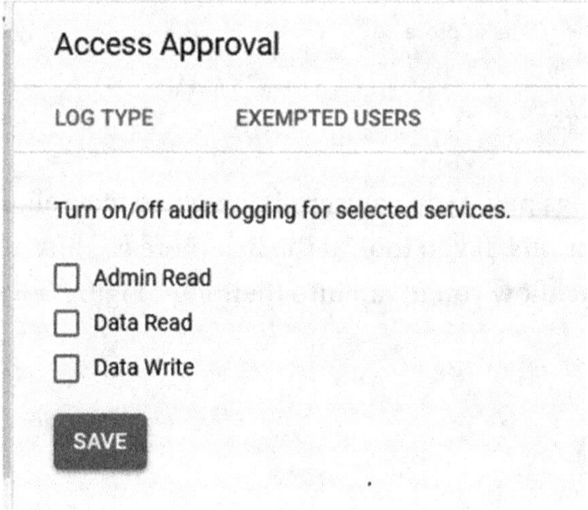

**Access Approval**

LOG TYPE        EXEMPTED USERS

Turn on/off audit logging for selected services.

☐ Admin Read
☐ Data Read
☐ Data Write

SAVE

*Figure 6-9.*  *Access Approval menu*

# Organization Administrators

In GCP, there are the following three levels of management:

- Organization

- Project

- Folder

In this book, we have discussed projects a great deal, which are the most common objects in GCP. However, in large GCP environments, you have the option to manage and set up policies on the organization level.

The organization level is the highest level of management in GCP, and any policy or setting that is configured on this level applies to all projects and folders. For that reason, you need to be very careful with how you handle permissions and who has permission to make org-level changes.

Let's go ahead and review the process that you need to use to give administrators organization-level permissions. In this example, I will go ahead and add a user to the Organization Administrator role, which gives permission to modify settings and policies on the organization level.

Open the IAM & Admin console and select the user you would like to add to the Organization Administrator role. Figure 6-10 shows the IAM & Admin console.

| 🛡 | IAM & Admin | IAM | +👤 ADD | -👤 REMOVE |
| :-: | :-- | :-- | :-- | :-- |
| +👤 | IAM | PERMISSIONS | RECOMMENDATIONS LOG | |
| 😀 | Identity & Organisation | These permissions affect this project and all of its resources. Learn more | | |
| ⚒ | Policy troubleshooter | View By:   MEMBERS    ROLES | | |

***Figure 6-10.***  *IAM & Admin console*

From the User Permission menu, click on the Add Another Role button and select "Organization Administrator" from the Role list. Click Save to apply the configuration, as shown in Figure 6-11.

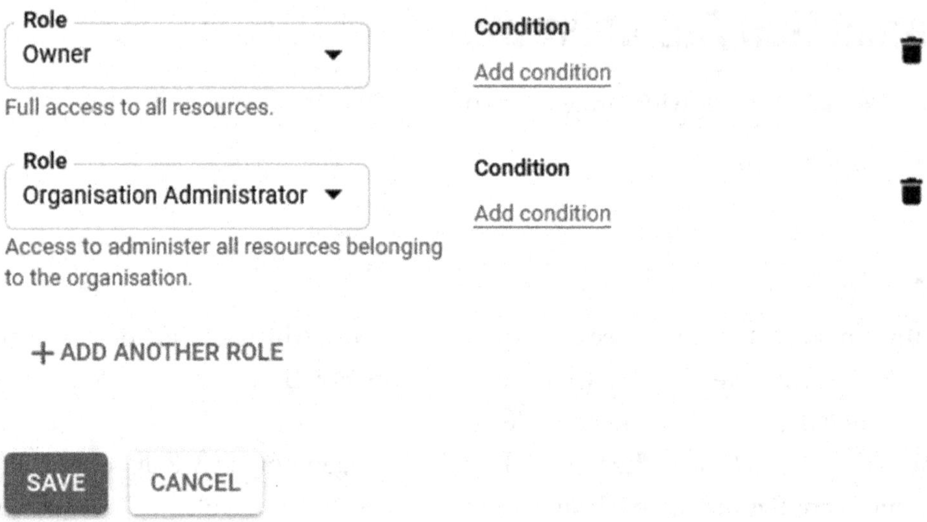

**Role**

Owner    ▼

Full access to all resources.

**Condition**

Add condition

🗑

**Role**

Organisation Administrator    ▼

Access to administer all resources belonging to the organisation.

**Condition**

Add condition

🗑

**+ ADD ANOTHER ROLE**

SAVE    CANCEL

**Figure 6-11.**  *Roles*

# Secret Manager API

GCP Secret Manager allows you to centralize all of your passwords, certificates, API secrets, login information, and sensitive data. Secret Manager accomplishes this by creating an encrypted security vault that protects all the data and thoroughly audits any read, write, or access request to the vault.

The cost of the service is based on the number of secret operations. The current cost is $0.02 USD per 10,000 operations, which is not much at all for such a valuable service.

Many businesses are struggling to maintain passwords, certificates, and other login information because the data is not centralized or protected. Secret Manager provides a secure, structured, and scalable solution for such a problem at a low price.

## Create a Secret

Let's go ahead and create a secret for a login password to a virtual machine or a service, which is a very common scenario. From the GCP console, search for Secret Manager API and open the console. From the Secret Manager API console, click Enable, as shown in Figure 6-12.

***Figure 6-12.*** *Enable Secret Manager API*

After enabling the service, go ahead and create a secret using the Create Secret button, as shown in Figure 6-13.

***Figure 6-13.*** *Create a secret*

Another thing you will notice is that on the left navigation menu of Secret Manager the many security services GCP offers are listed. Figure 6-14 shows the Security Services menu. We will not get to all of them in this chapter or book, but I believe it is good to know what GCP offers in terms of security.

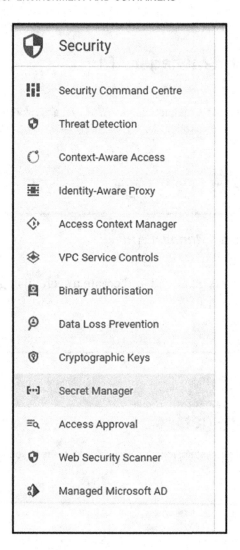

*Figure 6-14.* *GCP security services*

From the Create Secret page, you can add the password, username, or certificate information. In Figure 6-15, you have the option to upload a certificate, which can be a private key (PFX) or a public key (CER). You can also just type a password to a virtual machine, service, or application using the secret value.

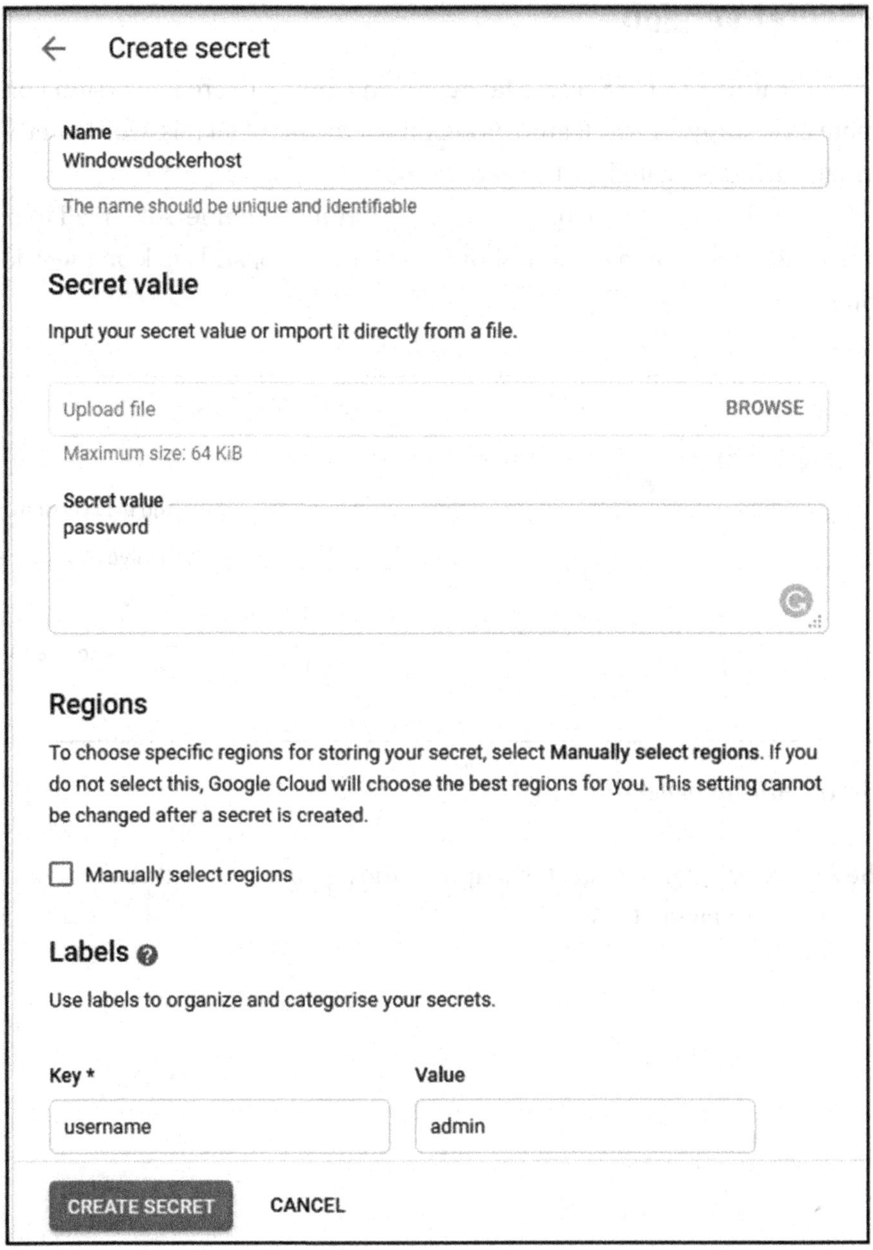

*Figure 6-15.*  *Create a secret*

You also have the option to select the region in which the secret will be stored, or to let GCP decide for you, which is the default option. You can also use the labels option to specify any setting that you like; in my case, I use the admin label for the username field.

# Create Secret Version

Another great feature of GCP Secret Manager is the ability to create version control. The ultimate case study for this feature is keeping a record of all passwords, certificates, and information that is related to the secret.

Let's say I need to update the password of my virtual machine. All I need to do is click on the action menu of my secret, shown in Figure 6-16, and click on the Add New Version option.

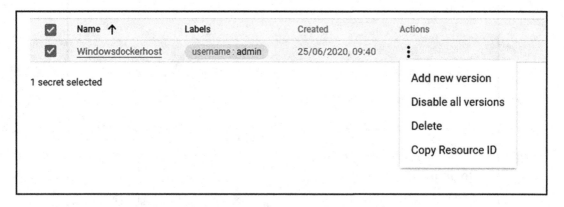

***Figure 6-16.***   *Add new version*

On the Add New Version page, I will update the secret value and click on Add New Version, as shown in Figure 6-17.

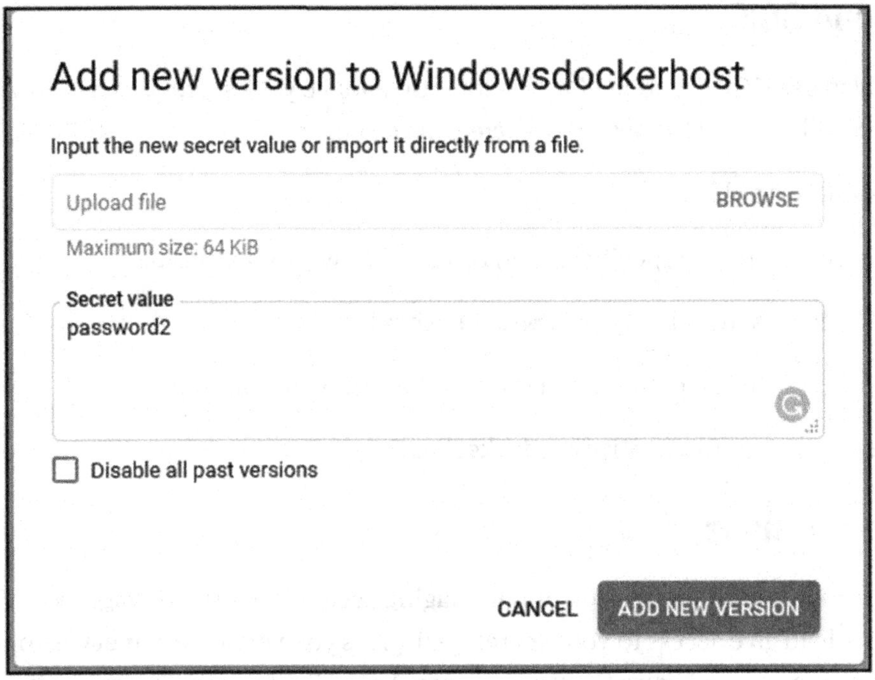

## Add new version to Windowsdockerhost

Input the new secret value or import it directly from a file.

| Upload file | BROWSE |
|---|---|

Maximum size: 64 KiB

Secret value
password2

☐ Disable all past versions

CANCEL    **ADD NEW VERSION**

***Figure 6-17.*** *Add new version*

If I go back and click on the Secret Details page, I will see all the versions of the secret with time and date.

This feature allows you to fully manage and understand the lifecycle of any secret you have. Figure 6-18 shows the versions of my secret.

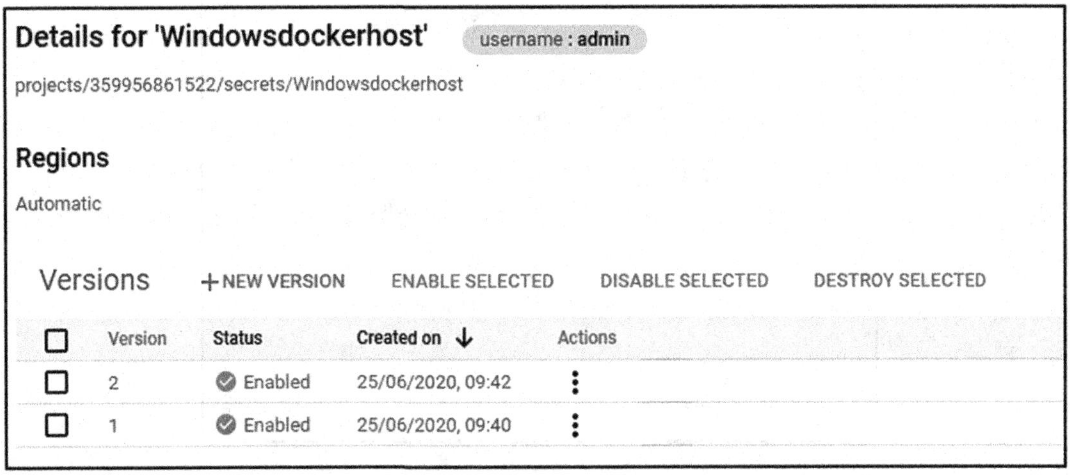

## Details for 'Windowsdockerhost'    username : admin

projects/359956861522/secrets/Windowsdockerhost

### Regions

Automatic

### Versions    + NEW VERSION    ENABLE SELECTED    DISABLE SELECTED    DESTROY SELECTED

| | Version | Status | Created on ↓ | Actions |
|---|---|---|---|---|
| ☐ | 2 | ✓ Enabled | 25/06/2020, 09:42 | ⋮ |
| ☐ | 1 | ✓ Enabled | 25/06/2020, 09:40 | ⋮ |

***Figure 6-18.*** *Versions*

## Use Cloud SDK

You can also use GCP Cloud SDK and gcloud to manage your secrets. The following command will show all the available secrets in your project.

```
$ gcloud secrets list
```

To list the details of a specific secret, run the following command:

```
$ gcloud secrets describe Windowsdockerhost
```

And finally, you can delete a secret using the following command:

```
$ gcloud secrets delete Windowsdockerhost
```

## IAM Permissions

When it comes to GCP permission and managing access to Secret Manager, you can use a built-in role to give access to your secret. GCP gives you very granular access options to Secret Manager, and in Figure 6-19 you can see the available roles. You can give viewer-only and edit permissions.

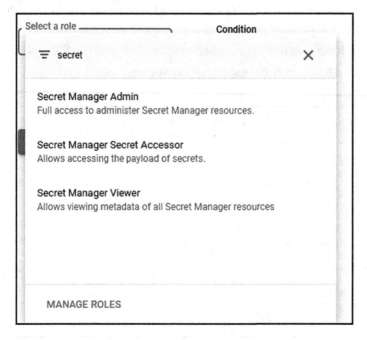

***Figure 6-19.*** *IAM roles for Secret Manager*

## Secret Manager Audit Logs

One of the most important features of Secret Manager is the ability to audit access to secrets with time, location, and data. Following our look at GCP audit logs earlier in this chapter, you can create a query that outputs all the operations of Secret Manager. Figure 6-20 shows the Secret Manager API audit logs, located in the Resource query menu. From the Resource menu, click on Audited Resource and select Secret Manager API.

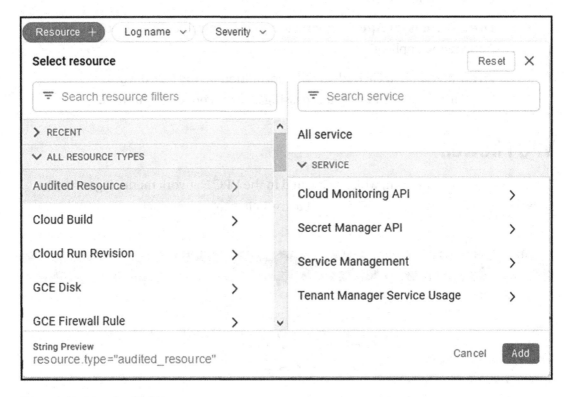

*Figure 6-20.* *Audit logs*

# Firewall

In this section, we are going to focus on GCP firewall services and see how to use the extra security layer to protect infrastructure.

By design, every GCP resource sits inside a virtual private network that is governed by a firewall that controls which traffic is allowed and denied. In GCP, all incoming traffic is disabled by default except ICMP traffic (ping).

Regardless of what changes you make on your tenant level, project level, or folder level, GCP has an infrastructure-level global firewall network that blocks malicious traffic. As a client, you have no control over this.

The GCP firewall offering is separated into the following services:

- **VPC firewall:** This firewall helps you create firewall rules that apply to your VPC.

- **Firewall policies:** These policies can be applied on a folder, project, or organization level.

- **Firewall rules for App Engine:** These rules control traffic into our App Engine applications.

- **Firewall Insights:** Gives detailed information on the logs of your firewall rules and traffic that is passing into and out of the firewall.

# VPC Firewall

Let's review the VPC firewall, which is located in the VPC Network menu. Figure 6-21 shows the VPC firewall, which is attached to my `Web-project` project.

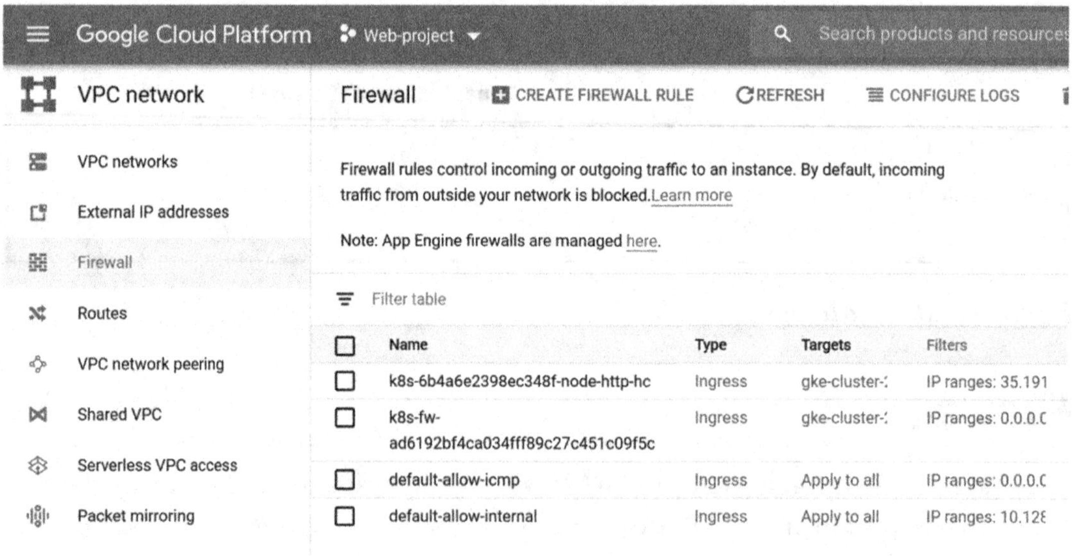

***Figure 6-21.*** *VPC firewall*

From the Firewall page, I can create a new firewall rule or delete existing rules that were created when provisioning the GCP service. In my case, and as shown in Figure 6-21, I can see the rules that were created for the GKE cluster deployed in Chapter 4.

---

**Note**    It is a good idea to review the firewall every few months and clean up unused rules.

---

By clicking on any of the rules, I will be redirected to the Firewall Rule Details page, where I have the option to modify the rule or enable logging. Figure 6-22 shows the Firewall Rule Details page.

←    Firewall rule details      ✏ EDIT     🗑 DELETE

**default-allow-icmp**

Description
Allow ICMP from anywhere

**Logs**
Turning on firewall logs can generate a large number of logs; this can increase costs in Stackdriver.Learn more
○ On
◉ Off

**Network**
default

Priority *
65534     ❓
Priority can be 0–65535Check priority of other firewall rules

**Direction**
Ingress

**Action on match**
Allow

Targets
All instances in the network     ▼

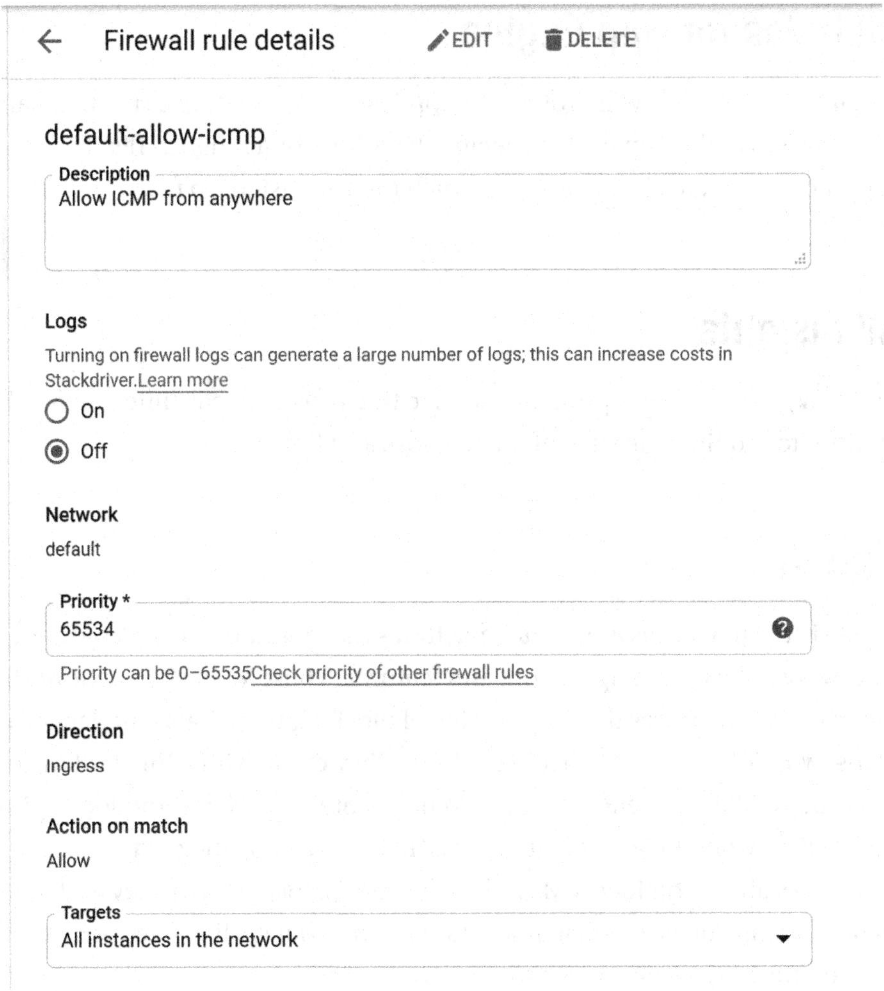

*Figure 6-22.* *Firewall Rule Details page*

It is important to note that, by default, Firewall logging is disabled. Enabling logging on a firewall rule can increase the cost of your GCP billing as logs consume a lot of data.

## Firewall Policies

Firewall policies allow you to expand the GCP firewall service and apply rules at the organization and folder levels. A firewall policy can allow, block, or defer connections from any network; once a rule has been created all resources in the organization will inherit it. A folder-level firewall policy will do the same thing but will apply at the folder level.

## Firewall Rules for App Engine

The App Engine firewall rules will protect the application by creating a rule that can block or allow access to the app from a specific IP address or a range of IPs. The most important part of these rules is the order in which they are listed, so make sure you order them correctly.

## Firewall Insights

The Firewall Insights service is a proactive service that provides real-time diagnostics, with capabilities to monitor the state of the network and firewall.

## Shielded VMs

GCP shielded virtual machines are virtual machines that contain and are configured with extra security policies, configuration, and features. These VMs offer state-of-the-art and advanced security features that are capable of blocking malicious and dangerous attacks against workloads running inside the VMs. They come with a Virtual Trusted Platform Module (vTPM) that encrypts the VM on a storage level; if someone copies the VHD of the VM they won't be able to attach it as a disk and copy the data.

The great news about shielded VMs is that they don't cost extra money and are charged as normal instances. It is also important to note that GKE worker nodes will start to use shielded VMs by default.

# Create Shielded VM

You create a shielded VM using the same steps you used to create a normal VM; however, to enable the shielded VM feature, you need to use the Security tab under the Firewall section. You can see the Shielded VM setting in Figure 6-23.

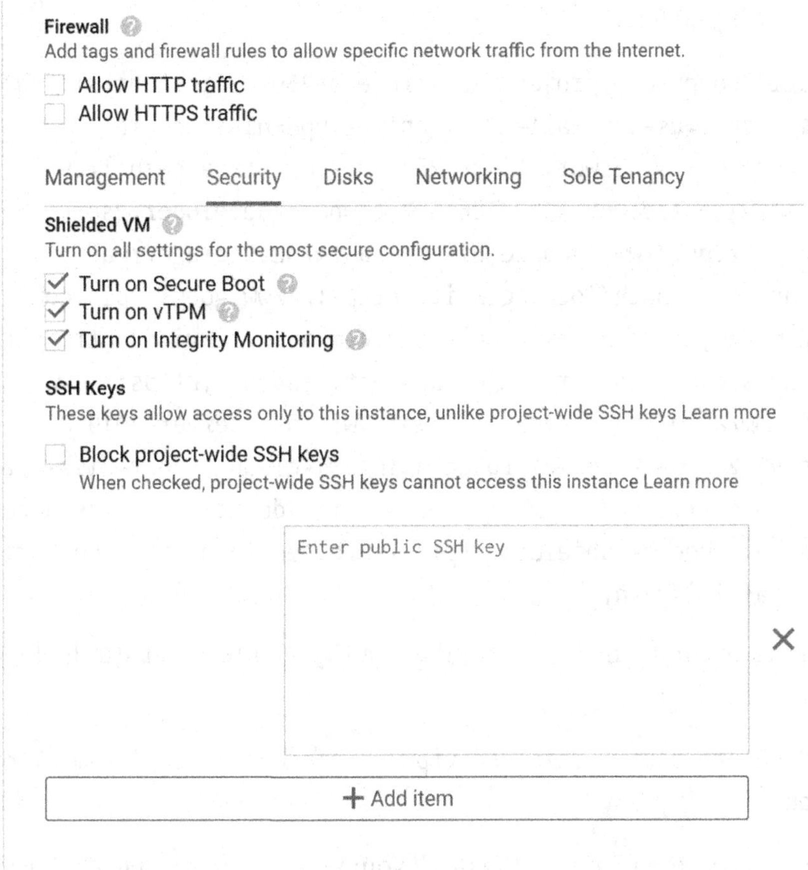

**Firewall** ⑦
Add tags and firewall rules to allow specific network traffic from the Internet.

☐ Allow HTTP traffic
☐ Allow HTTPS traffic

Management   Security   Disks   Networking   Sole Tenancy

**Shielded VM** ⑦
Turn on all settings for the most secure configuration.

☑ Turn on Secure Boot ⑦
☑ Turn on vTPM ⑦
☑ Turn on Integrity Monitoring ⑦

**SSH Keys**
These keys allow access only to this instance, unlike project-wide SSH keys Learn more

☐ Block project-wide SSH keys
   When checked, project-wide SSH keys cannot access this instance Learn more

```
Enter public SSH key
```
✕

＋ Add item

*Figure 6-23.*  *Shielded VM*

The main features appear under Security and are as follows:

- **Secure Boot:** Prevents any malicious code from accessing the boot sequence of the VM and accessing data.

- **vTPM:** As mentioned earlier, this allows you to encrypt your data and prevent it from being mapped as the virtual disk.

- **Integrity monitoring:** Using GCP monitoring tools, the boot process is monitored in case someone tries to access the data during boot time.

## Create a Shielded VM Using Cloud Shell

You can also use the Cloud Shell and gcloud command line to create a shielded VM using the following code:

```
$ gcloud beta compute --project=web-project-269903 instances create
instance-1 --zone=us-central1-a --machine-type=n1-standard-
2 --subnet=default --network-tier=PREMIUM --maintenance-policy=
MIGRATE --service-account=359956861522-compute@developer.gserviceaccount.
com --scopes=https://www.googleapis.com/auth/devstorage.read_only,https://
www.googleapis.com/auth/logging.write,https://www.googleapis.com/auth/
monitoring.write,https://www.googleapis.com/auth/servicecontrol,https://
www.googleapis.com/auth/service.management.readonly,https://www.
googleapis.com/auth/trace.append --image=windows-server-2019-dc-for-
containers-v20200609 --image-project=windows-cloud --boot-disk-size=
50GB --boot-disk-type=pd-standard --boot-disk-device-name=instance-1 --
shielded-secure-boot --shielded-vtpm --shielded-integrity-monitoring --
reservation-affinity=any
```

The important commands to enable the security feature to make a shielded VM, in gcloud code, are as follows:

```
--shielded-secure-boot --shielded-vtpm --shielded-integrity-monitoring --
reservation-affinity=any
```

It is highly recommended you deploy all your workloads as shielded VMs; however, I think that in the future the default VM option will be shielded. These VMs provide excellent security features at the same cost as a normal VM, so there is no reason not to use it unless you have an application limit that prevents you from enabling it.

## Admin Best Practices

In the last section of this chapter, I would like to outline some best practices that can help you keep your GCP admin account or accounts safe and sound from malicious access.

# Use Separate Organizations Admin Account

It is highly recommended that you create a separate user account with organization administrator permissions and another account for day-to-day administration. Using one account with org admin permissions and admin permissions to all the GCP services gives the account too much access that spreads across the organization, project, and folder levels. If an account with that level of permissions gets compromised, the entire tenant data and configuration is in major danger.

In large organizations, two people should have org admin permissions, and no more than five users will have admin permissions to all resources. All other accounts should utilize role-level permissions, which will reduce the attack surface of the organization.

# Multi-Factor Authentication

Without any exceptions, all users that have access to the GCP management console should have MFA enabled. It has been proven time after time that MFA prevents 80 percent of security and identity failures in the environment.

# User Roles

When setting up new users like developers, admins, DBs, and more, you should use the built-in roles that GCP offers. The roles allow users to work on the workloads they are supposed to work on without accessing GCP resources that are beyond their job role.

# Summary

In this chapter, we learned about some of the GCP security features that span services like identity, virtual machines, logs, and secret management.

I encourage you to review all the security services GCP has to offer to better safeguard your GCP infrastructure, as more and more features are being introduced to the platform.

In the next chapter, we will move on to scaling containers and applications.

# CHAPTER 7

# Scaling

In this chapter, we are going to learn how to scale containers, workloads, and hosts in GCP. Scaling is a very important part of any deployment and infrastructure, and these days the process has become easier as more services offer dynamic scaling, also known as auto-scaling.

The main focus of this chapter will be on scaling, primarily examining auto-scaling and not manual scaling of hosts and workloads. During this chapter, we are going to look at the following topics:

- Scaling Google Kubernetes Service (GKE)

- Scaling Cloud Run and Cloud Build containers

- Scaling GCP Container Registry

- Scaling Compute Engine hosts

## Scale Google Kubernetes Service (GKE)

If you remember Chapter 4, we have learned about GKE and how to deploy applications to a GKE cluster. We also covered the deployment process for a GKE cluster using the GCP console and Cloud SDK.

When it comes to GKE clusters, Google gives you the option to use auto-scaling and let your cluster manage the process of scaling up or down based on the utilization of the cluster.

## GKE Cluster Autoscaler

Google calls the process of automatically and dynamically scaling a GKE cluster GKECluster Autoscaler. Autoscaler resizes the number of nodes in the node pool of a cluster without our doing anything. This process is seamless, hands-free, human-free, and accurate in resource allocation.

189

© Shimon Ifrah 2021
S. Ifrah, *Getting Started with Containers in Google Cloud Platform*,
https://doi.org/10.1007/978-1-4842-6470-6_7

Any IT or software architect will tell you that manual scaling is a challenging process, and in most cases, organizations over-scale their infrastructure.

When using Autoscaler, the GKE cluster is resized up or down when needed. It also allows you to better manage your costs and resource allocation. When you configure Autoscaler, you have the option to set the minimum and the maximum number of nodes in the node pool.

## Auto-Scaling Profiles

The Autoscaler's decision to scale resources is also based on the auto-scaling profile you configure. Scaling profiles are based on the following two profiles:

- **Balanced:** This is the default profile that GKE will use when using Autoscaler.

- **Optimize-utilization:** This profile is very cost oriented and will try to keep the cost of running your cluster as low as possible by scaling down the cluster as soon as possible; however, this is not recommended for most environments, because of the aggressive nature of the profile, which prioritizes cost and not performance.

## Enable GKE Cluster Autoscaler Using GKE Console

Now that we understand the concept of Autoscaler, let's see where and how to configure it. The Autoscaler configuration is located in the Create a Kubernetes cluster window, in the default-pool configuration, as shown in Figure 7-1. In the default-pool configuration, you need to tick the checkbox next to "Enable auto-scaling." Once you do so, you will see the option to set the minimum and maximum number of nodes in the cluster. The default configuration is 0 and 3 nodes.

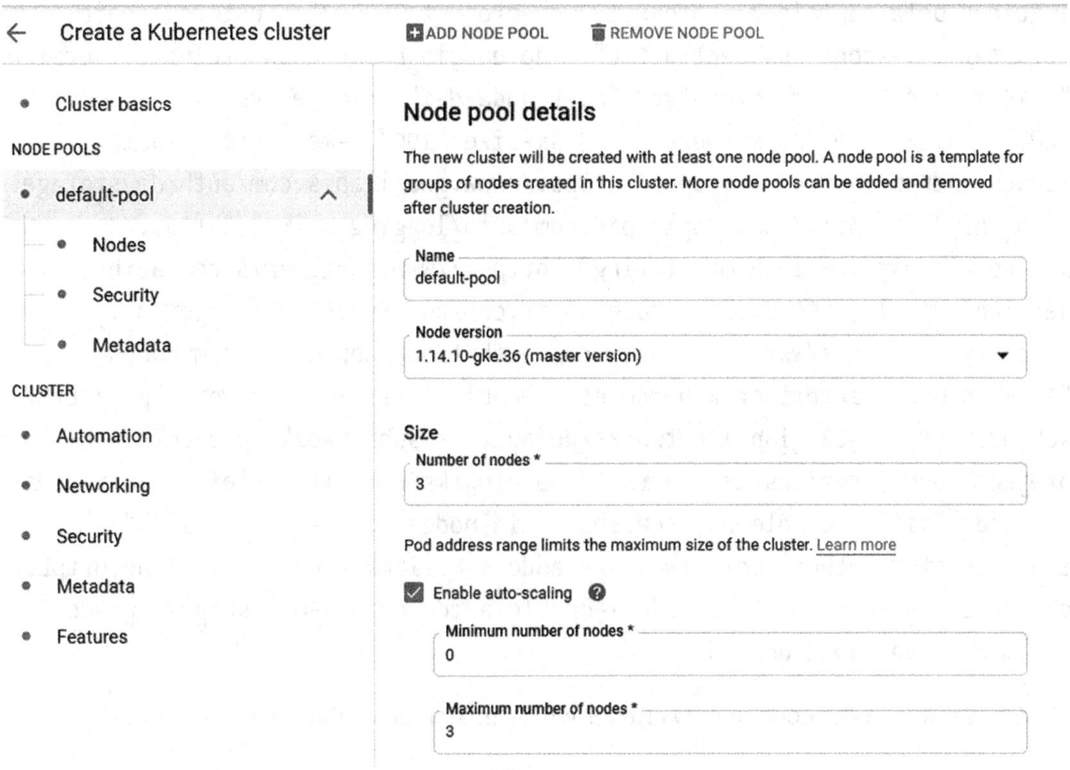

**Figure 7-1.**  *Auto-scaling*

If you were to use Cloud SDK and gcloud to enable Autoscaler, you would use the following command switches:

```
--enable-autoscaling --min-nodes 0 --max-nodes 3
```

# Enable Autoscaler Using Cloud SDK and gcloud

To create a new GKE cluster with Autoscaler configured, use the following command:

---

**Note**   The following code is located in the code library under the name 7.1.GKE_ Autoscaler.

---

```
$ gcloud beta container --project "web-project-269903" clusters create
"cluster-1" --zone "us-central1-c" --no-enable-basic-auth --cluster-version
"1.14.10-gke.36" --machine-type "n1-standard-1" --image-type
"COS" --disk-type "pd-standard" --disk-size "100" --metadata disable-
legacy-endpoints=true --scopes "https://www.googleapis.com/auth/devstorage.
read_only","https://www.googleapis.com/auth/logging.write","https://
www.googleapis.com/auth/monitoring","https://www.googleapis.com/auth/
servicecontrol","https://www.googleapis.com/auth/service.management.
readonly","https://www.googleapis.com/auth/trace.append" --num-nodes
"3" --enable-stackdriver-kubernetes --enable-ip-alias --network "projects/
web-project-269903/global/networks/default" --subnetwork "projects/web-
project-269903/regions/us-central1/subnetworks/default" --default-max-pods-
per-node "110" --enable-autoscaling --min-nodes "0" --max-nodes "3" --no-
enable-master-authorized-networks --addons HorizontalPodAutoscaling,HttpLoa
dBalancing --enable-autoupgrade --enable-autorepair --max-surge-upgrade
1 --max-unavailable-upgrade 0
```

Once you run the code, a new cluster with Autoscaler enabled will be created.

## Enable Autoscaler on Existing GKE Cluster

Can you enable Autoscaler on an existing GKE cluster? Yes, you can; however, please note that enabling Autoscaler will cause the master node to restart, so please schedule this change to after hours.

## Horizontal vs. Vertical Pod Autoscaler

Before we get into the details of each of the two scalings (horizontal and vertical), let's first understand what they do.

Horizontal Scaling: Scale the number of pods in the deployment

Vertical Scaling: Scale the actual pod resources (CPU and memory)

The main difference between the two is that horizontal scaling increases the number of pods in the deployment, while vertical will increase the resources of the existing pods without adding more pods.

# Vertical Pod Auto-scaling

Moving from nodes to pods, GKE has another great feature that removes the need to figure out a pod's load and resource allocation. With Vertical Pod Autoscaling (VPA), GKE handles the resource allocation of pods and automatically scales pods up and down.

It is highly important and recommended you use VPA with GKE Cluster Autoscaler otherwise your cluster will run out of resources.

# Enable VPA on GKE Cluster Using Console

To enable VPA on a GKE cluster, you need to enable it during the setup stage or after. The VPA configuration is located under the Cluster Automation section, as shown in Figure 7-2.

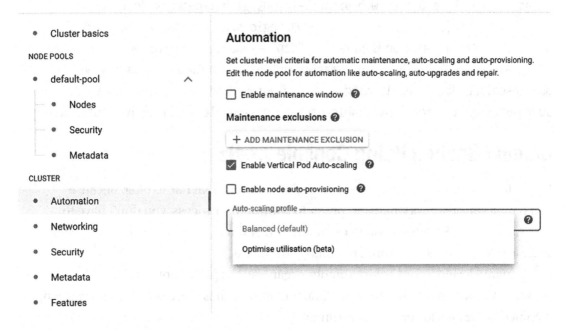

***Figure 7-2.***  *Auto-scaling profile*

You will also use the Auto-scaling profile section under the VPA settings, and, as shown, the Balanced profile is the default profile.

# Enable VPA Using Cloud SDK and gcloud

The following code, which also appears in the code library under 7.2.GKE_VPA, will create a new GKE cluster with both GKE Cluster Autoscaler and VPA enabled:

```
$ gcloud beta container --project "web-project-269903" clusters create
"cluster-1" --zone "us-central1-c" --no-enable-basic-auth --cluster-version
"1.14.10-gke.36" --machine-type "n1-standard-1" --image-type "COS" --disk-type
"pd-standard" --disk-size "100" --metadata disable-legacy-endpoints=
true --scopes "https://www.googleapis.com/auth/devstorage.read_only","https://
www.googleapis.com/auth/logging.write","https://www.googleapis.com/auth/
monitoring","https://www.googleapis.com/auth/servicecontrol","https://www.
googleapis.com/auth/service.management.readonly","https://www.googleapis.com/
auth/trace.append" --num-nodes "3" --enable-stackdriver-kubernetes --enable-ip-
alias --network "projects/web-project-269903/global/networks/default" --
subnetwork "projects/web-project-269903/regions/us-central1/subnetworks/
default" --default-max-pods-per-node "110" --enable-autoscaling --min-nodes
"0" --max-nodes "3" --no-enable-master-authorized-networks --addons HorizontalP
odAutoscaling,HttpLoadBalancing --enable-autoupgrade --enable-autorepair --max-
surge-upgrade 1 --max-unavailable-upgrade 0 --enable-vertical-pod-autoscaling
```

# Manual Scaling Using Console (resize)

If you don't want to use any of the auto-scaling options GKE has to offer, because you have a sensitive workload and prefer to control this process, you don't have to use Autoscaler. GKE allows you to manually add and remove nodes from the cluster whenever you want and without too many limitations.

In many development environments, organizations prefer not to use auto-scaling because the workloads are not important, and many times there is a focus on cost when it comes to the development environment.

Either way, the choice is yours, and you can start with or without auto-scaling.

---

**Note**    The correct terminology for GKE cluster manual scaling is resizing.

---

To resize a cluster using the console, open the GKE console and click on the edit symbol (the pencil) located on the right side of the cluster, as shown in Figure 7-3.

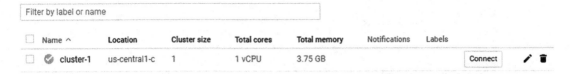

***Figure 7-3.*** *Edit cluster*

From the Edit Cluster page, scroll down to the Node Pools section and click on the pool name, as shown in Figure 7-4.

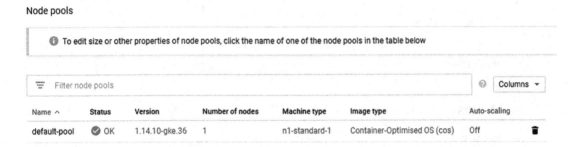

***Figure 7-4.*** *Node pool*

From the Node Pool Details page, click on the edit icon, as shown in Figure 7-5.

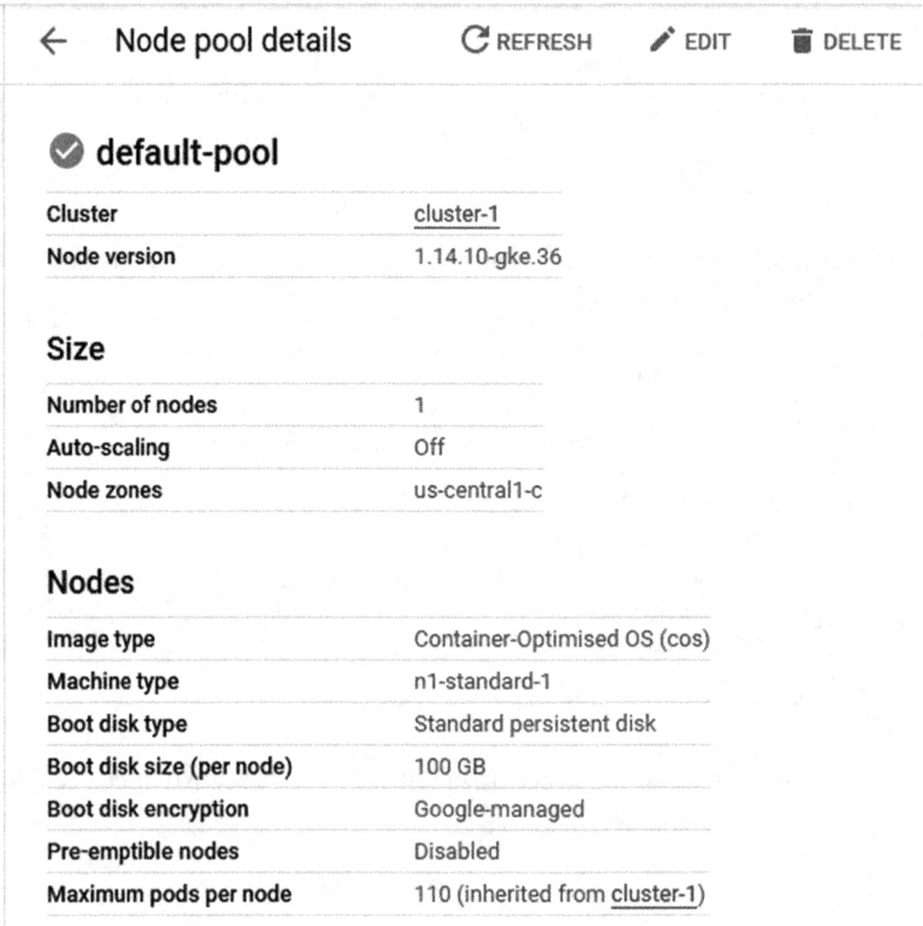

**Figure 7-5.** *Node pool details*

After you click on the edit icon, you will see two options. First, you have the option to change the value for number of nodes; in my case, and as shown in Figure 7-6, I have one node, which I will change to two.

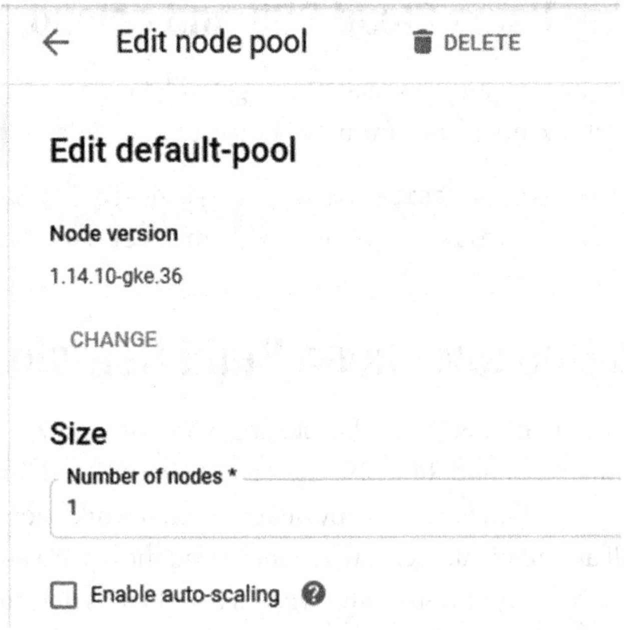

**Figure 7-6.** *Number of nodes*

This is a good opportunity to point out the location to enable the auto-scaling option, which will enable auto-scaling on the cluster.

After your resizing of the node pool, it will take a few minutes for the cluster to resize. In my case, I changed the number of nodes to two, as shown in Figure 7-7, and in the next section, I will resize it back to one node using Cloud SDK and gcloud.

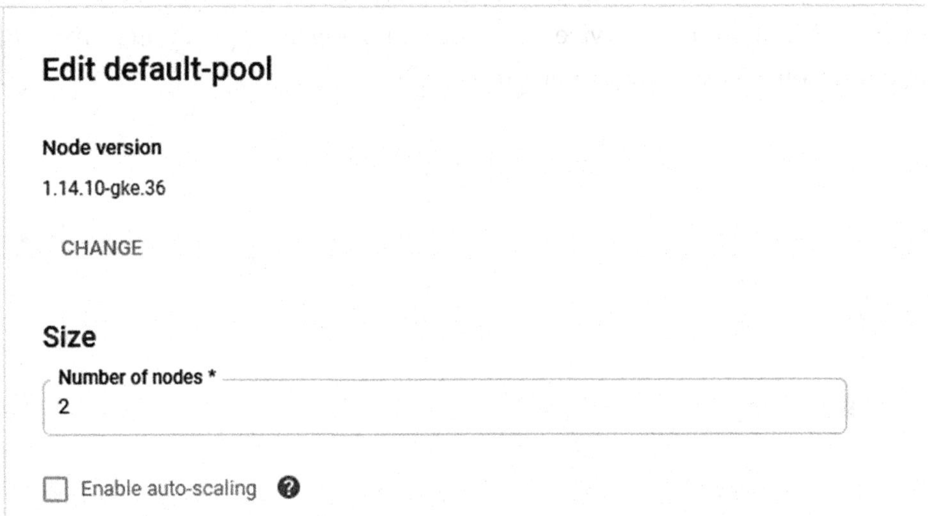

**Figure 7-7.** *Resize*

## Manual Scaling Using Cloud SDK and gcloud

To resize an existing cluster using Cloud SDK and gcloud, I will use the following example, which will resize my cluster from two nodes to one node:

```
$ gcloud container clusters resize cluster-1 --node-pool default-pool --num-
nodes 1 --region us-central1-c --project web-project-269903
```

# Scale Cloud Run and Cloud Build Containers

In this section, we will learn how Cloud Run scaling works and how to manage scaling with workloads running in Cloud Run. The good news about Cloud Run and scaling is that auto-scaling in Cloud Run is enabled by default. When workloads are deployed to Cloud Run, they will automatically scale when they need more CPU and RAM. In Cloud Run, applications are being monitored, and when a high load is detected, the application will automatically scale.

It is important to note that Cloud Run will scale applications horizontally, which means that GCP will add more pods to the application and will not add more CPU or RAM to existing pods.

## Configure Auto-scaling with Cloud Run

Let's go ahead and deploy an application to Cloud Run and review the auto-scaling features that are built into the service. I start by deploying an application from GCR using the Cloud Run console, as shown in Figure 7-8.

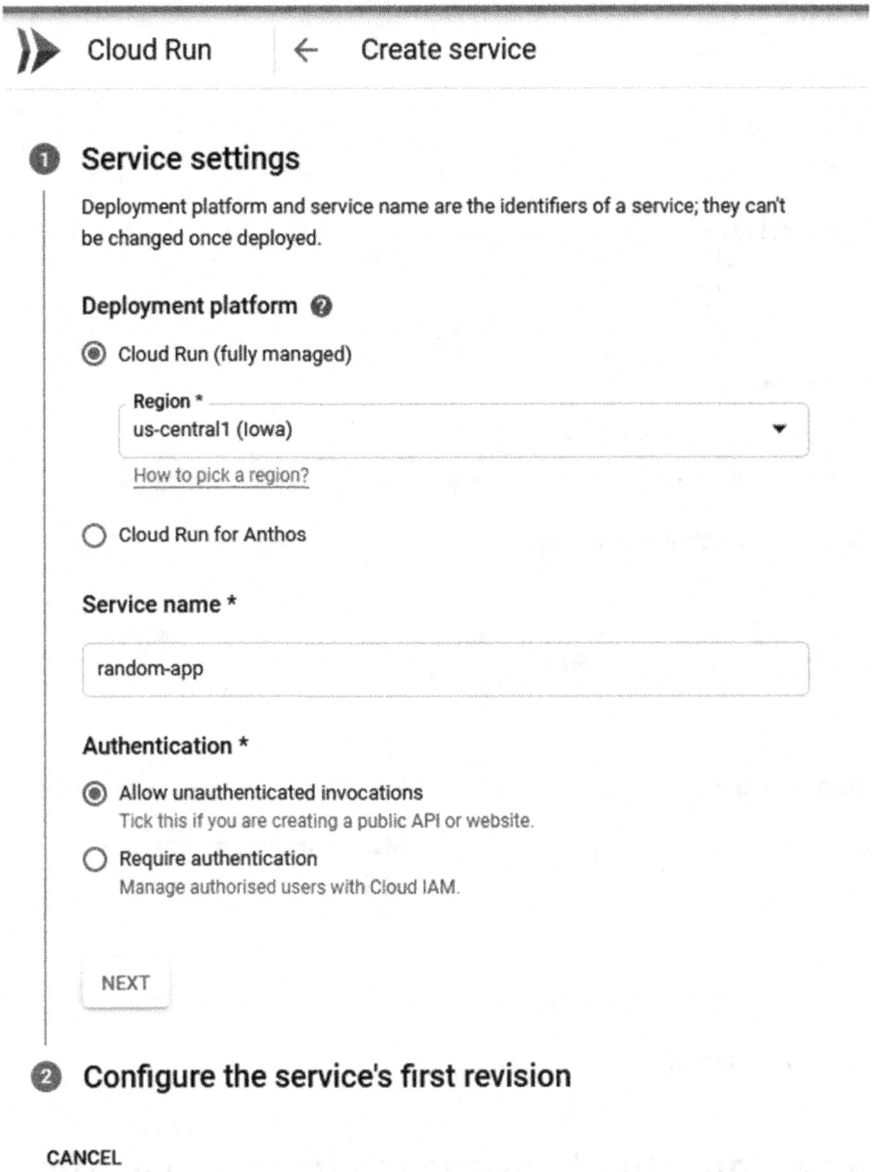

**Figure 7-8.** *Create service*

In the Create Service wizard, I fill in the details of the application and click Next. The auto-scaling feature appears in the second part of the wizard.

In the second part of the wizard, I scroll down to the Auto-scaling section, and as shown in Figure 7-9, I have the option to set the maximum number of instances. There is no option to set the minimum number of instances.

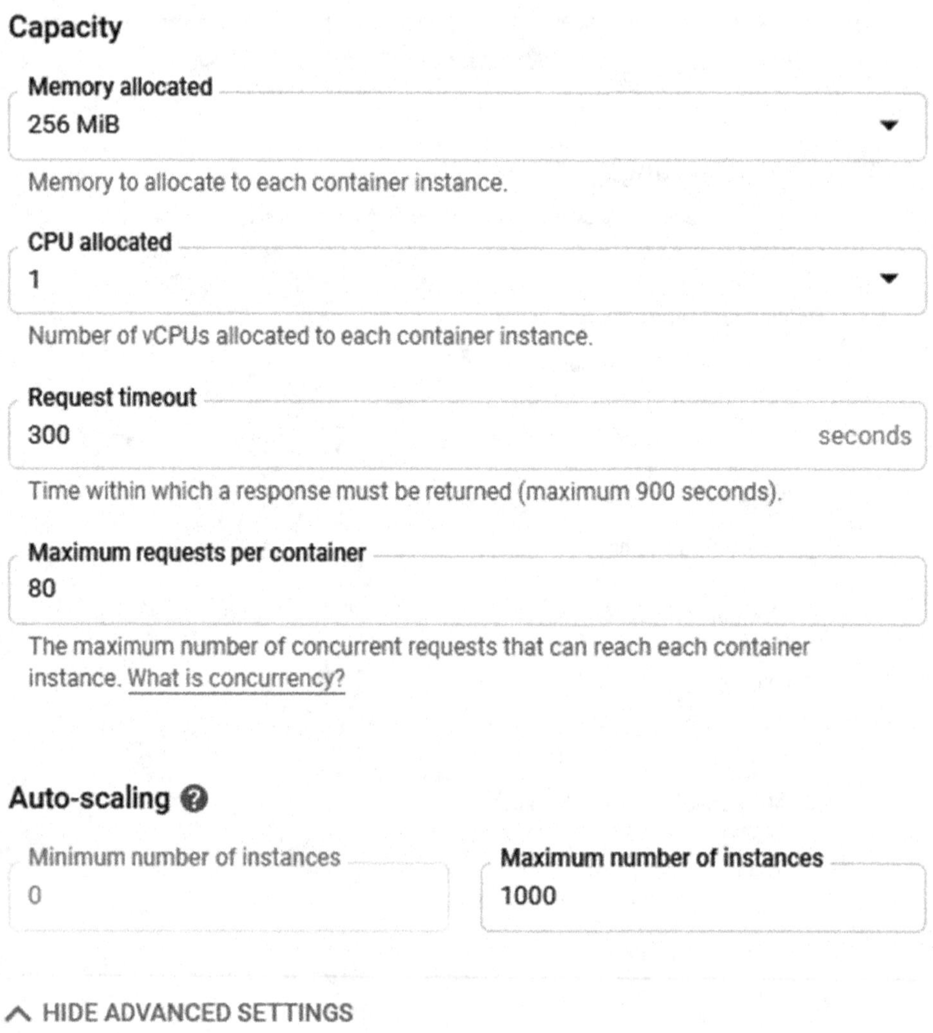

## Capacity

**Memory allocated**

256 MiB    ▼

Memory to allocate to each container instance.

**CPU allocated**

1    ▼

Number of vCPUs allocated to each container instance.

**Request timeout**

300                                                              seconds

Time within which a response must be returned (maximum 900 seconds).

**Maximum requests per container**

80

The maximum number of concurrent requests that can reach each container
instance. What is concurrency?

## Auto-scaling ❷

Minimum number of instances          Maximum number of instances

0                                    1000

∧ HIDE ADVANCED SETTINGS

***Figure 7-9.*** *Auto-scaling*

# Configure Cloud Run Auto-scaling Using Cloud SDK and gcloud

If you prefer to use Cloud SDK and gcloud to deploy your Cloud Run application, you
can use the following code. The important part in the following code is the `--max-instances` value, which sets the auto-scaling feature to scale up to ten containers.

```
$ gcloud run deploy random  --port 80 --platform=managed --allow-
unauthenticated --region=us-central1--image=gcr.io/web-project-269903/
random@sha256:15baf8ffa7c4f53200f56899b082a6bd4ed8c3cc25884a76181a4970cdc68
99c --max-instances 10
```

## Cloud Run Limit

The maximum number of containers Cloud Run can scale is 1,000 per deployment;
however, this number can be increased to a greater number.

## Increase Limits

If you need to increase the limit of your Cloud Run auto-scaling, you can perform the
following process:

- Open the GCP management console.

- Click on IAM & Admin from the left navigation menu.

- From the extended menu, click on Quotas. In Figure 7-10, you can
  see the Quotas menu.

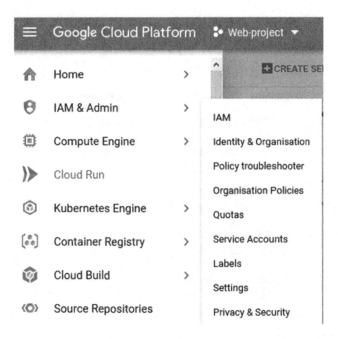

***Figure 7-10.*** *Quotas*

- On the Quotas page, use the Service drop-down menu to locate "Cloud Run Admin API" and select it.

- The Quotas page will show all the Cloud Run limits, and the one we are after is the Cloud Run Admin API, Container instances per day, which is set to 1,000 per day.

Figure 7-11 shows the Cloud Run quotas.

| Quota type | | Service | | Metric | | Location | |
|---|---|---|---|---|---|---|---|
| All quotas | ▼ | Cloud Run Admin API | ▼ | All metrics | ▼ | All locations | ▼ | Clear |

| Service | Location | Current Usage | 7-Day Peak Usage ^ | Limit |
|---|---|---|---|---|
| Cloud Run Admin API <br> Read requests per 100 seconds | Global | 0.587 | 26 | 1,000 |
| Cloud Run Admin API <br> Write requests per 100 seconds | Global | 0.006 | 1 | 100 |
| Cloud Run Admin API <br> Container instances per day | Global | 0 | 0 | 1,000 |

***Figure 7-11.*** *Cloud Run quotas*

To create a request to increase the quotas, select the quota and click on the "Edit quotas" link, as shown in Figure 7-12.

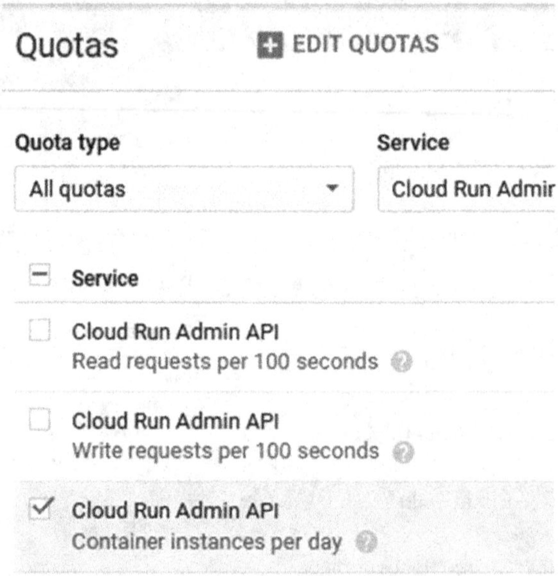

***Figure 7-12.*** *Edit quotas*

On the Edit Quotas page, confirm your details and click Next, as shown in Figure 7-13.

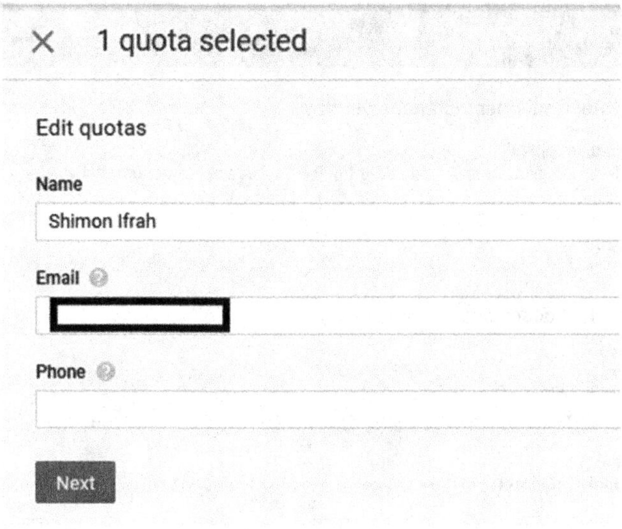

***Figure 7-13.*** *Quota selected*

On the final screen, enter a new limit for the maximum number of containers that you would like to run. Fill in the details and click on the Submit Request button. Figure 7-14 shows the final screen.

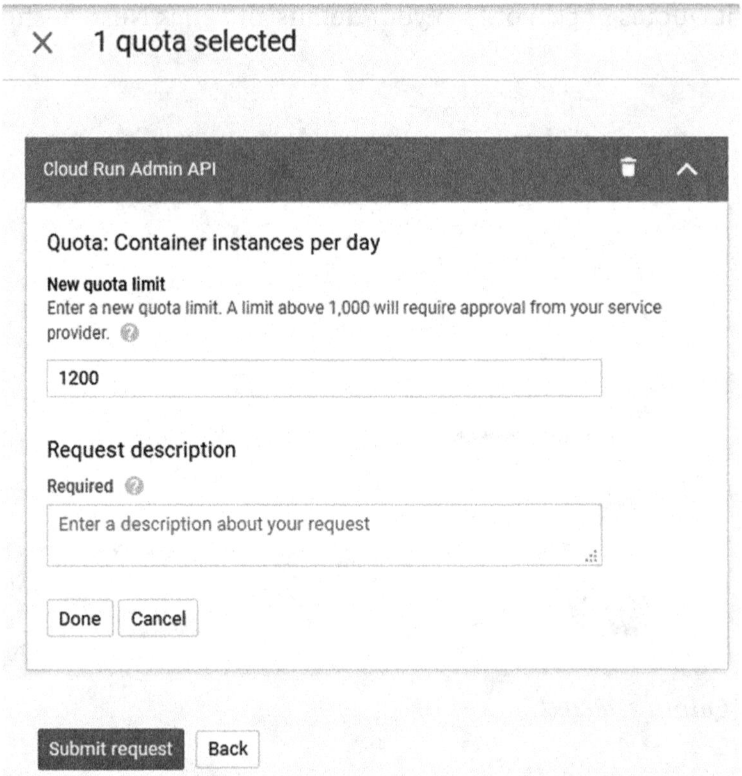

*Figure 7-14.* *Container instances per day limit*

# Domain Mapping

Another option that is not directly related to scaling but more to productionizing your Cloud Run application is to use domain mapping. Domain mapping can map a top-level domain to a Cloud Run application. To do just that, from the Cloud Run console, click on the "Manage Custom Domains" link, as shown in Figure 7-15.

*Figure 7-15.* *Manage Custom Domains*

From the Manage Custom Domains page, click on the "Add Mapping" link, as shown in Figure 7-16.

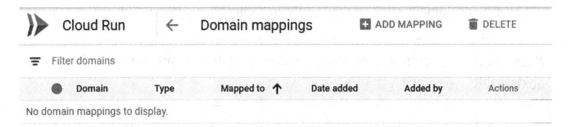

**Figure 7-16.** *Add mapping*

From the Add Mapping page, select your Cloud Run application from the menu. From the Select a Verified Domain drop-down menu, select a new domain. In the Base Domain to Verify option, type the URL of the domain.

In my case, the domain name is `www.ictweekly.com`, as shown in Figure 7-17.

# Add mapping BETA

You can map domains and subdomains to the selected Cloud Run service. Learn more

**①** Select or enter domain  —  **②** Verify  —  **③** Update DNS records

Select a service to map to *
randon-app2 (us-central1)  ▼

Select a verified domain
Verify a new domain...  ▼

Base domain to verify *
www.ictweekly.com

e.g. to map 'api.example.com', you need to verify 'example.com'.

CANCEL       VERIFY IN WEBMASTER CENTRAL ☑

**Figure 7-17.** *App mapping menu*

To verify the domain, click on the "Verify-in Webmaster Central" link.

---

**Note**    With some domain registries, you might not need to add the www in the domain URL.

---

To verify the domain, you need to create a TXT record in the root DNS zone of the domain. Figure 7-18 shows the verification page and the value of the TXT record.

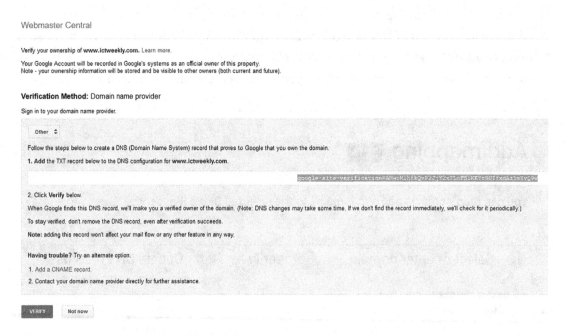

*Figure 7-18.* *Verify domain ownership*

In my case, I am using AWS Route 53 as my domain registry, and in Figure 7-19, you can see the TXT entry.

**Edit Record Set**

**Name:** ictweekly.com.

**Type:**  TXT – Text    ⌄

**Alias:** ○ Yes  ◉ No

**TTL (Seconds):**    300  | 1m | 5m | 1h | 1d |

**Value:**  "google-site-
verification=ANwoMlhfkQvP2JjY2xILoF
SINK8rBUlfxdAz5mYvQ9w"

A text record. Enter multiple values
on separate lines. Enclose text in
quotation marks.
Example:
"Sample Text Entries"
"Enclose entries in quotation marks"

**Routing Policy:**   Simple    ⌄

Route 53 responds to queries based only on the values in this record. Learn
More

***Figure 7-19.*** *AWS Route 53 TXT DNS record*

Once you add the record to Route 53, click on the Verify button.

**Note**    You might need to wait for ten to fifteen minutes for the verification to work.

After the verification process is complete, you will see a configuration message
similar to that shown in Figure 7-20.

Webmaster Central

Great job, **ictweekly.com** is now verified! You can now use Google services for your property such as Search Console .

- Add additional owners to **ictweekly.com** .
- Verify another property.
- View your list of verified properties.

***Figure 7-20.*** *Domain verified*

In the final step of the configuration, go back to the Add Mapping wizard and click Refresh. Then, click on the Continue button to add DNS records for Cloud Run.

On the Update DNS Record page, note down the DNS records and add them to the DNS zone. These records will create the mapping from the DNS zone registry to Cloud Run, as shown in Figure 7-21.

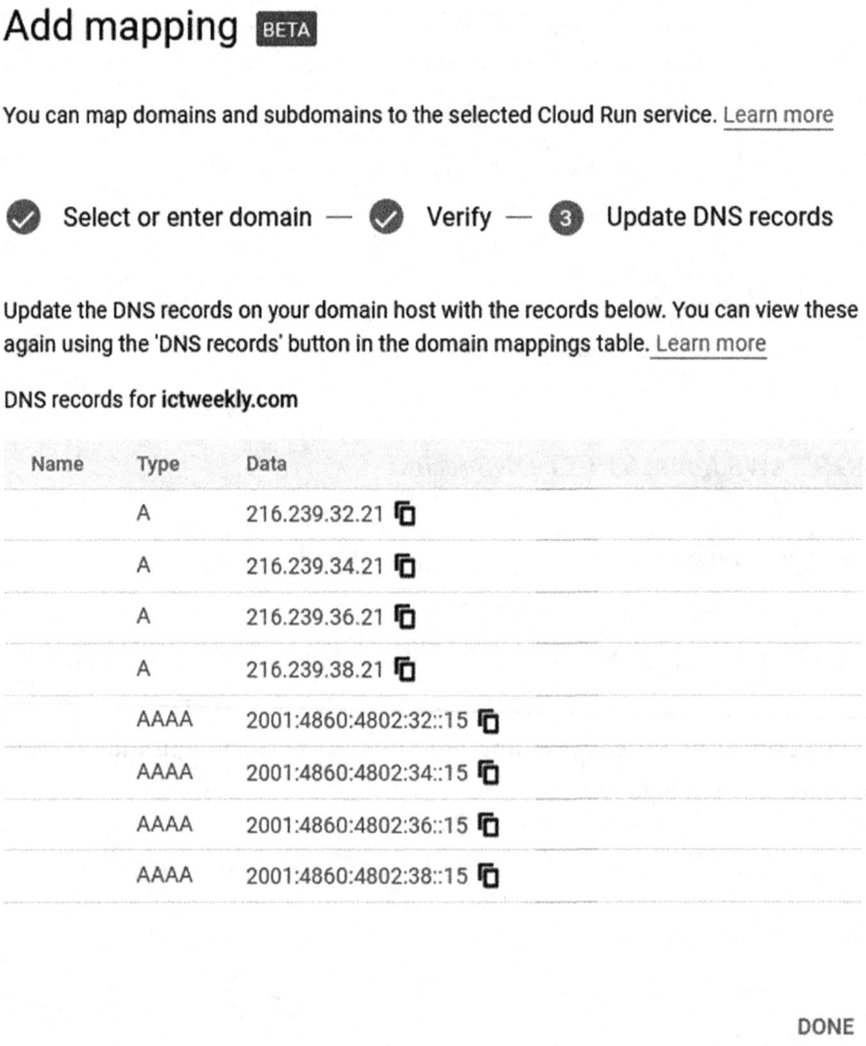

# Add mapping BETA

You can map domains and subdomains to the selected Cloud Run service. Learn more

✓ Select or enter domain — ✓ Verify — ③ Update DNS records

Update the DNS records on your domain host with the records below. You can view these again using the 'DNS records' button in the domain mappings table. Learn more

DNS records for **ictweekly.com**

| Name | Type | Data |
|------|------|------|
|  | A | 216.239.32.21 📋 |
|  | A | 216.239.34.21 📋 |
|  | A | 216.239.36.21 📋 |
|  | A | 216.239.38.21 📋 |
|  | AAAA | 2001:4860:4802:32::15 📋 |
|  | AAAA | 2001:4860:4802:34::15 📋 |
|  | AAAA | 2001:4860:4802:36::15 📋 |
|  | AAAA | 2001:4860:4802:38::15 📋 |

DONE

***Figure 7-21.*** *Add DNS records*

Once the DNS records are in place, open your browser and navigate to URL (http://ictweekly.com) and check the result, as shown in Figure 7-22.

788086833366

**Figure 7-22.** *Result*

# Scale GCP Container Registry

In this section, we will learn about Google Container Registry (GCR) and the options that are available for us to scale the service. When it comes to GCR, we cannot scale the actual service for the simple reason that GCR is a storage service that has no limit. GCR is a managed service where we only pay for network traffic and for the underline storage space our images are taking up.

There is one thing that we can do to optimize the performance of GCR, and it is choosing the location of our GCR registry. It is highly recommended you set the registry region to be the same as your applications.

There is no point in using the U.S. region to store your images when your applications are in Europe. So, make sure you follow this rule.

For added security, you can opt-in and use vulnerability scanning to add an extra layer of security to your images.

Please review Chapter 2, where we learned how to enable vulnerability scanning.

# Scale Compute Engine Hosts

In the last section of this book, we will learn about scaling Compute Engine hosts, also known as virtual machines. In the following example, we will scale an existing Compute Engine virtual machine.

From the GCP Compute Engine console, select the VM instance you would like to scale and stop it.

---

**Note**    You must shut down your VM before scaling it.

---

The Stop button is located at the top-right corner of the VM Instances page, as shown in Figure 7-23.

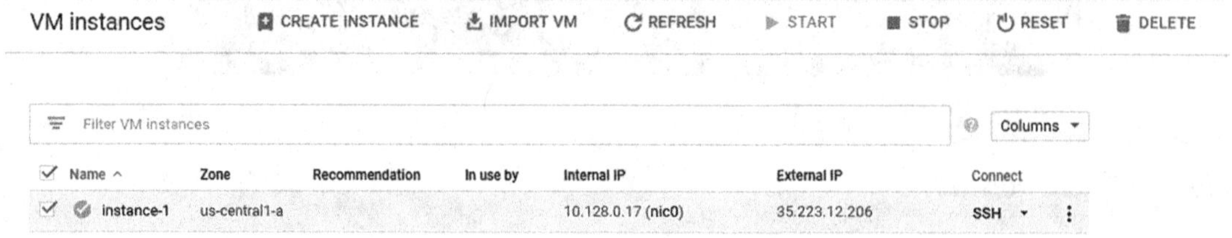

VM instances    ⊡ CREATE INSTANCE    ⬇ IMPORT VM    ⟳ REFRESH    ▶ START    ■ STOP    ⏻ RESET    🗑 DELETE

| ✓ | Name ∧ | Zone | Recommendation | In use by | Internal IP | External IP | Connect | |
|---|--------|------|----------------|-----------|-------------|-------------|---------|---|
| ✓ ⊚ | instance-1 | us-central1-a | | | 10.128.0.17 (nic0) | 35.223.12.206 | SSH ▾ | ⋮ |

Filter VM instances    ⊘ Columns ▾

**Figure 7-23.** *VM instances*

After the VM is off, click on it and click on the Edit button. Under Machine Configuration, you will have the option to select the machine family type and how many resources you need the machine to have. See Figure 7-24.

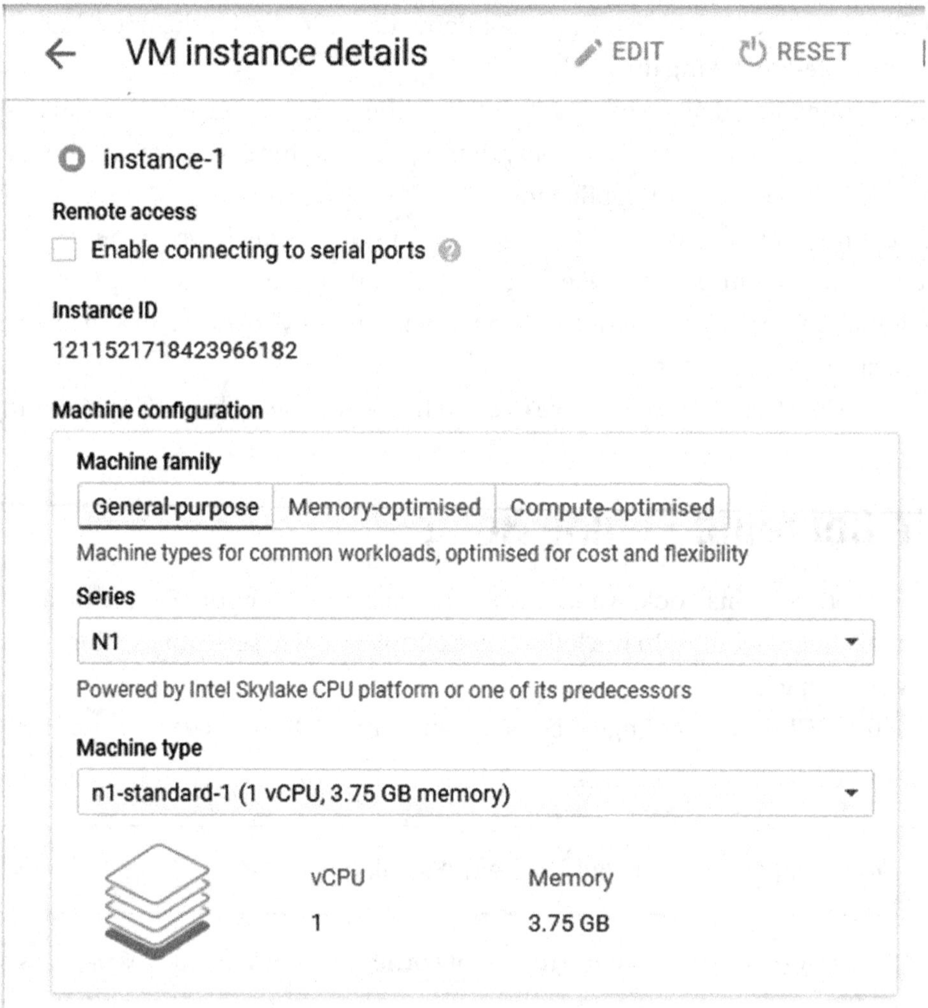

← **VM instance details**    ✎ EDIT    ⏻ RESET    |

⊚ instance-1

**Remote access**
☐ Enable connecting to serial ports ⊘

**Instance ID**
1211521718423966182

**Machine configuration**

**Machine family**

| General-purpose | Memory-optimised | Compute-optimised |
|-----------------|------------------|-------------------|

Machine types for common workloads, optimised for cost and flexibility

**Series**

N1 ▾

Powered by Intel Skylake CPU platform or one of its predecessors

**Machine type**

n1-standard-1 (1 vCPU, 3.75 GB memory) ▾

vCPU          Memory

1             3.75 GB

**Figure 7-24.** *Machine configuration*

# Machine Types

When it comes to selecting the size of your VM instance, it is not as simple as you might think. GCP offers machine types that are based on the type of workload the machine is going to run. As of writing these lines, GCP offers the following four machine types.

## General-purpose

General-purpose machines are good for web applications, backend processing, Docker hosts, and development workload. These machines are good for general stuff and applications that need a good balance of RAM and CPU. They are also good for development and testing purposes and offer good pricing and an easy entry point to GCP VMs.

## Memory-optimized

These VM types are good for applications that consume and need RAM memory for processing data or workloads. A good example of this type is database servers.

## Compute-optimized

The compute-optimized machines are good for applications that use a lot of CPU, like gaming and calculations.

## Shared-core

The last machine type is very good for development and testing purposes only and is not recommended for running production workloads.

When you select your VM instance for production purposes, make sure you understand what your application is doing and which machine type will fit it.

# Auto-scaling Compute Engine Hosts

Another great option for scaling Compute Engine hosts is to use auto-scaling, which is much more efficient and automatic.

With Compute Engine auto-scaling, we set and forget our configuration and let GCP handle the process of scaling up or down hosts. Setting up auto-scaling in Compute Engine is not as simple as in GKE, because the core technology is different; however, once you set it up and understand the concept, you will be able to do it more easily.

## Instance Group

The concept of auto-scaling in Compute Engine is based on what we call an Instance Group. Inside a managed group, we create a machine template, which can be based on a public image or an existing VM image.

For example, we can create a VM with our preferred applications and configuration. After everything is loaded and working, we can create a golden image—or an instance template, in GCP terminology.

During the managed group configuration, we can specify a scaling limit, which is the number of hosts we would like to have as a maximum number and a threshold to which to scale (CPU based).

Let's start by creating an instance template using a public image or existing instance (VM).

## Create Instance Template

To create an instance template, open the Compute Engine console from the left-side navigation, then click on Instance Templates. To create a new template from a public image, click on the Create Instance Template button, as shown in Figure 7-25.

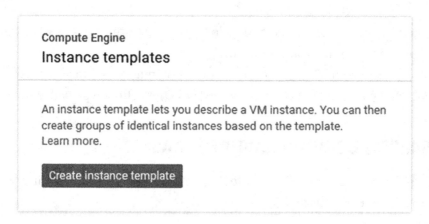

*Figure 7-25. Create instance template*

**Note**    In most cases, you will probably create a template from the existing instance which you will see soon.

From the template, the wizard selects the instance machine configuration and gives the instance a name, as shown in Figure 7-26.

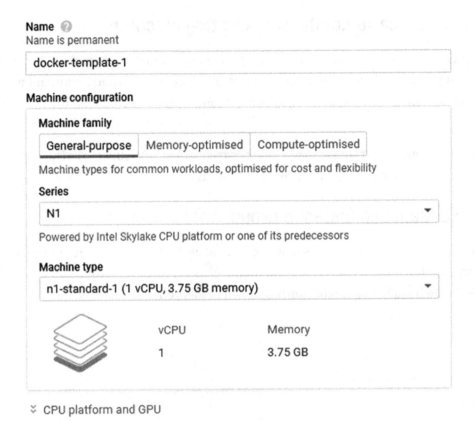

Name 🕐
Name is permanent

> docker-template-1

**Machine configuration**

> **Machine family**
>
> | General-purpose | Memory-optimised | Compute-optimised |
>
> Machine types for common workloads, optimised for cost and flexibility
>
> **Series**
>
> > N1
>
> Powered by Intel Skylake CPU platform or one of its predecessors
>
> **Machine type**
>
> > n1-standard-1 (1 vCPU, 3.75 GB memory)
>
> |        | vCPU | Memory  |
> |--------|------|---------|
> |        | 1    | 3.75 GB |

≫ CPU platform and GPU

***Figure 7-26.*** *Machine configuration*

Create the template and save, then confirm that it appears under Instance Templates, as shown in Figure 7-27.

| ☰ | Filter instance templates | | | | |
|---|---|---|---|---|---|
| ☐ | Name ^ | Machine type | Image | Disk type | In use by |
| ☐ | docker-template-1 | 1 vCPU, 3.75 GB | debian-10-buster-v20200618 | Standard persistent disk | |

***Figure 7-27.*** *Instance template*

## Create Instance Template from Existing Machine

If you prefer to create an instance from an existing instance (virtual machine), you can do so using Cloud SDK and gcloud commands. The following gcloud command will create a template from a VM called `instance-1`, and it will be saved with the name of docker:

```
$ gcloud compute instance-templates create docker --source-instance
instance-1 --source-instance-zone us-central1-a
```

## Create a Managed Instance Group

Now that you have your templates ready, go ahead and create an instance group. From the Compute Engine left-side navigation menu, click on Instance Groups and then click on the Create Instance Group button, as shown in Figure 7-28.

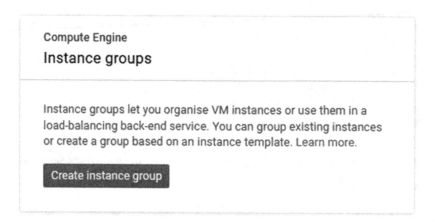

***Figure 7-28.*** *Create instance group*

From the wizard page, name the group and use the Instance Template drop-down menu to select the template you created, as shown in Figure 7-29.

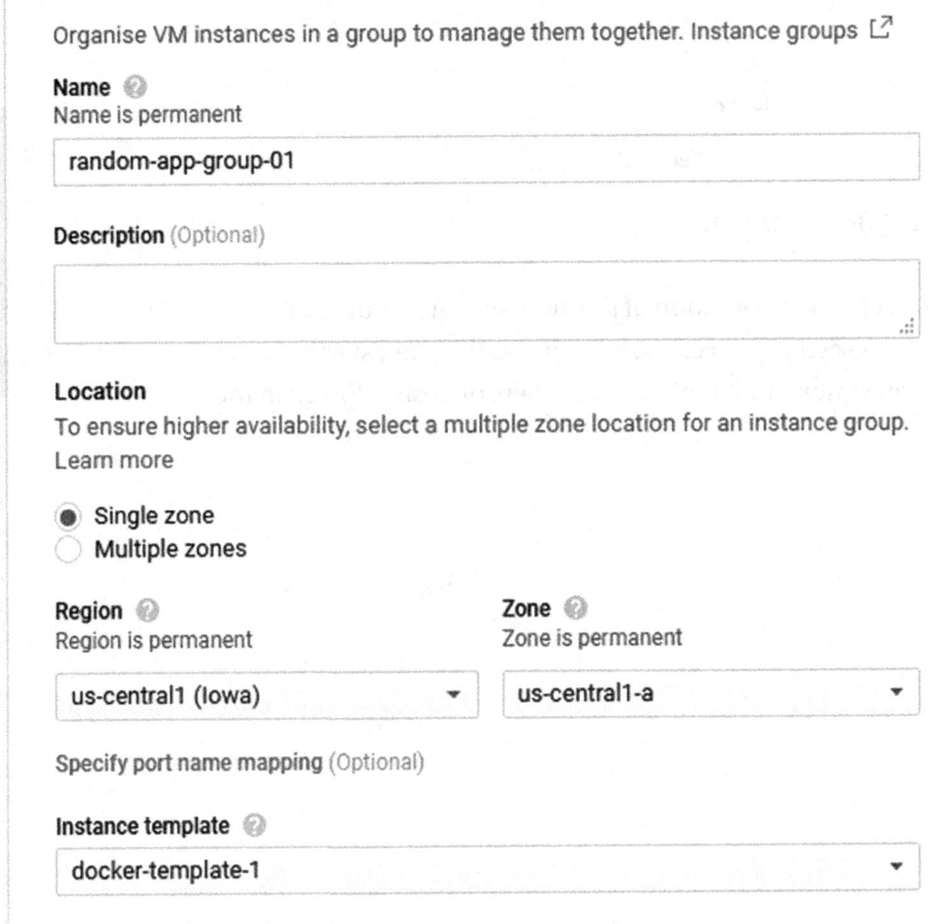

Organise VM instances in a group to manage them together. Instance groups [↗]

**Name** ⓘ
Name is permanent

    random-app-group-01

**Description** (Optional)

**Location**
To ensure higher availability, select a multiple zone location for an instance group.
Learn more

● Single zone
○ Multiple zones

**Region** ⓘ
Region is permanent

    us-central1 (Iowa)          ▼

**Zone** ⓘ
Zone is permanent

    us-central1-a               ▼

Specify port name mapping (Optional)

**Instance template** ⓘ

    docker-template-1                              ▼

***Figure 7-29.*** *Instance group*

In Figure 7-30, you can see both templates; the docker template is the one I created from an existing instance.

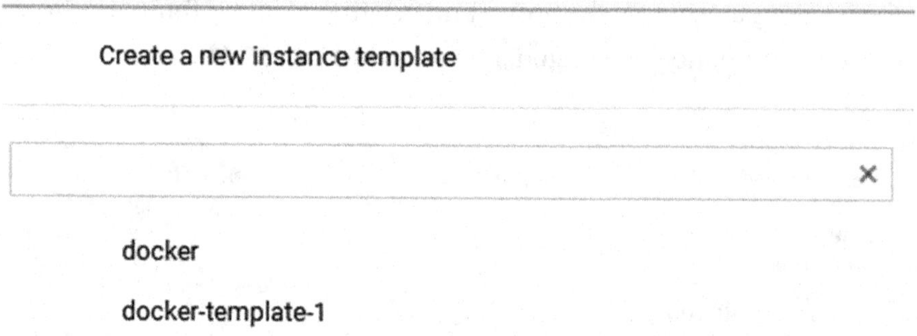

Create a new instance template

docker

docker-template-1

**Figure 7-30.** *Templates*

The actual configuration of the auto-scaling feature is shown in Figure 7-31. Under the Metrics section, you can set the threshold when starting a new instance. You can also set the maximum and minimum numbers of hosts allowed in the group.

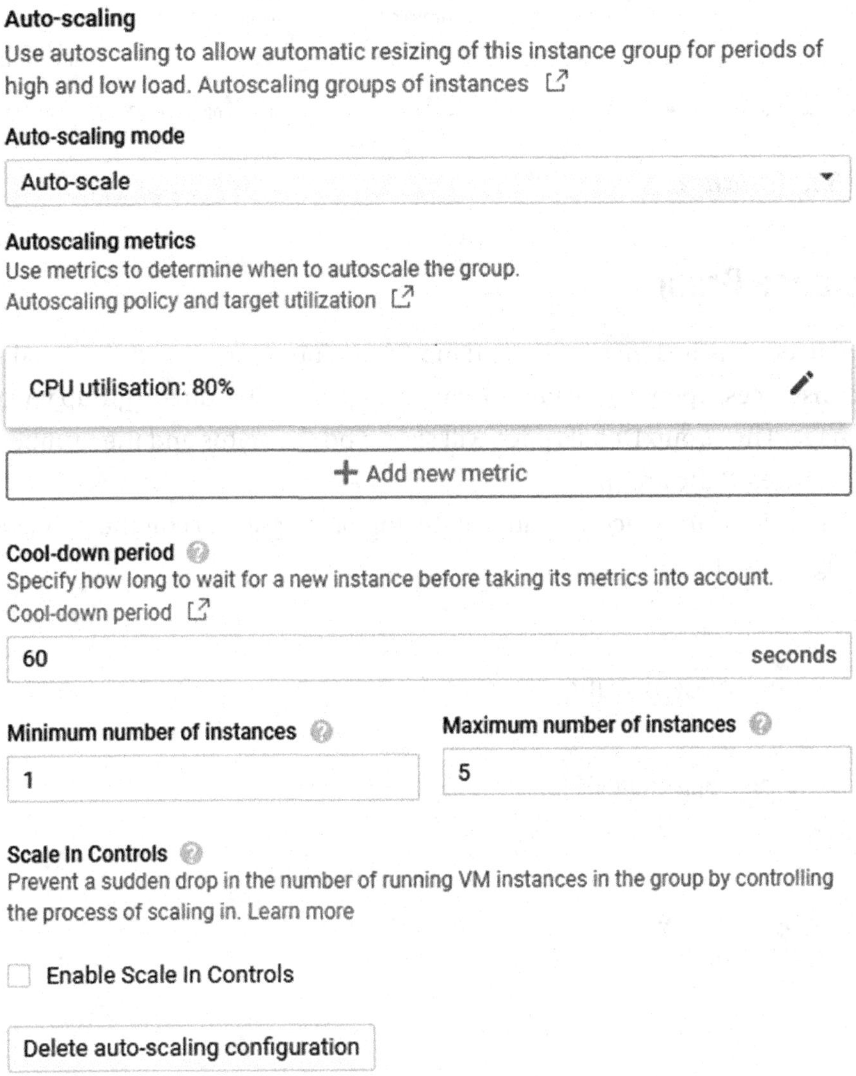

**Auto-scaling**

Use autoscaling to allow automatic resizing of this instance group for periods of high and low load. Autoscaling groups of instances 🗗

**Auto-scaling mode**

| Auto-scale | ▼ |
|---|---|

**Autoscaling metrics**

Use metrics to determine when to autoscale the group.
Autoscaling policy and target utilization 🗗

| CPU utilisation: 80% | ✎ |
|---|---|

| ➕ Add new metric |
|---|

**Cool-down period** ❓

Specify how long to wait for a new instance before taking its metrics into account.
Cool-down period 🗗

| 60 | seconds |
|---|---|

**Minimum number of instances** ❓    **Maximum number of instances** ❓

| 1 | | 5 |
|---|---|---|

**Scale In Controls** ❓

Prevent a sudden drop in the number of running VM instances in the group by controlling the process of scaling in. Learn more

☐ Enable Scale In Controls

| Delete auto-scaling configuration |
|---|

***Figure 7-31.*** *Auto-scaling configuration*

Once the group is ready, it will appear both under VM Instances (as an instance) and under Instance Groups. Figure 7-32 shows the instance, which is part of the managed group.

| | Name ⌃ | Zone | Recommendation | In use by | Internal IP |
|---|---|---|---|---|---|
| ☐ ◯ | instance-1 | us-central1-a | | | 10.128.0.17 (nic0) |
| ☐ ✅ | random-app-group-01-wf46 | us-central1-a | | random-app-group-01 | 10.128.0.19 (nic0) |

***Figure 7-32.*** *Instance*

## Edit Instance Group

If you need to edit the instance group and modify the number of maximum and minimum instances, open the Instance Groups page and click on the group you would like to manage. The Group Details page will show you the status and the number of running instances of the group.

Click on the Edit Group icon located at the top of the page to edit the group, as shown in Figure 7-33.

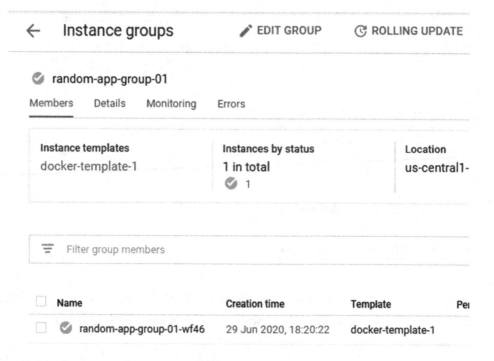

***Figure 7-33.*** *Instance Group Details page*

Go ahead and change the minimum number of instances and save the configuration. Figure 7-34 shows the minimum and the maximum number of instances option.

**Cool-down period** ⊙
Specify how long to wait for a new instance before taking its metrics into account.
Cool-down period ⬈

| 60 | seconds |
|----|---------|

| Minimum number of instances ⊙ | Maximum number of instances ⊙ |
|-------------------------------|-------------------------------|
| 2 | 5 |

*Figure 7-34. Minimum and maximum number of instances*

After changing the number of instances, a new instance will show up under VM instances, as shown in Figure 7-35.

| ☐ | ✓ random-app-group-01-hxwt | us-central1-a | random-app-group-01 | 10.128.0.20 (nic0) | 34.71.155.68 |
|---|----------------------------|---------------|---------------------|--------------------|--------------|
| ☐ | ✓ random-app-group-01-wf46 | us-central1-a | random-app-group-01 | 10.128.0.19 (nic0) | 35.223.12.206 |

*Figure 7-35. Instances*

# Summary

In this chapter, we have learned how to scale GKE, Cloud Run, GCR, and Compute Engine services. The main focus of this chapter was to use auto-scaling when it was possible. As shown in the chapter, auto-scaling is available across all services.

In the next chapter, we will cover monitoring.

# CHAPTER 8

# Monitoring

In this chapter, we are going to learn about Google Cloud Platform monitoring tools and how to use them with the container services. GCP offers a wide range of monitoring tools that can fit in with any deployment, like virtual machines, application monitoring, uptime, storage, and networking.

Our focus in this chapter will be on the following topics:

- Cloud Monitoring Overview

- Monitor Google Kubernetes Service (GKE)

- Monitor Cloud Run Containers

- Monitor Compute Engine Resources

- GCP Cost Management and Tools

## Cloud Monitoring Overview

Google Cloud Platform's main monitoring service is called Cloud Monitoring, and offers monitoring services not only for GCP services but also for other public cloud providers, like AWS, though you are limited to GCP resources.

Cloud Monitoring can provide 360-degree monitoring services for virtual machines by installing a monitoring agent that collects information from the virtual machine. You can also use the Cloud Monitoring agent to monitor on-premises servers.

## Alerting

Using Cloud Monitoring alerting, you can create uptime checks that monitor VM instances, websites, and cloud services and follow up with an alert if the services are down.

221

© Shimon Ifrah 2021
S. Ifrah, *Getting Started with Containers in Google Cloud Platform*,
https://doi.org/10.1007/978-1-4842-6470-6_8

# Alerting Policies

With alerting policies, you can define conditions that control when an alert is triggered and what happens after an alert is triggered.

# Metrics

GCP also offers extensive access to metrics using Metrics Explorer, which allows you to create dashboards and charts.

# GKE Monitoring

When it comes to Kubernetes clusters on Google Cloud Platform, there is a dedicated service that helps to monitor them, which you will see next.

# Monitor Google Kubernetes Service (GKE)

When it comes to GKE cluster monitoring, GCP has dedicated services called Operations Suite for GKE. The Operations Suite for GKE is enabled by default when you create a GKE cluster and gives insight into your GKE cluster.

# Pricing

Operations Suite pricing is based on the following items:

> **Log ingestions:** Every GB of logs is charged at $0.50 per GB, while the first 50 GB are free every month.
>
> **Logging storage:** Logs stored longer than the default retention period are charged per GCP regional storage price.
>
> **Monitoring data:** This charge is based on ingested metrics data and starts at $0.2580 per 100 to 150 MB.

# Enable Monitoring

I told you earlier that monitoring is enabled by default; however, if you prefer not to use monitoring because it is not needed—and reasons can be the fact that it is a development environment and the higher cost—you can disable monitoring during the cluster configuration stage.

If you look at Figure 8-1, you will see where the GKE monitoring settings are located. You will find them in the Features section under Telemetry; by default the feature is enabled.

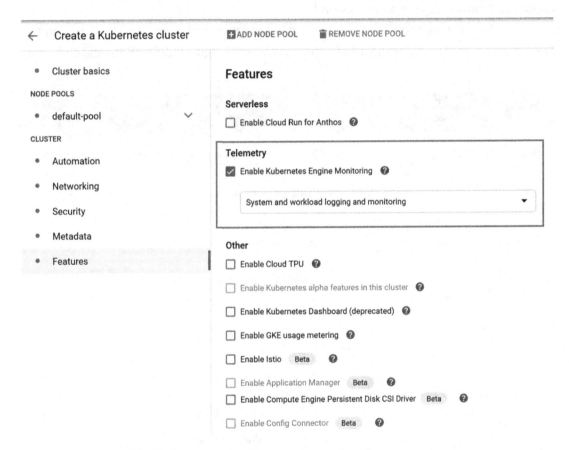

***Figure 8-1.***  *Enable Kubernetes logging and monitoring*

If you click on the drop-down menu, you will see that you have the option to monitor just the system without the pods (workloads). By default, monitoring of the system (cluster) and workloads (pods) is enabled and recommended.

**Note**    Monitoring can be enabled on existing clusters if it was disabled initially.

# GKE Operations Suite Dashboard

The Operations Suite dashboard is where all of the GKE monitoring data, metrics, and alerts are located, and from there you can monitor your cluster. The Operations Suite is available for you from the GKE Monitoring page. From the left-hand navigation menu, locate the Monitoring icon and click on it.

In the Monitoring console's left-hand navigation menu, click on Dashboards, and the Kubernetes Engine (new) dashboard will open, as shown in Figure 8-2. Go ahead and click on it.

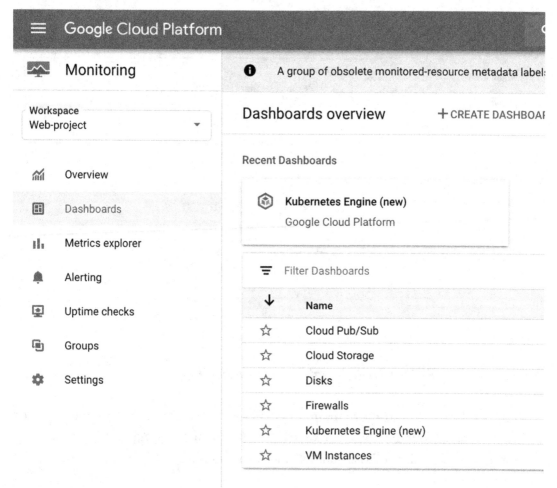

*Figure 8-2.* *Kubernetes Engine (new)*

The GKE dashboard, as shown in Figure 8-3, focuses on three main monitoring areas, and they are:

Infrastructure - These are the worker nodes and master node

Workloads - Pods that are running inside the cluster

Services - These are system services that are running in the cluster like DNS and HTTP server.

You will see them on the bottom section of the main console in the tabs.

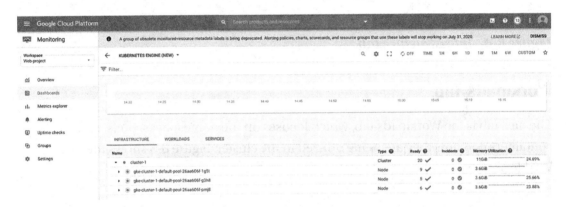

***Figure 8-3.*** *Dashboard*

Let's go ahead and explore each tab.

# Infrastructure

The first tab in the Operations suite is the Infrastructure tab, which gives you the opportunity to drill down and monitor the health of your cluster's worker nodes and everything that runs on them.

In my case, I have three worker nodes. Using the Infrastructure tab, I can see how many pods are running on each node and what the CPU and memory utilization are for each node. Figure 8-4 shows the Infrastructure tab and the worker nodes I have in my cluster.

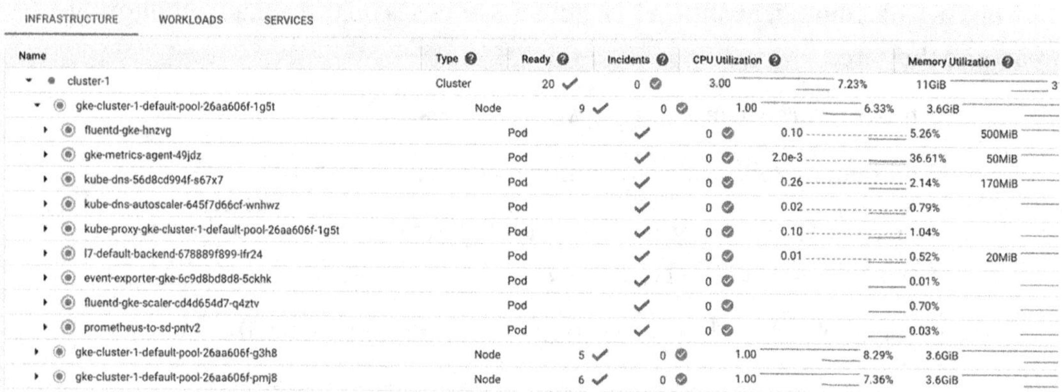

INFRASTRUCTURE WORKLOADS SERVICES

| Name | Type | Ready | Incidents | CPU Utilization | Memory Utilization |
|---|---|---|---|---|---|
| cluster-1 | Cluster | 20 ✓ | 0 | 3.00 7.23% | 11GiB 3 |
| gke-cluster-1-default-pool-26aa606f-1g5t | Node | 9 ✓ | 0 | 1.00 6.33% | 3.6GiB |
| fluentd-gke-hnzvg | Pod | ✓ | 0 | 0.10 5.26% | 500MiB |
| gke-metrics-agent-49jdz | Pod | ✓ | 0 | 2.0e-3 36.61% | 50MiB |
| kube-dns-56d8cd994f-s67x7 | Pod | ✓ | 0 | 0.26 2.14% | 170MiB |
| kube-dns-autoscaler-645f7d66cf-wnhwz | Pod | ✓ | 0 | 0.02 0.79% | |
| kube-proxy-gke-cluster-1-default-pool-26aa606f-1g5t | Pod | ✓ | 0 | 0.10 1.04% | |
| l7-default-backend-678889f899-lfr24 | Pod | ✓ | 0 | 0.01 0.52% | 20MiB |
| event-exporter-gke-6c9d8bd8d8-5ckhk | Pod | ✓ | 0 | 0.01% | |
| fluentd-gke-scaler-cd4d654d7-q4ztv | Pod | ✓ | 0 | 0.70% | |
| prometheus-to-sd-pntv2 | Pod | ✓ | 0 | 0.03% | |
| gke-cluster-1-default-pool-26aa606f-g3h8 | Node | 5 ✓ | 0 | 1.00 8.29% | 3.6GiB |
| gke-cluster-1-default-pool-26aa606f-pmj8 | Node | 6 ✓ | 0 | 1.00 7.36% | 3.6GiB |

***Figure 8-4.*** *Infrastructure tab*

# Workloads Tab

The next tab is the Workloads tab, which focuses on the namespaces, pods, and containers and how they are being utilized in the cluster. Figure 8-5 shows the main Workloads tab.

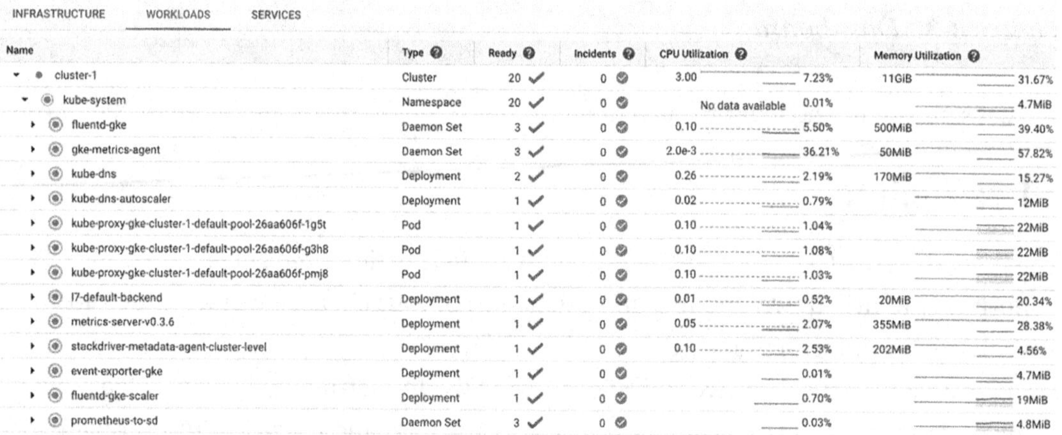

INFRASTRUCTURE WORKLOADS SERVICES

| Name | Type | Ready | Incidents | CPU Utilization | Memory Utilization |
|---|---|---|---|---|---|
| cluster-1 | Cluster | 20 ✓ | 0 | 3.00 7.23% | 11GiB 31.67% |
| kube-system | Namespace | 20 ✓ | 0 | No data available 0.01% | 4.7MiB |
| fluentd-gke | Daemon Set | 3 ✓ | 0 | 0.10 5.50% | 500MiB 39.40% |
| gke-metrics-agent | Daemon Set | 3 ✓ | 0 | 2.0e-3 36.21% | 50MiB 57.82% |
| kube-dns | Deployment | 2 ✓ | 0 | 0.26 2.19% | 170MiB 15.27% |
| kube-dns-autoscaler | Deployment | 1 ✓ | 0 | 0.02 0.79% | 12MiB |
| kube-proxy-gke-cluster-1-default-pool-26aa606f-1g5t | Pod | 1 ✓ | 0 | 0.10 1.04% | 22MiB |
| kube-proxy-gke-cluster-1-default-pool-26aa606f-g3h8 | Pod | 1 ✓ | 0 | 0.10 1.08% | 22MiB |
| kube-proxy-gke-cluster-1-default-pool-26aa606f-pmj8 | Pod | 1 ✓ | 0 | 0.10 1.03% | 22MiB |
| l7-default-backend | Deployment | 1 ✓ | 0 | 0.01 0.52% | 20MiB 20.34% |
| metrics-server-v0.3.6 | Deployment | 1 ✓ | 0 | 0.05 2.07% | 355MiB 28.38% |
| stackdriver-metadata-agent-cluster-level | Deployment | 1 ✓ | 0 | 0.10 2.53% | 202MiB 4.56% |
| event-exporter-gke | Deployment | 1 ✓ | 0 | 0.01% | 4.7MiB |
| fluentd-gke-scaler | Deployment | 1 ✓ | 0 | 0.70% | 19MiB |
| prometheus-to-sd | Daemon Set | 3 ✓ | 0 | 0.03% | 4.8MiB |

***Figure 8-5.*** *Workloads*

If you drill down from the cluster level to the pod level, you will see how much CPU and memory each pod is using (Figure 8-6).

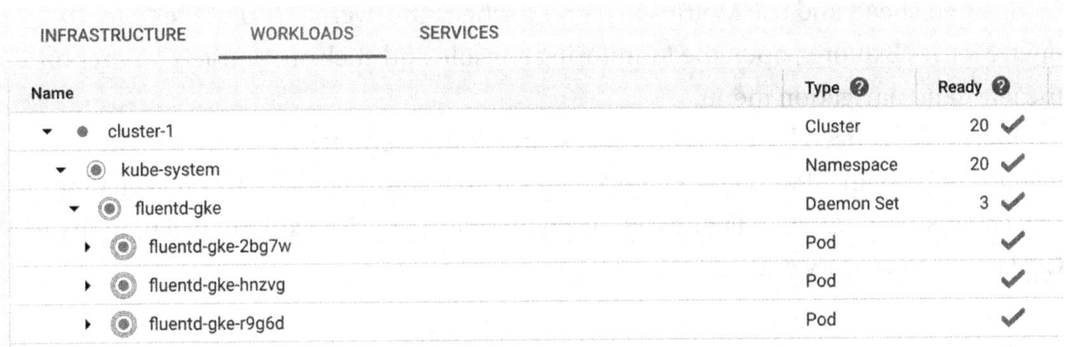

**Figure 8-6.** *Pods view*

## Services Tab

The last tab we will review is the Services tab, which is where you can monitor built-in services you have running on your cluster, including custom services. This tab also goes from cluster-level monitoring down to namespace and services.

Figure 8-7 shows the Services tab.

**Figure 8-7.** *Services tab*

## View Metrics

The next thing to explore is the GKE Metrics explorer, which allows you to zoom in and monitor the overall performance of your GKE cluster. The monitoring tabs are good for drill-down performance monitoring on a resource level, but sometimes you need to be able to review the overall performance of the cluster.

Let's go ahead and use Metrics Explorer to check the overall CPU usage time. To open Metrics Explorer, open the Monitoring console and click on Metrics Explorer on the left-hand navigation menu.

To check the overall CPU usage time, search for Kubernetes containers in the resource type search box. Next, in the Metrics search box, search for CPU usage time. The end result is shown in Figure 8-8. Using this view, Metrics Explorer will update the CPU usage view every one minute.

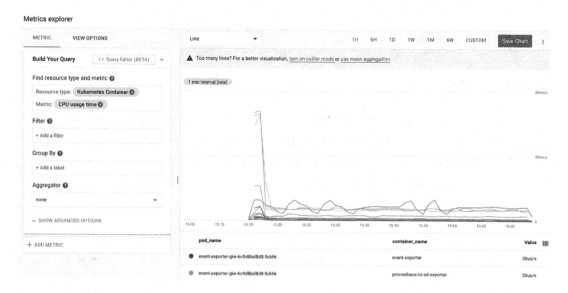

***Figure 8-8.*** *Kubernetes cluster CPU monitoring*

# Monitor Cloud Run Containers

In this section, we will learn how to monitor workload in Cloud Run and how to use Cloud Monitoring with Cloud Run.

Like GKE and other GCP services, by default and at no extra cost, Cloud Run comes with free monitoring capabilities you can use out of the box. These monitoring tools help you keep an eye on Cloud Run and understand if you need to optimize your deployment.

If you remember from Chapter 7, where we talked about scaling, we learned that Cloud Run has a built-in auto-scaling feature that will scale Cloud Run workloads, which means that we don't need to spend too much time scaling and understanding how many resources we need to give our Cloud Run deployment.

If we monitor our workloads in Cloud Run, we can figure out how many resources our workloads need in the initial deployment, which also prevents Cloud Run from scaling our deployment.

## Service Details

The first area in Cloud Run that allows you to monitor your workloads is the Service Details page, which is accessible when you click on your Cloud Run deployment. The Details page allows you to use the Cloud Monitoring metrics feature and display aggregated data.

Figure 8-9 shows the Service Details page and the Metrics page, where you can see the count of the number of requests the workload is receiving, which is updated every minute.

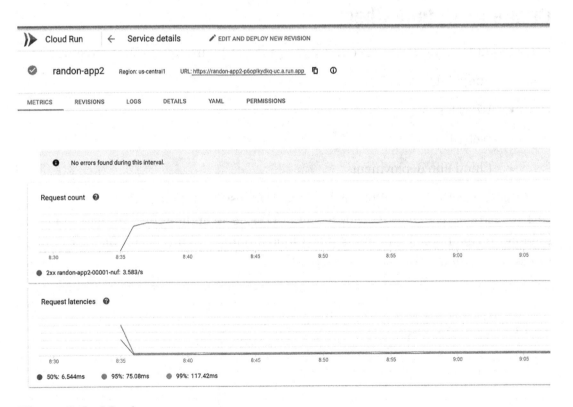

***Figure 8-9.***  *Metrics*

By default, the following metrics are found on the Main Service Details, Metrics page:

**Container CPU utilization:** Overall CPU usage of the workload

**Container memory utilization:** RAM memory usage

**Billable container instance time:** Cost of running the Cloud Run workloads based on millisecond

**Request latencies:** Overall network latency

**Request count:** Number of network requests to the workload endpoint

For a container as a service, Cloud Monitoring provides great monitoring power at zero cost.

# Create an Uptime Check

Using Cloud Monitoring uptime checks, you can monitor the uptime of the following:

- Endpoints

- Websites

- Web APIs

- Cloud Run deployments

Uptime checks can monitor anything that is accessible over the internet or in the GCP infrastructure. In the following example, I create an uptime check for my Cloud Run random app endpoint. I start by opening Cloud Monitoring and clicking on the Uptime Checks menu item, as shown in Figure 8-10.

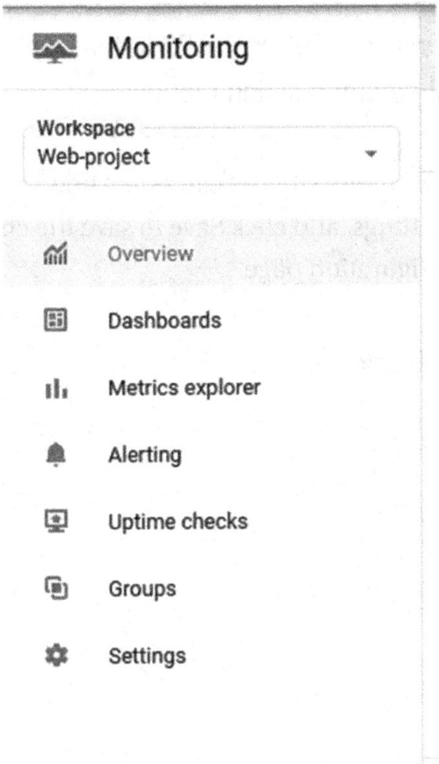

*Figure 8-10.* *Uptime checks monitoring*

From the Uptime Check management console's top menu, I click on Create Uptime Checks to create my first uptime check. Figure 8-11 shows the Create Uptime Check menu.

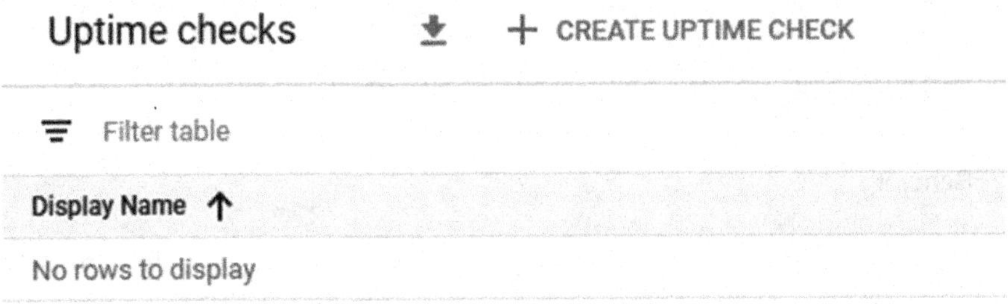

*Figure 8-11.* *Create an uptime check*

From this menu, I fill in some details. For Title of Uptime Check I choose a meaningful name that belongs to my random app. For Check Time, I leave it HTTP. I also have the option to use HTTPS or any TCP/IP port number that my application is listening on. In the Hostname box, I type the URL of my application.

231

**Note**   Please don't use www, HTTP, or HTTPS in the front of the URL; GCP is smart enough to figure the best communication method.

I check every drop-down menu, where I can select how often I would like the check to run. I go over the other settings, and click Save to save the check. Figure 8-12 shows the New Uptime Check configuration page.

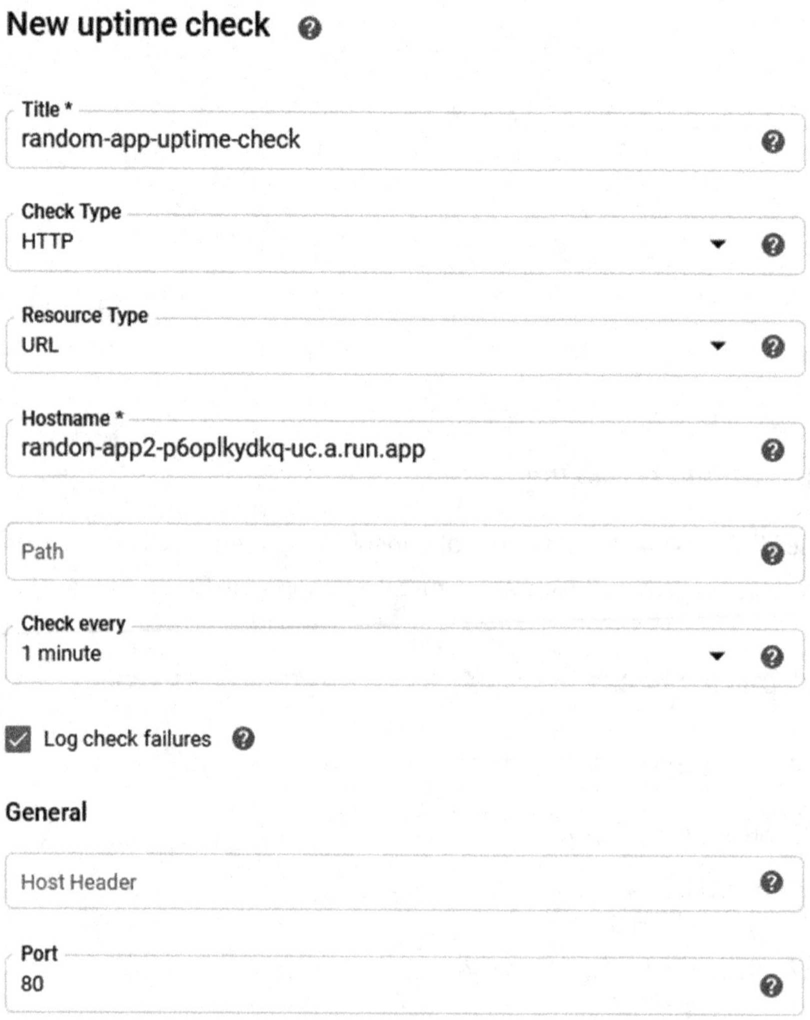

**New uptime check**  ❷

Title *
random-app-uptime-check                                                    ❷

Check Type
HTTP                                                                  ▼   ❷

Resource Type
URL                                                                  ▼   ❷

Hostname *
randon-app2-p6oplkydkq-uc.a.run.app                                        ❷

Path                                                                       ❷

Check every
1 minute                                                             ▼   ❷

☑ Log check failures  ❷

**General**

Host Header                                                                ❷

Port
80                                                                         ❷

*Figure 8-12.*  *New uptime check*

Once the uptime check has been configured, I wait a minute and then check the status. Figure 8-13 shows the Uptime Check Status page. You will notice that GCP is doing the checks from four different locations.

| Asia Pacific | Europe | North America | South America | Policies |
| :---: | :---: | :---: | :---: | :---: |
| ✓ | ✓ | ✓ | ✓ | 1 |

*Figure 8-13.* *Uptime checks locations*

# Alerting

It is great that GCP gives you the capability to create uptime checks using a simple and well-driven user interface; however, an uptime check without an alerting capability will not do any good. After all, the main purpose of creating a check is to let you know when your website is down. The Cloud Monitoring alerting service gives you the option to turn your uptime checks into alerts.

## Create an Alert

To create an uptime alert, from the Cloud Monitoring page, click on the Alerting menu item located on the left-hand navigation menu. Figure 8-14 shows the alerting menu item.

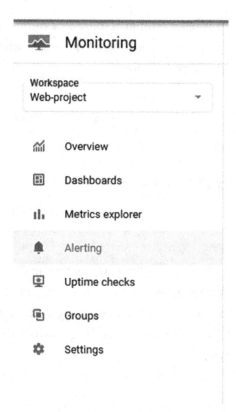

**Figure 8-14.** *Alerting*

From the Alerting management console's top menu, click on Create Policy, as shown in Figure 8-15.

**Figure 8-15.** *Create a policy*

From the Create an Alerting Policy page, name your alert with a meaningful name and click on the Add Condition button, as shown in Figure 8-16.

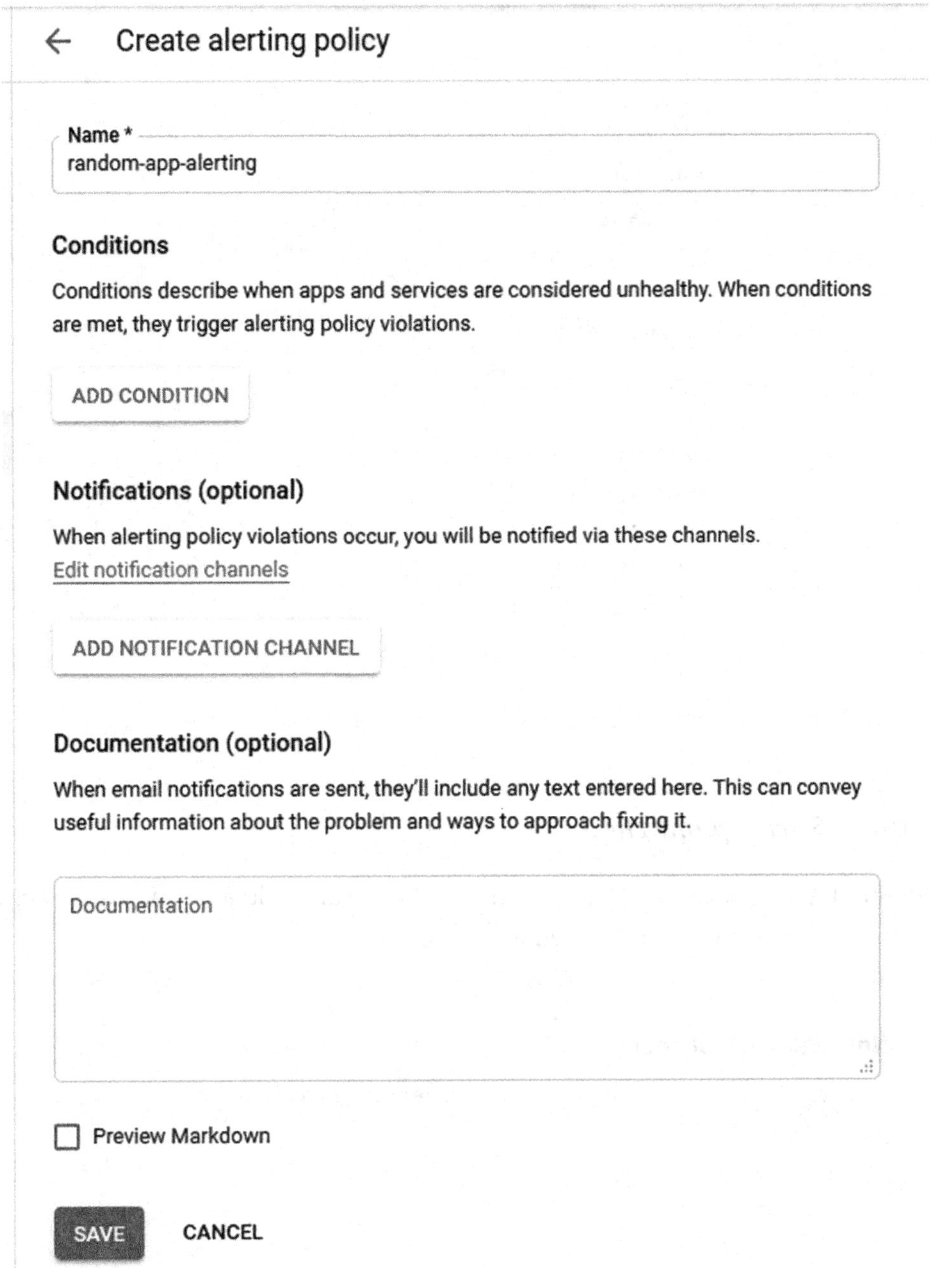

←     Create alerting policy

Name *
random-app-alerting

**Conditions**

Conditions describe when apps and services are considered unhealthy. When conditions are met, they trigger alerting policy violations.

ADD CONDITION

**Notifications (optional)**

When alerting policy violations occur, you will be notified via these channels.
Edit notification channels

ADD NOTIFICATION CHANNEL

**Documentation (optional)**

When email notifications are sent, they'll include any text entered here. This can convey useful information about the problem and ways to approach fixing it.

Documentation

☐ Preview Markdown

SAVE     CANCEL

***Figure 8-16.*** *Create alerting policy*

From the conditions menu, click on the second tab, which is called Uptime Check, as shown in Figure 8-17. From the Uptime Check ID drop-down menu, select you check; in my case, the random-app-uptime-check I created before.

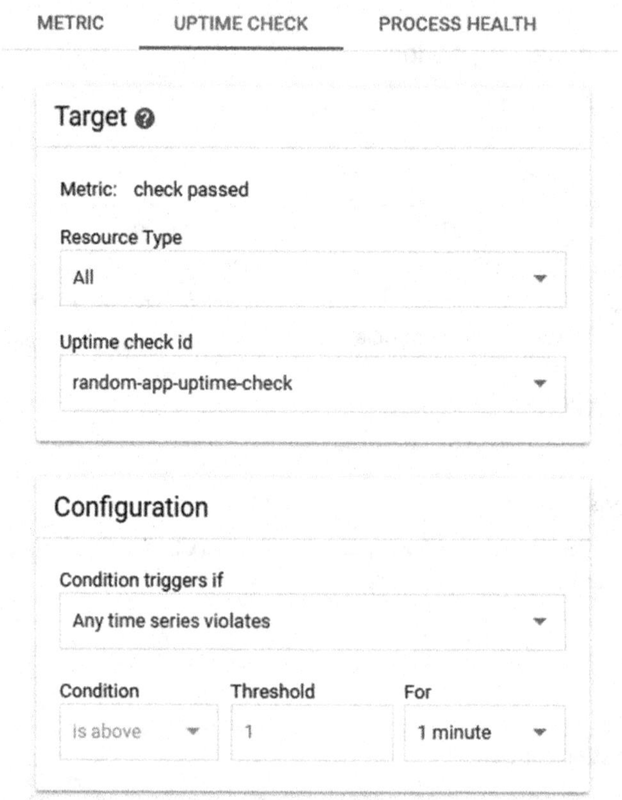

METRIC          UPTIME CHECK          PROCESS HEALTH

**Target** ❓

Metric:   check passed

Resource Type

All                                                           ▼

Uptime check id

random-app-uptime-check                                      ▼

**Configuration**

Condition triggers if

Any time series violates                                     ▼

Condition              Threshold              For

is above        ▼     1                      1 minute    ▼

***Figure 8-17.***  *Select uptime check*

After adding the condition, return to the Alert page and add a notification by clicking on Edit Notification Channel, as shown in Figure 8-18.

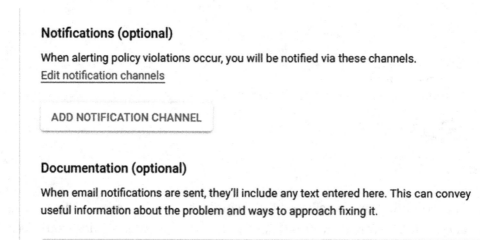

**Notifications (optional)**

When alerting policy violations occur, you will be notified via these channels.
Edit notification channels

ADD NOTIFICATION CHANNEL

**Documentation (optional)**

When email notifications are sent, they'll include any text entered here. This can convey useful information about the problem and ways to approach fixing it.

***Figure 8-18.***  *Notifications*

236

From the Notification Channels page, you have the option to add a notification from a very large selection, which is really good. I have to say that the flexibility GCP gives us in terms of notifications is very special.

My favorite one is the Slack Channel notification, which can help an entire DevOps or operations team to get notified when an application is not responding. Figure 8-19 shows the Notification Channels page.

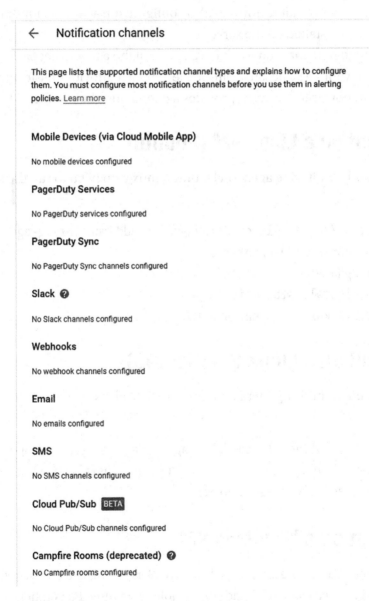

*Figure 8-19. Notifications*

# Monitor Compute Engine Resources

In this section, we will learn how to monitor Google Compute Engine VM instances using Cloud Monitoring. In GCP, you monitor VM instances using a Cloud Monitoring agent, which is a software daemon that collects metrics regarding the performance of the VM and passes them to Cloud Monitoring.

By default, the agent collects information about the CPU usage, network usage and traffic, and memory information. You can also configure the agent to monitor third-party applications that are installed on the server.

It is important to note that you don't have to install the agent to get basic monitoring information about your VMs, because out-of-the-box GCP provides basic information without the agent; however, the agent provides a deeper insight into the VM.

## Install Agent on a Linux VM (Ubuntu)

To install the Cloud Monitoring agent on Ubuntu Linux, you need to run the following commands:

```
$ curl -sSO https://dl.google.com/cloudagents/add-monitoring-agent-repo.sh
$ sudo bash add-monitoring-agent-repo.sh
$ sudo apt-get update
 $ sudo apt-get install stackdriver-agent
$ sudo service stackdriver-agent start
```

## Install Agent on a Linux VM (CentOS)

To install the Cloud Monitoring agent on Linux CentOS, please run the following commands:

```
$ curl -sSO https://dl.google.com/cloudagents/add-monitoring-agent-repo.sh
$ sudo bash add-monitoring-agent-repo.sh$  sudo yum install -y stackdriver-agent
$ sudo service stackdriver-agent start
```

## Install Agent on a Windows VM

To install the Cloud Monitoring agent on a Windows Server VM, use the following process. Log in to the VM instance using RDP and run the following three PowerShell cmdlets.

**Note**    You don't need to run PowerShell as administrator.

```
cd $env:UserProfile;
(New-ObjectNet.WebClient).DownloadFile("https://repo.stackdriver.com/
windows/StackdriverMonitoring-GCM-46.exe", ".\StackdriverMonitoring-GCM-46.
exe")
.\StackdriverMonitoring-GCM-46.exe
```

After you run the last cmdlet, the agent installation process will start, as shown in Figure 8-20.

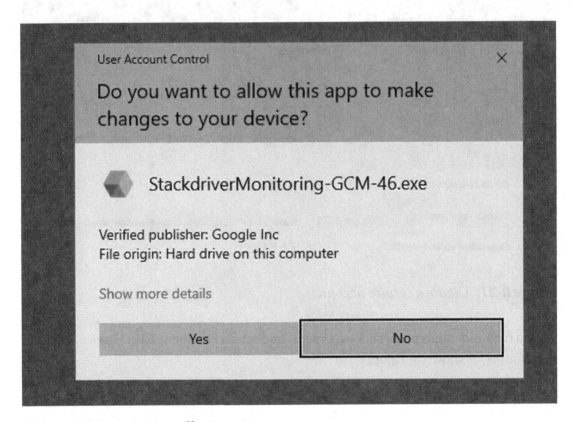

***Figure 8-20.*** *Agent installation*

Follow the installation steps and complete the installation.

# Create Service Account for Authorizing Agent

After installing the Cloud Monitoring agent, you need to create a service account with enough permissions to read and write events from the VM instance to Cloud Monitoring. This process is built from the two following steps:

1. Create a service account.

2. Authorize account from the VM instance.

Let's start with creating a service account. From the GCP console, open the API & Services management console and click on Credentials, as shown in Figure 8-21.

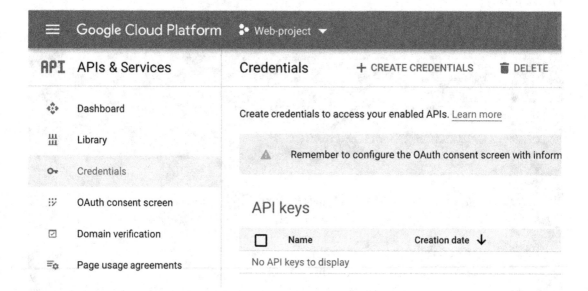

***Figure 8-21.*** *Create a service account*

On the Credentials page, click on Create Credentials and then select Service Account from the list, as shown in Figure 8-22.

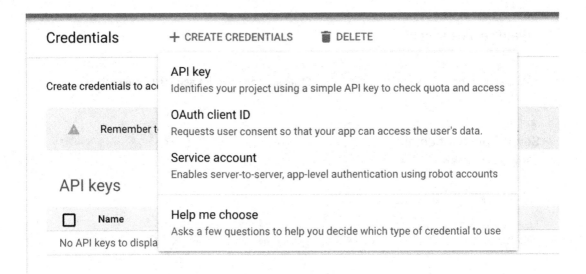

**Figure 8-22.** *Service account*

On the Create Service Account page, fill in the following details:

Service account name

Service account ID

Click Create to continue, as shown in Figure 8-23.

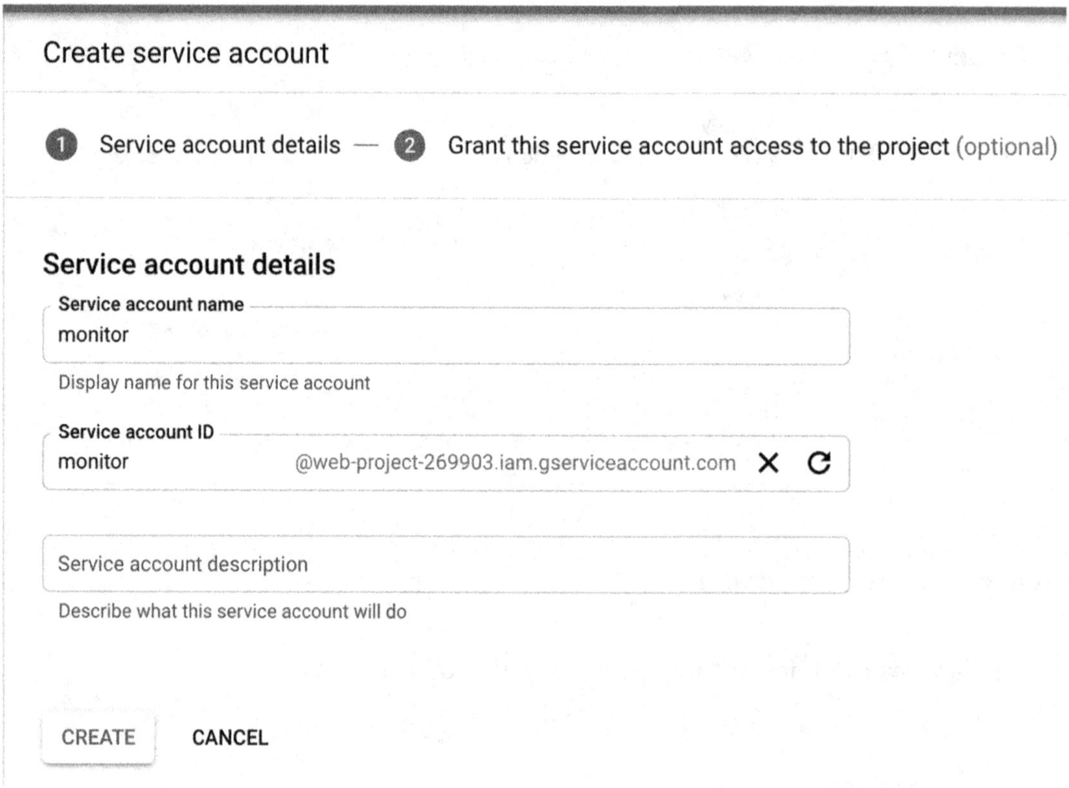

Create service account

①  Service account details  —  ②  Grant this service account access to the project (optional)

## Service account details

Service account name
monitor

Display name for this service account

Service account ID
monitor                              @web-project-269903.iam.gserviceaccount.com  ✕  ⟳

Service account description

Describe what this service account will do

CREATE      CANCEL

*Figure 8-23.*  *Create a service account*

After clicking Create, you need to grant the service account permissions to write monitoring metrics and logs. From the Select Role menu, search for the Monitoring Metric Writer permissions and add them. Figure 8-24 shows the monitoring permissions.

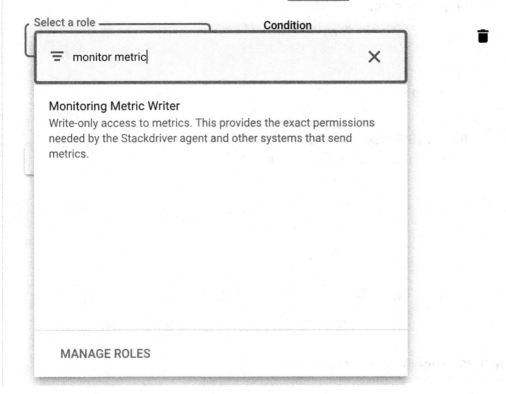

**Figure 8-24.** *Monitoring Metric Writer*

Go ahead and add another role, but this time use Logs Configuration Writer. Figure 8-25 shows the log role.

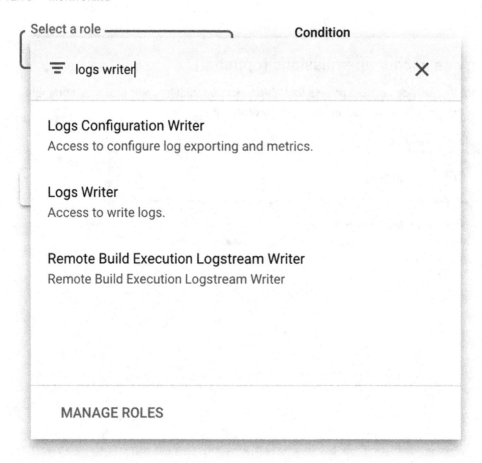

***Figure 8-25.*** *Logs Configuration Writer*

When you finish, go back to the Credentials page and click on the newly created service account. From the Account Details page, scroll down to the Keys sections and click on Add Key. Figure 8-26 shows the Keys section.

## Service account status

Disabling your account allows you to preserve your policies without having to delete it.

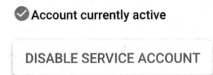 Account currently active

DISABLE SERVICE ACCOUNT

∨ SHOW DOMAIN-WIDE DELEGATION

## Keys

Add a new key pair or upload a public key certificate from an existing key pair. Please note that public certificates need to be in RSA_X509_PEM format.Learn more about upload key formats

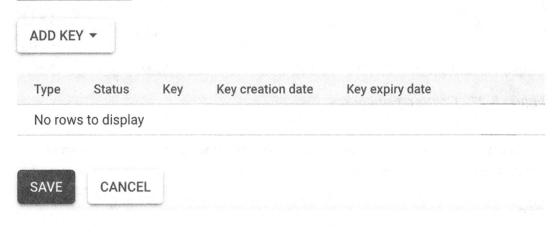

| Type | Status | Key | Key creation date | Key expiry date |
|------|--------|-----|-------------------|-----------------|
| No rows to display | | | | |

SAVE     CANCEL

***Figure 8-26.*** *Add Key*

From the Add Key page, select JSON as the key type and click Create to save, as shown in Figure 8-27. Save the file in a safe place, and as you will use it next.

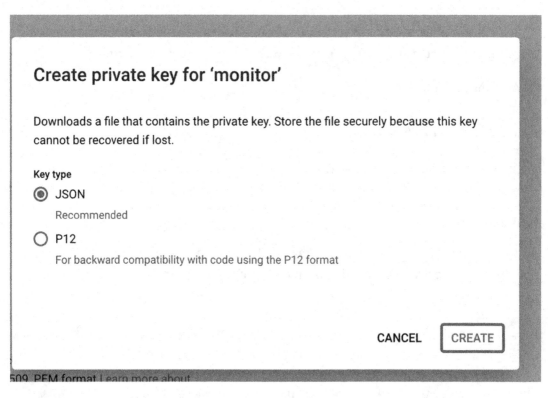

***Figure 8-27.*** *Create a private key*

After you create the key, the status of the key will show up as Active, as shown in Figure 8-28.

***Figure 8-28.*** *Key status*

# Copy Authorization File

After creating the key, you need to upload it to your VM instance. The authorization process is done by copying the authorization file to the VM.

## Upload Path for Linux VM

To authorize a Linux VM, copy the file (.JSON) to the following path on the VM. If the path doesn't exist, go ahead and create it.

```
/etc/google/auth/
```

## Upload Path for Windows VM

To authorize a Windows VM, copy the file (.JSON) to the following path on the VM. If the path doesn't exist, go ahead and create it.

```
C:\ProgramData\Google\Auth
```

# Monitor VM Instances

Now, that you have the agent installed, you can learn how to access the monitoring data of your virtual machines in GCP. The first place to start is in the Compute Engine management console.

Go ahead and open the console and click on VM instances. Click on a VM instance and then click on the Monitoring tab in the middle of the screen, as shown in Figure 8-29. The Monitoring tab will show you CPU, networking, memory, and other data related to the performance of the virtual machine.

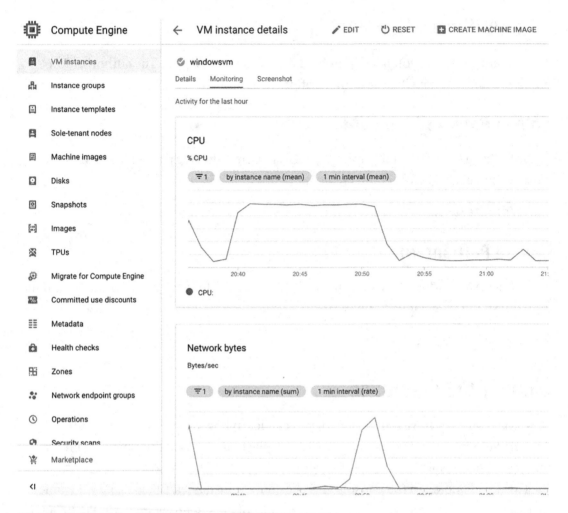

*Figure 8-29.*  *Monitoring tab*

Another method to monitor VM instances is from the Cloud Monitoring console. Go ahead and open the Cloud Monitoring console, and if you have installed the Cloud Monitoring agent on your VM, the Install Agent task will have a green tickbox, as shown in Figure 8-30.

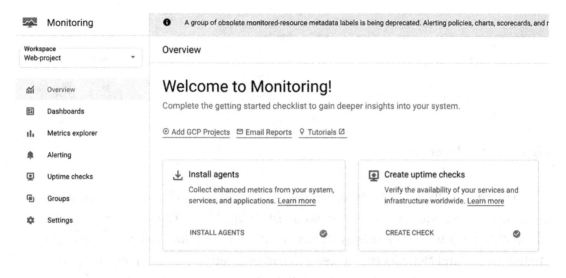

*Figure 8-30.* *Welcome to Cloud Monitoring*

From the Cloud Monitoring console, click on Dashboards and select VM Instances from the Dashboards list, as shown in Figure 8-31.

| ↓ | Name |
|---|---|
| ☆ | Cloud Pub/Sub |
| ☆ | Cloud Storage |
| ☆ | Disks |
| ☆ | Firewalls |
| ☆ | VM Instances |

*Figure 8-31.* *Dashboards*

On the main screen of the VM Instances dashboard, you will see the Inventory tab, which lists all the VMs that you have running under the project the dashboard is located under. The Inventory page gives you a great look into the overall performance and details of the VMs, with IP information, zone, CPU, and memory usage. Figure 8-32 shows the Inventory tab.

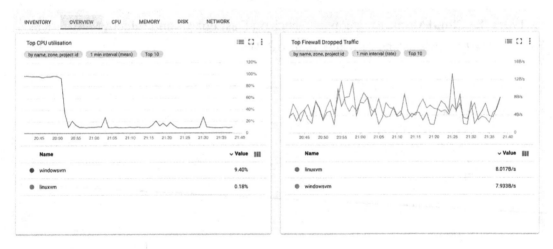

| Name ∧ | Zone | Public IP | Private IP | CPU utilisation | Memory utilisation |
|---|---|---|---|---|---|
| linuxvm | us-central1-a | 35.225.100.37 | 10.128.0.25 | 0.18% | 2.74% |
| windowsvm | us-central1-a | 34.69.190.21 | 10.128.0.24 | 9.26% | 47.64% |

***Figure 8-32.*** *Inventory*

If you click on the Overview tab, you will start to drill down into more detailed information about the performance of your virtual machines. The overview pages list all the VMs in the inventory, using a different color for each one. You can use the CPU, Memory, Disk, and Network tabs to get rich and detailed information regarding the performance of your VM instances. Figure 8-33 shows the Overview tab.

***Figure 8-33.*** *Overview tab*

# GCP Cost Management

In the last section of this chapter, we will focus on how to manage costs in Google Cloud Platform and how to prevent waste. Google has done an excellent job with helping us understand how much we are paying for our resources, and also what exactly we are paying for.

In every cloud, platform cost plays a critical part in the overall administration and management of the infrastructure. Without keeping an eye on cost and resource waste, the point of using a cloud platform is missed.

For our benefit and ease of management, Google has created a central area in the GCP management console called Billing where we can see our costs and for what we are paying. To access the Billing console, locate it in the left-hand navigation menu or search for Billing from the search box in the portal.

Figure 8-34 shows the Billing navigation menu.

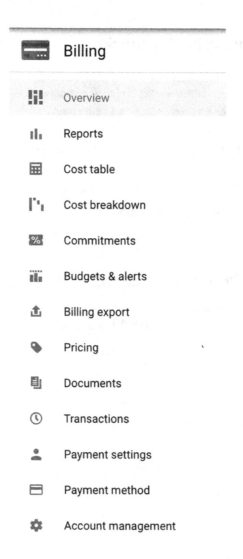

*Figure 8-34.  Billing*

The first things I would like to point out when you look at the Billing console are the following two things:

Billing health checks

Credit and cost

These two items show us if there are any quick fixes or recommendations that will help us optimize or reduce the cost of our GCP subscription. Figure 8-35 shows them.

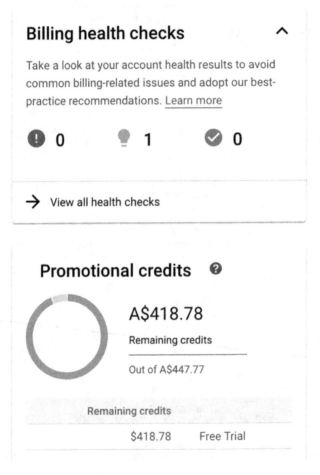

*Figure 8-35.* *Billing recommendations and credits*

# Create Billing Alert

The first thing I would like to recommend you do is set up a billing alert. A billing alert can help you set up a budget and apply an alert that will alert you before reaching the budget.

To create a billing alert, from the Billing left-hand navigation menu, click on Budgets and Alerts and then click on Create Budget. Figure 8-36 shows that GCP has a recommendation for me to create a billing alert.

---

←    **Billing health checks**

---

Take a look at your account health results to avoid common billing-related issues and adopt our best-practice recommendations. Learn more

💡 **Set up budget alerts**

Set up budgets with multiple alert thresholds to reduce spending surprises and unexpected cost overruns.

You haven't set up budget alerts for this billing account.      CREATE BUDGET

---

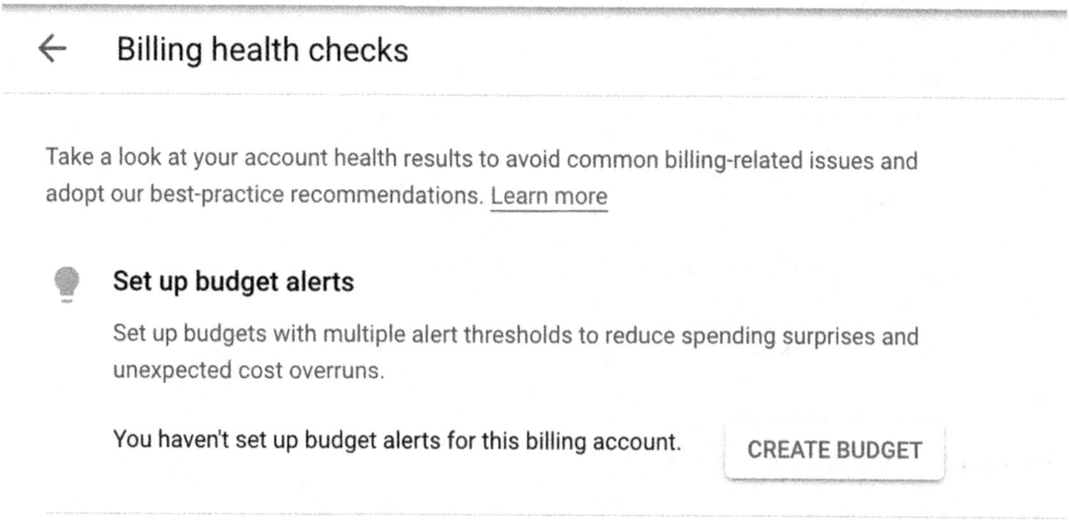

***Figure 8-36.*** *Create a budget*

From the Scope page of the Create Alert console, fill in the following details:

> **Alert name:** This can be any name you like.

> **Projects:** Here, you can set up an alert for the entire subscription or for specific projects.

Figure 8-37 shows the Scope page.

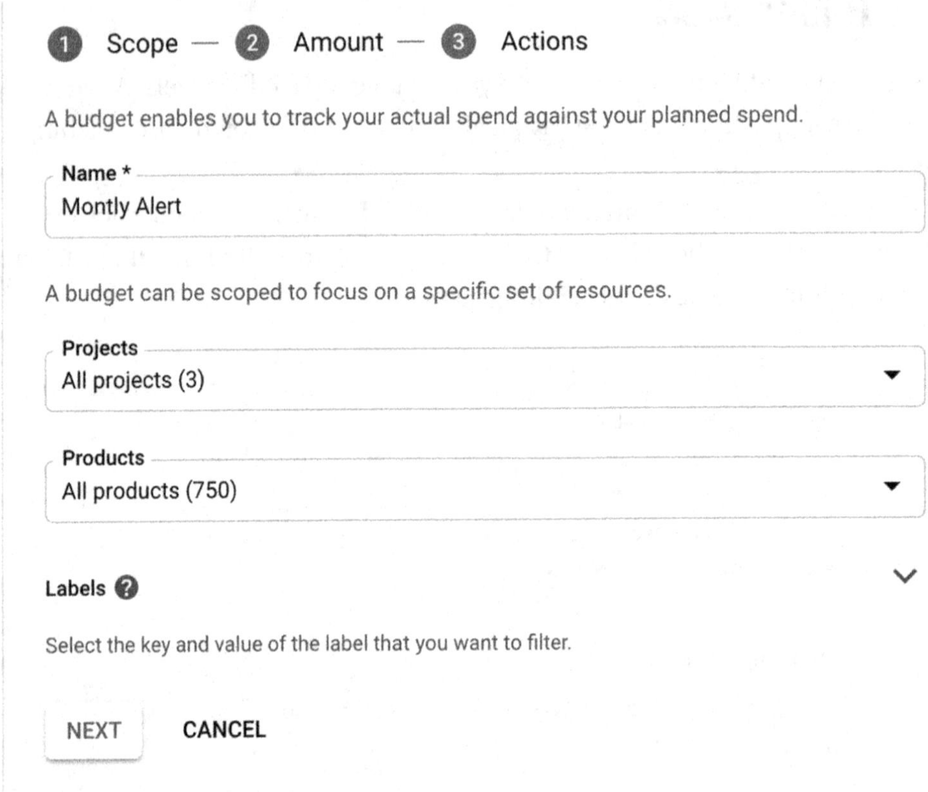

**1** Scope — **2** Amount — **3** Actions

A budget enables you to track your actual spend against your planned spend.

Name *
Montly Alert

A budget can be scoped to focus on a specific set of resources.

Projects
All projects (3)                                                          ▼

Products
All products (750)                                                       ▼

Labels ?                                                                  ⌄

Select the key and value of the label that you want to filter.

NEXT    CANCEL

*Figure 8-37.* *Scope page*

On the next page, set up budget type and amount of the budget. I will use the specified amount of $100, so every time my GCP usage gets to $100, I will be notified. By default, GCP will set an alert when the budget reaches 50, 90, and 100 percent of the budget.

Figure 8-38 shows the Amount configuration page.

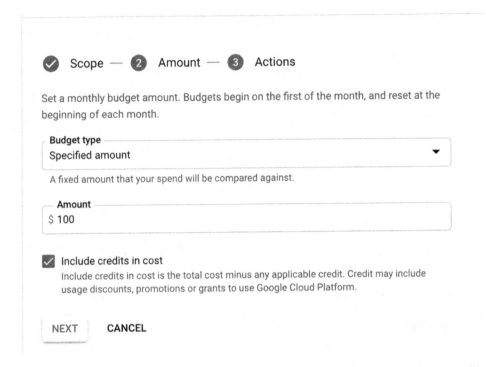

**Figure 8-38.** *Amount configuration*

# Cost Table

Another helpful feature in GCP is the cost table, which allows you to review how much each project cost you and what it is costing in terms of services. You can access the cost table feature from the Billing navigation menu.

As shown in Figure 8-39, I can see the cost of my project web-project and all the services that are running in it, like the following:

- Cloud Run

- VM instances

- Cloud Storage

- Secret Manager

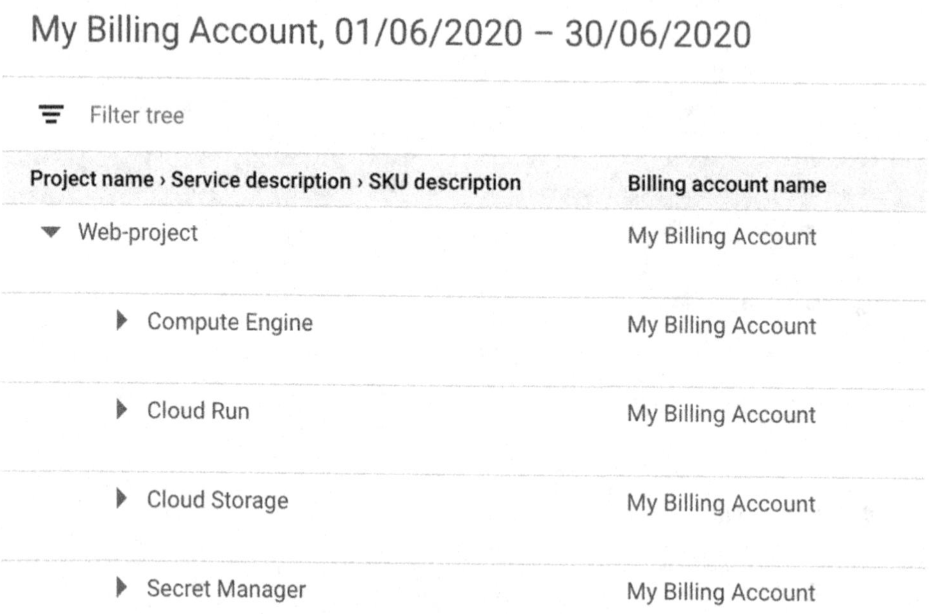

## My Billing Account, 01/06/2020 – 30/06/2020

| Filter tree | |
|---|---|
| **Project name › Service description › SKU description** | **Billing account name** |
| ▼ Web-project | My Billing Account |
| ▶ Compute Engine | My Billing Account |
| ▶ Cloud Run | My Billing Account |
| ▶ Cloud Storage | My Billing Account |
| ▶ Secret Manager | My Billing Account |

***Figure 8-39.*** *Cost table*

In the far-right column, you can see the cost of each service.

# Cost Breakdown

Another great billing feature is Cost Breakdown, which allows you to see the breakdown of your costs based on the following:

- Credits

- Taxes

- Total costs

- Adjustments

With Cost Breakdown, you can review how credits affect your overall GCP billing compared to the total cost of the account. You can access Cost Breakdown from the Billing left-hand navigation menu. Figure 8-40 shows the main Cost Breakdown screen.

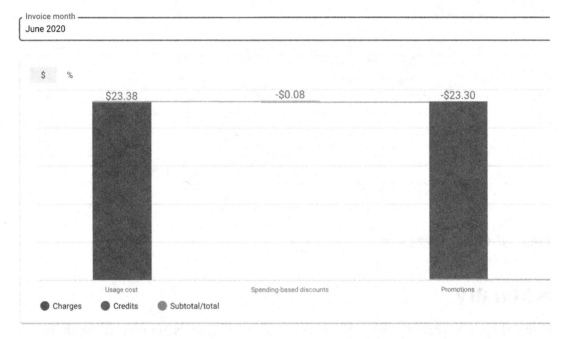

**Figure 8-40.** *Cost Breakdown*

# Pricing

The last and most important feature that I believe will help you to figure out how much each service actually costs is the Pricing feature located on the left-hand navigation menu. The Pricing page shows the latest price for each GCP service and how it is charged (by time or unit).

This feature is excellent because you don't need to search the internet for calculators for each cloud service that you are using. Each service is listed with the latest pricing details, and you can scroll down or search for the service pricing you are after.

As of writing this section, there are 1440 SKU to search from, which include every service, API, or object that has a cost. Figure 8-41 shows the Pricing page.

Pricing for My Billing Account

| Google service ↑ | Service description | Service ID | SKU ID ↑ | SKU description | Product taxonomy ❷ | Unit description | Per-unit quantity ❷ | Tiered usage start ❷ | List price ($) |
|---|---|---|---|---|---|---|---|---|---|
| GCP | Cloud Pub/Sub | A1E8-BE35-7EBC | 027D-B6C7-CCA2 | Message Delivery Basic | GCP > Analytics > Pub/Sub > Message | tebibyte | 1 | 0 | 0.00 |
| GCP | Cloud Pub/Sub | A1E8-BE35-7EBC | 027D-B6C7-CCA2 | Message Delivery Basic | GCP > Analytics > Pub/Sub > Message | tebibyte | 1 | 0.01 | 57.421999999 |
| GCP | Cloud Run | 152E-C115-5142 | 02A2-9231-36A6 | Memory Allocation Time | GCP > Serverless > Cloud Run > Other | gibibyte second | 1 | 0 | 0.000003588 |
| GCP | Compute Engine | 6F81-5844-456A | 0C5C-D8E4-38C1 | Licensing Fee for Debian 10 Buster (CPU cost) | GCP > Marketplace Services | hour | 1 | 0 | 0.00 |
| GCP | Cloud Run | 152E-C115-5142 | 0CCB-7057-48DE | Cloud Run GOOGLE-API Egress | GCP > Network > Egress > Cloud Run | gibibyte | 1 | 0 | 0.00 |
| GCP | Cloud Storage | 95FF-2EF5-5EA1 | 0D5D-6E23-4250 | Standard Storage US Multi-region | GCP > Storage > GCS > Storage > Standard > Multi-gibibyte month Regional and Dual-Regional | | 1 | 0 | 0.037324299 |
| GCP | Compute Engine | 6F81-5844-456A | 123C-0EFC-B7C8 | Network Google Ingress from Americas to Americas | GCP > Compute > GCE > Ingress > Premium | gibibyte | 1 | 0 | 0.00 |
| GCP | Stackdriver Logging | 5490-F7B7-8DF6 | 143F-A1B0-E0BE | Log Volume | GCP > Ops Tools > Cloud Logging > Logs | gibibyte | 1 | 0 | 0.00 |
| GCP | Stackdriver Logging | 5490-F7B7-8DF6 | 143F-A1B0-E0BE | Log Volume | GCP > Ops Tools > Cloud Logging > Logs | gibibyte | 1 | 50 | 0.717774999 |
| GCP | Compute Engine | 6F81-5844-456A | 14F9-7705-2FD4 | Network Intra Zone Egress | GCP > Network > Egress > GCE > Intra-zone | gibibyte | 1 | 0 | 0.00 |

***Figure 8-41.*** *Pricing page*

# Summary

In this chapter, we have learned about Google Cloud Platform's monitoring capabilities and, most important, the Cloud Monitoring service that enables us to monitor resources and workloads in GCP.

We also explored how to install the Cloud Monitoring Agent on Linux and Windows machines.

In the last section, we learned about GCP Billing features, which allow us to keep an eye on the cost of our GCP subscription.

In the next chapter, we will move on to backing up and restoring containers and applications.

# CHAPTER 9

# Backup and Restore

In this chapter, we will learn how to back up and restore workloads in Google Cloud Platform (GCP). Backing up and restoring workloads in any infrastructure (self-hosted or cloud-hosted) is one of the most critical operations you will need to make sure you have under control. Many organizations neglect this part of the operation, only to find out when it is too late how important having a backup is.

The second important thing in any environment is to make sure your backups are working by testing your restore process. Over my sixteen years in IT I have heard too many horror stories about companies backing up workloads for years only to find out they are not working because no one tested the restore process and everyone assumed the restore would work.

In this chapter, we will cover the following topics:

- Back Up and Restore Compute Engine VM Instances
- Back Up GKE Persistent Storage Disks
- Manage Cloud Storage and File Store

## Back Up Compute Engine VM Instances

I would like to start with VM instances, which will help you understand the concept of backups in GCP.

## Snapshots

In Google Cloud Platform, backups are done using snapshots of persistent disk volumes that are attached to resources like VM instances and GKE hosts. When it comes to VM instances, you run a backup by taking snapshots either manually or by using a scheduler, which is the recommended method.

© Shimon Ifrah 2021
S. Ifrah, *Getting Started with Containers in Google Cloud Platform*,
https://doi.org/10.1007/978-1-4842-6470-6_9

When you run your first snapshot, GCP will take a full disk backup; however, after the first snapshot, any further backups will only contain the changes that were made to the instance. Using this method, backup size is smaller and so are the costs of running backups and keeping them for a long period of time.

# Create Snapshot

Go ahead and create your first snapshot to learn by example and understand how back up and restore works in GCP. In my case, I have a running VM instance of which I will take a snapshot.

To create a snapshot of an existing machine, use the following process:

- Open the GCP console and navigate to the Compute Engine console.

- In the Compute Engine console's left-hand navigation menu, click on Snapshots.

Figure 9-1 shows the Snapshots page.

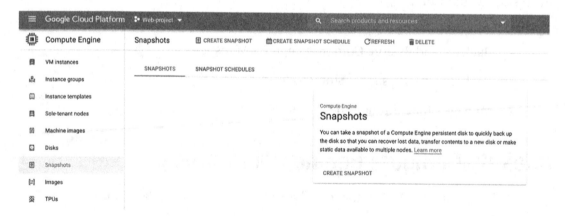

***Figure 9-1.***  *Snapshots*

- On the Snapshots page, click on Create Snapshot.

- On the Create Snapshot page, fill in the following details:

  - **Name:** This the name of the backup set.

  - **Source Disk:** This is the present storage disk of the VM instance you are backing up, so make sure you get this value right. If you are not sure, click on the VM instance and scroll down to the Boot Disk section and note the name of your disk or disks.

  - **Location:** This is very important. By default, GCP will backup your data to multiple regions for high-availability reasons; however, the cost will double since two backup sets are kept, plus there are network traffic charges.

  - If the workloads belong to a development environment, it might be smarter to use a regional zone. If you select a regional zone, make sure the backup is in the same location as the VM; otherwise, you will pay for network traffic.

- When you are ready, click on Create to start the backup process.

Figure 9-2 shows the Create a Snapshot screen.

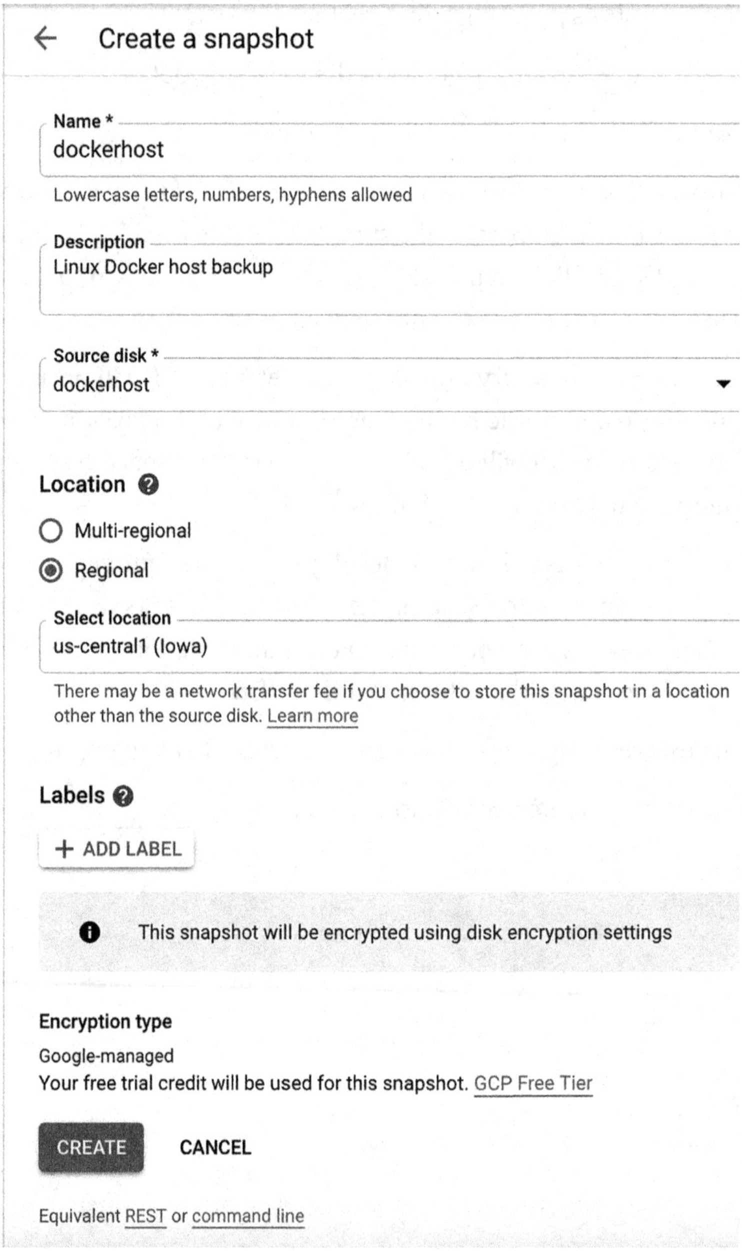

*Figure 9-2.* *Create a snapshot*

After creating the backup, GCP will start the snapshotting process, regardless if the VM is running or not. When the process is complete, you will see the snapshot in the Snapshots page, as shown in Figure 9-3.

If you look at Figure 9-3, my snapshot has completed, and it is 369.86 MB in size.

| | Name ↑ | Location | Snapshot size | Creation time | Creation type | Source disk | Disk size |
|---|---|---|---|---|---|---|---|
| ☐ | ✅ dockerhost | us-central1 | 369.86 MB | 8 Jul 2020, 20:31:47 | Manual | dockerhost | 10 GB |

*Figure 9-3.  Snapshot*

# Create a Snapshot Using Cloud SDK and gcloud

You can also create a VM instance snapshot using Cloud SDK and gcloud. The process is the same as running any gcloud command from Cloud Shell and Cloud SDK. The following code will take a snapshot of my dockerhost VM instance:

```
$ gcloud compute disks snapshot dockerhost --project=web-project-
269903 --description=Linux\Docker\ host\ backup --snapshot-names=
dockerhost --zone=us-central1-a --storage-location=us-central1
```

To view existing snapshots, using the following command:

```
$ gcloud compute snapshots list
```

# Schedule Snapshots

To schedule the operation of your backup infrastructure in GCP so as to not worry about taking backups, it is smart to automate the entire process. Using a snapshot schedule, you can configure the backup process to take place on specific days and times.

The process to use the snapshot schedule is simple. First, you create a schedule in the Snapshot Schedule console. Second, you configure the VM to use the schedule. Let's see how this process works.

From the Snapshot Scheduler tab, located in the Snapshots console, click on Create Snapshot Schedule, as shown in Figure 9-4.

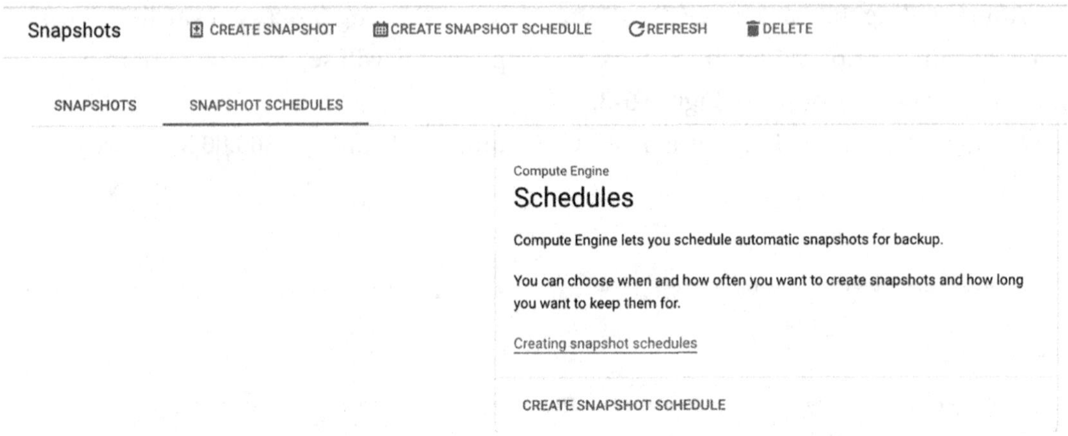

Snapshots      ⊕ CREATE SNAPSHOT      ▦ CREATE SNAPSHOT SCHEDULE      ↻ REFRESH      🗑 DELETE

SNAPSHOTS        SNAPSHOT SCHEDULES

Compute Engine
## Schedules

Compute Engine lets you schedule automatic snapshots for backup.

You can choose when and how often you want to create snapshots and how long you want to keep them for.

Creating snapshot schedules

CREATE SNAPSHOT SCHEDULE

***Figure 9-4.*** *Create a schedule*

On the Create a Snapshot Schedule page, you need to name the schedule and configure the following settings:

- **Name:** Use a meaningful name that will help identify what type of backup it is.

- **Region:** Select a region where the schedule will be located.

- **Snapshot location:** Select a region where the backup data will be.

- **Schedule options:** This is where we configure the schedule details (day and time).

When you finish, save the configuration. You can see the Create a Snapshot Schedule page in Figure 9-5.

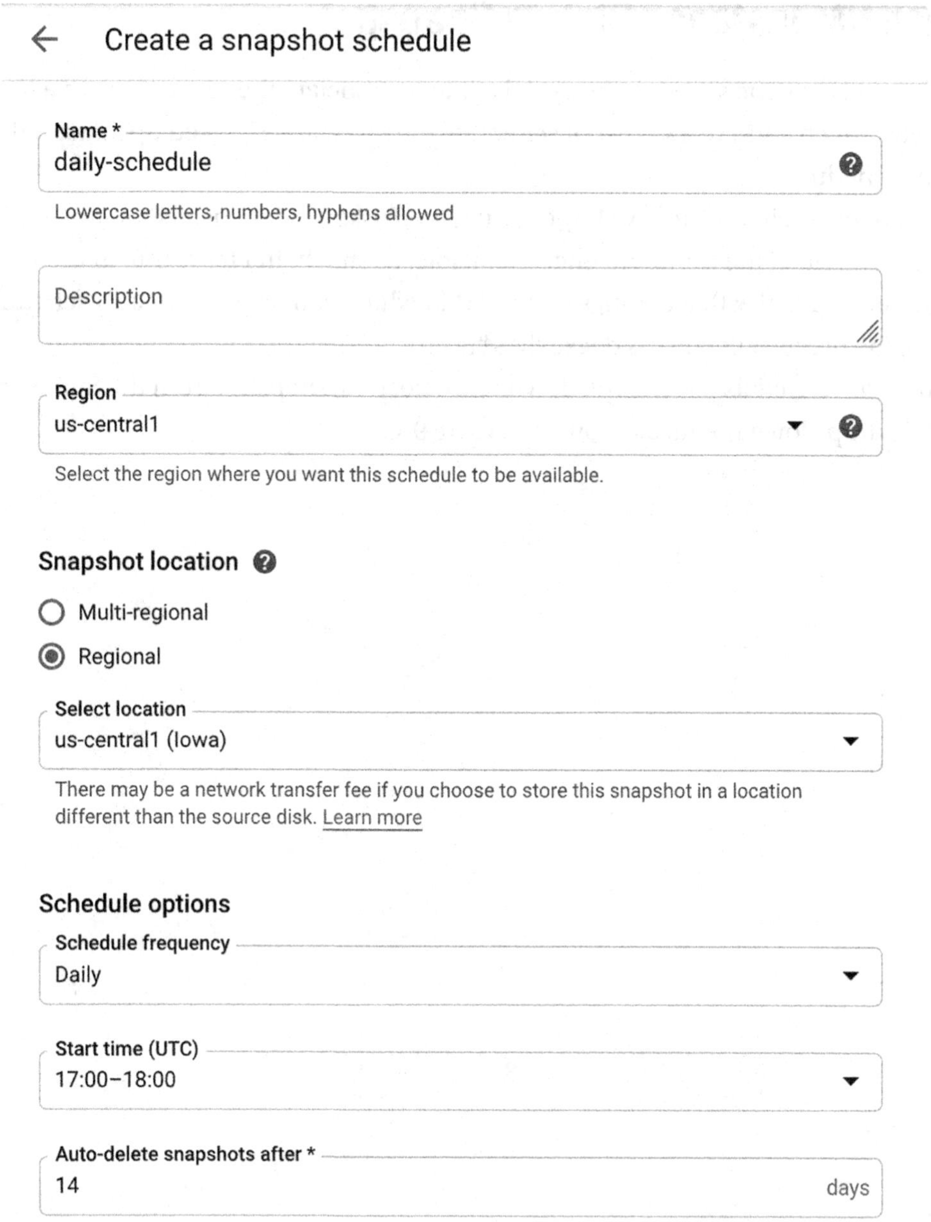

← Create a snapshot schedule

**Name ***

daily-schedule                                                    ❓

Lowercase letters, numbers, hyphens allowed

Description                                                        ⁄⁄.

**Region**

us-central1                                                  ▼   ❓

Select the region where you want this schedule to be available.

**Snapshot location** ❓

○ Multi-regional

◉ Regional

**Select location**

us-central1 (Iowa)                                            ▼

There may be a network transfer fee if you choose to store this snapshot in a location different than the source disk. Learn more

**Schedule options**

**Schedule frequency**

Daily                                                         ▼

**Start time (UTC)**

17:00–18:00                                                   ▼

**Auto-delete snapshots after ***

14                                                         days

***Figure 9-5.*** *Create a schedule*

# Attach VM Instance Disk to Snapshot

Now that you have the schedule ready, it is time to associate the schedule with a VM. When you attach a VM to a snapshot schedule, the VM will be backed up in accordance with the schedule.

You attach a schedule to a VM by opening the Disks section located on the left-hand navigation menu of the Compute Engine console, as shown in Figure 9-6. In the Disks section, select the disk that belongs to the VM to which you need to attach a schedule. In my case, the name of the disk is dockerhost.

On the Disk Details page, scroll down and select the snapshot from the Snapshot Schedule drop-down menu, as shown in Figure 9-6.

**Figure 9-6.** *Snapshot schedule*

If you go back to the Snapshot Schedules page, you will see that the schedule is attached or being used by my dockerhost machine, as shown in Figure 9-7.

| | Name ↑ | Region | Schedule frequency (UTC) | Auto-delete snapshots after | In use by |
|---|---|---|---|---|---|
| ☐ | ✓ daily-schedule | us-central1 | Every day between 17:00 and 18:00 | 14 days | dockerhost |

SNAPSHOTS     SNAPSHOT SCHEDULES

≡ Filter table

*Figure 9-7.* *Used by*

# Restore Compute Engine VM Instance

When it comes to restoring your snapshots, GCP gives you a few options, as follows:

- **Create a new VM from an existing snapshot:** This option is good if you would like to have a copy of a running instance and compare or test the configuration of the instance in a sandbox environment.

- **Replace existing disk with a snapshot:** This is probably what most people will use if they need to restore the VM. In this case, we first create a disk from a snapshot and attach it as a boot disk.

Let's go ahead and start with the first option.

## Create a New Instance from a Snapshot

To create a new VM instance from a disk snapshot, open the Snapshots console and click on the snapshot you would like to spin a VM from. Figure 9-8 shows my snapshots.

| | Name ↑ | Location | Snapshot size |
|---|---|---|---|
| ☐ | ✓ dockerhost | us-central1 | 369.86 MB |
| ☐ | ✓ dockerhost-us-central1-a-20200708170456-5oteuisw | us-central1 | 7.78 MB |
| ☐ | ✓ dockerhost-us-central1-a-20200709170457-a909so83 | us-central1 | 52.11 MB |
| ☐ | ✓ dockerhost-us-central1-a-20200710170459-rjzetb5t | us-central1 | 47.6 MB |

≡ Filter table

*Figure 9-8.* *Snapshots*

On the Snapshot Details page, click on the Create Instance button located on the top menu, as shown in Figure 9-9. Follow the Create Instance wizard to deploy a VM.

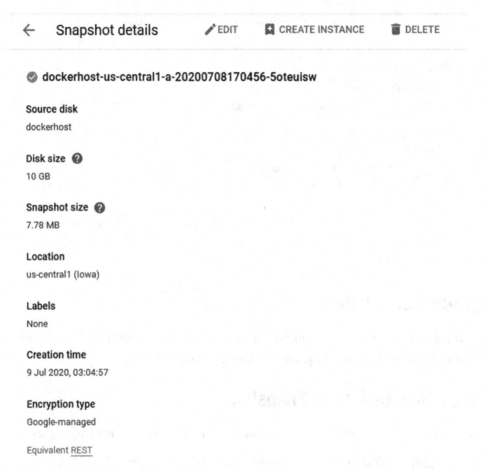

*Figure 9-9.* *Create instance*

In the wizard under Boot Disk, you will notice that the disk will be created from a snapshot, as shown in Figure 9-10.

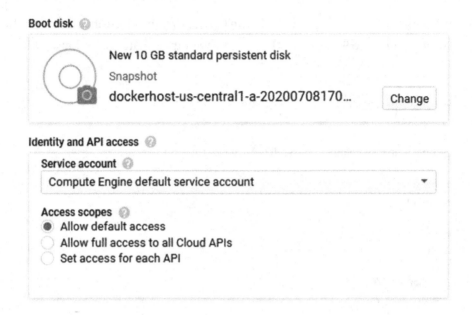

*Figure 9-10.* *Boot disk*

# Replace Boot Disk

The second restore option is handier if you need to restore a running VM instance, because it will replace an existing boot disk or a secondary disk.

## Create a New Disk from Snapshot

To use this option, you need to create a new disk first using the following process:

- Open the Disks section from the Compute Engine console and click on Create Disk.

- Name the disk.

- On the Create Disk wizard, in the Source Type section, click on Snapshot and select the snapshot you would like to use.

Figure 9-11 shows the source type options.

**Source type** ⓘ

| Blank disk | Image | Snapshot |

**Source snapshot** ⓘ

dockerhost-us-central1-a-20200708170456-5oteuisw    ▼

**Size (GB)** ⓘ (Optional)

10

*Figure 9-11.* *Source type*

## Replace Disk of an Existing VM

Now it is time to attach the disk to an existing VM. Do so as follows:

- First, stop the VM and click on it.

- From the VM Details page, click on Edit and scroll down to the Boot Disk section, as shown in Figure 9-12.

- Remove the existing disk using the X sign and click on the Add Item button.

  From the Add Item menu, click on the drop-down box under Name and select the disk you created in the previous subsection. In my case, the disk is called disk-1, and it appears in the list, as shown in Figure 9-12.

- When you finish, save the settings and start the VM.

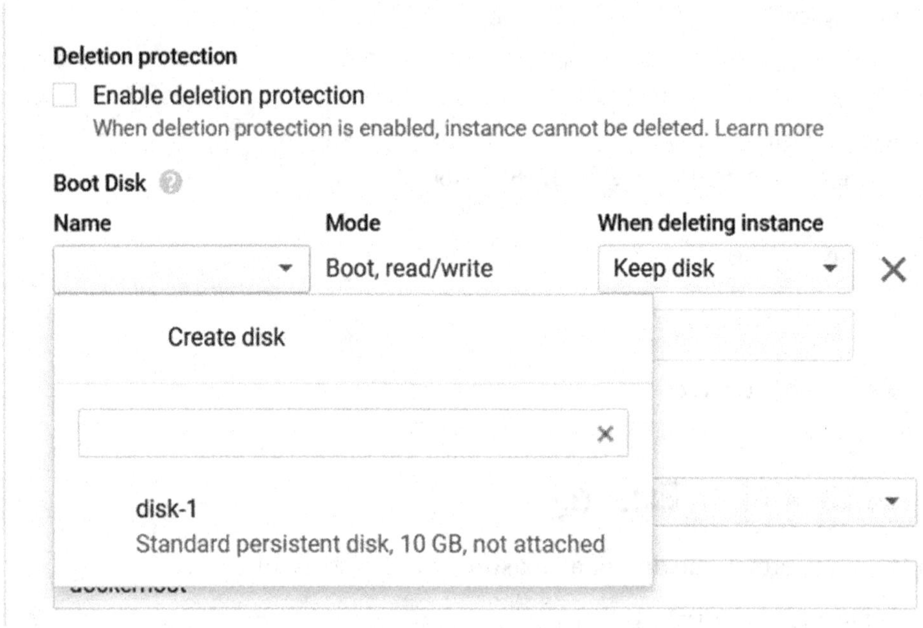

**Deletion protection**

☐ Enable deletion protection

When deletion protection is enabled, instance cannot be deleted. Learn more

**Boot Disk** ⓘ

| Name | Mode | When deleting instance |
|---|---|---|
| ▼ | Boot, read/write | Keep disk ▼ ✕ |

Create disk

✕

disk-1
Standard persistent disk, 10 GB, not attached

*Figure 9-12.  Add disk*

# Back Up Persistent Storage Disks (GKE)

When it comes to Google Kubernetes Engine (GKE) backups and recovery, the process to manage GKE data is very similar to that for Compute Engine VM instances. Since GKE uses persistent storage (same as VM), we actually use the same interface and process to back up and restore data as we used in the previous section.

Let's go ahead and deploy a stateful GKE application using the process we learned in Chapter 4. To deploy a stateful application, connect to your GKE cluster from the Shell terminal using the following gcloud command:

---

**Note**   You can find the connect command, on the GKE cluster page, by clicking on the Connect button next to the cluster name.

---

```
$ gcloud container clusters get-credentials cluster-1 --zone us-central1-
c --project web-project-269903
```

After connecting to the GKE cluster, deploy a stateful application using the following line:

**Note**   This is the same random app we deployed in Chapter 4.

```
$ kubectl apply -f deploy_storage.yaml
```

After deploying the stateful application, from the GKE cluster console, click on Storage. On the Storage page, you will see the newly created volume, as shown in Figure 9-13.

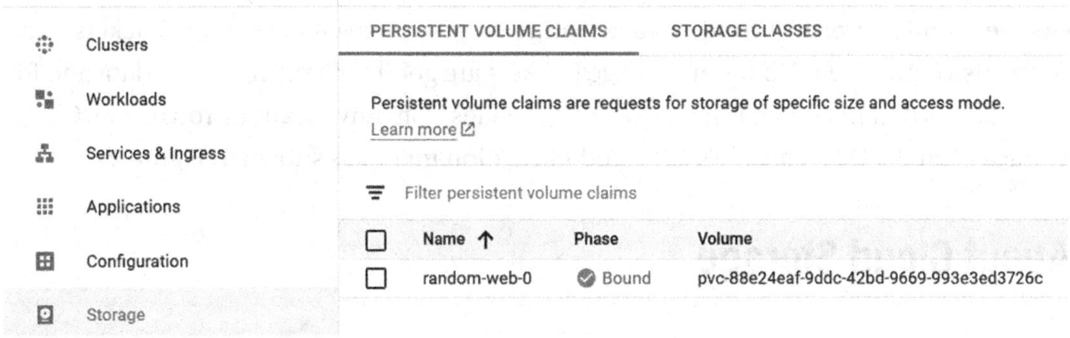

*Figure 9-13.*  *GKE storage*

If you click on the Disks section under Compute Engine, you will see the volume that belongs to the stateful application. Figure 9-14 shows the GKE volumes under Disks.

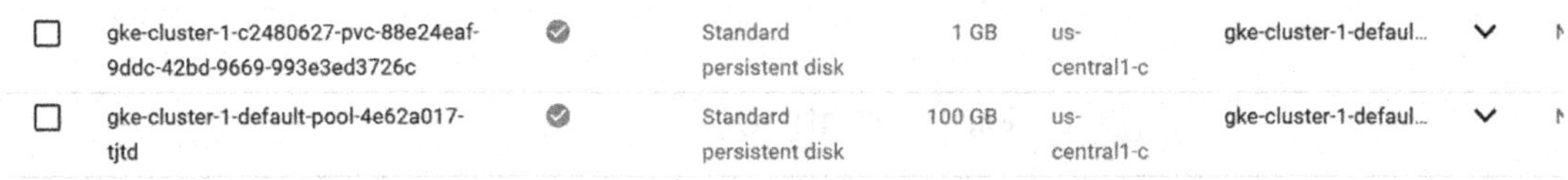

*Figure 9-14.*  *GKE disks*

If you click on the disk, you will see to which application it belongs in the cluster. This part is very important when you need to back up and restore applications that are running on GKE.

In Figure 9-15, you can see that the volume belongs to the random-web-0 application in my example.

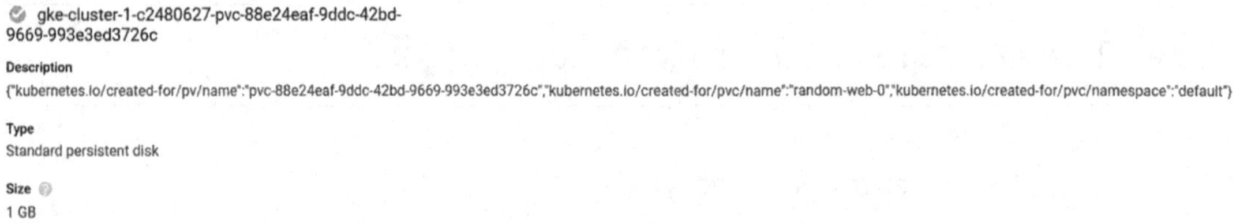

gke-cluster-1-c2480627-pvc-88e24eaf-9ddc-42bd-9669-993e3ed3726c
Description
{"kubernetes.io/created-for/pv/name":"pvc-88e24eaf-9ddc-42bd-9669-993e3ed3726c","kubernetes.io/created-for/pvc/name":"random-web-0","kubernetes.io/created-for/pvc/namespace":"default"}
Type
Standard persistent disk
Size
1 GB

***Figure 9-15.*** *Disk details*

# Manage Cloud Storage

Google Cloud Platform's Cloud Storage feature allows you to create storage buckets and store unstructured data in them. Storage buckets are good for storing simple data and for applications that need to dump data or retrieve files from any location. You access Cloud Storage from the GCP console's left-hand navigation menu, as shown in Figure 9-16.

## About Cloud Storage

Storage
SQL
Spanner
Memorystore
Data Transfer

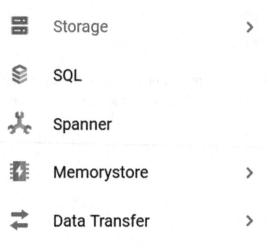

***Figure 9-16.*** *Cloud Storage*

## Create Bucket

To create a storage bucket, you need to use the Create Bucket button on the top menu, as shown in Figure 9-17.

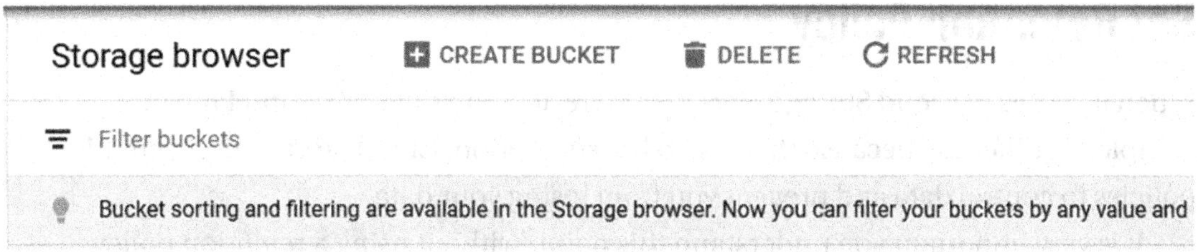

**Figure 9-17.** *Create storage*

On the Create Storage Bucket page, start by giving the bucket a name. You also need to set the bucket location. As previously advised, always place the storage next to your applications for quick access. Figure 9-18 shows the name and region selection.

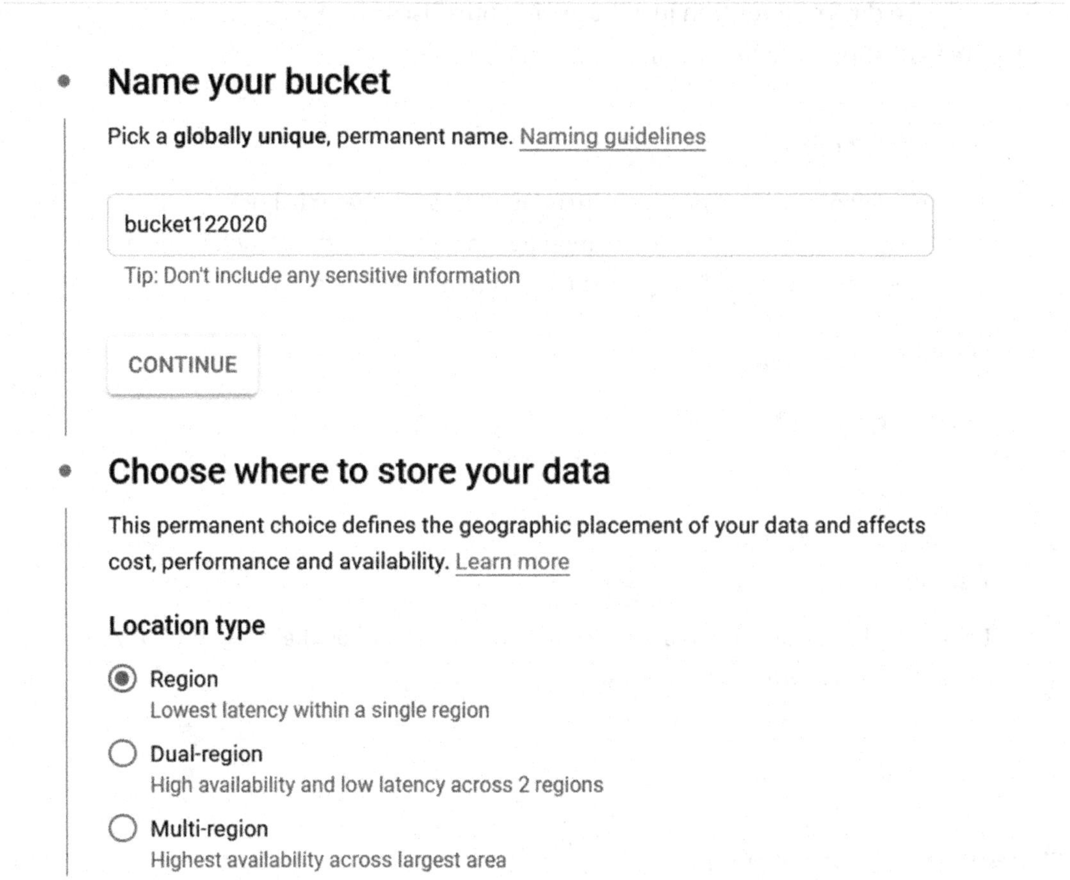

**Figure 9-18.** *Location*

# Set Retention Policy

When it comes to Cloud Storage, backup and restore are different—and I mean completely different, because there is no backup option. Cloud Storage uses retention policies to control data and prevent you from losing your data.

It is very important you understand this point: without using a retention policy, deleted data is gone forever and cannot be restored. The retention policy will keep any deleted data in the storage bucket for the life of the configured retention policy.

For example, if I set a retention policy of two years, deleted data would be kept in the bucket and be visible for two years before being deleted automatically.

Set a retention policy in the Retention Policy section on the Create Bucket setup page. By default, the retention policy is disabled. In my case, I will enable the retention policy with two days of retention just for testing purposes.

Figure 9-19 shows the Retention Policy section.

## Retention policy

Set a retention policy to specify the minimum duration that this bucket's objects must be protected from deletion or modification after they're uploaded. You might set a policy to address industry-specific retention challenges. Learn more

☑ Set a retention policy

Retain objects for *

| 2 | days ▼ |

## Labels

Labels are key:value pairs that allow you to group related buckets together or with other Cloud Platform resources. Learn more

    + ADD LABEL

***Figure 9-19.*** *Retention policy*

# Add and Delete Files from Cloud Storage

To add files to Cloud Storage, you can use the GUI for GCP API tools by using the following link:

https://cloud.google.com/storage/docs/uploading-objects#rest-upload-objects

For the purpose of this demo, we will use the GUI.

Click on the bucket name on the Cloud Storage console and then click on the Upload Files button. You can also upload a folder using the Upload Folder button. In Figure 9-20 you can see that I have uploaded a file.

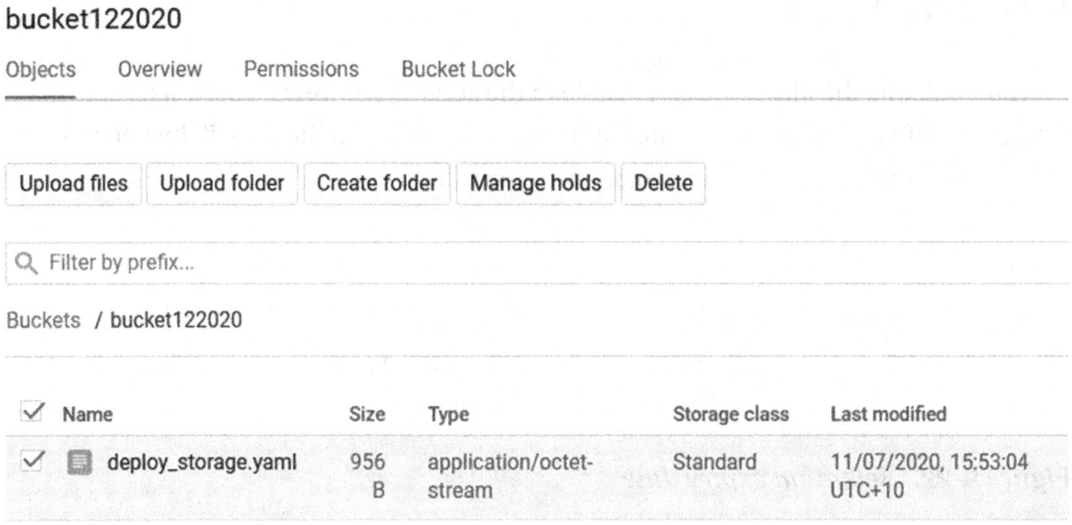

## bucket122020

Objects    Overview    Permissions    Bucket Lock

| Upload files | Upload folder | Create folder | Manage holds | Delete |

Q  Filter by prefix...

Buckets  / bucket122020

| | Name | Size | Type | Storage class | Last modified |
|---|---|---|---|---|---|
| ☑ | 📄 deploy_storage.yaml | 956 B | application/octet-stream | Standard | 11/07/2020, 15:53:04 UTC+10 |

***Figure 9-20.***   *Upload files and folders*

I will go ahead and delete the file by selecting it and clicking the Delete button that is located on the top menu. Figure 9-21 shows the Delete File menu.

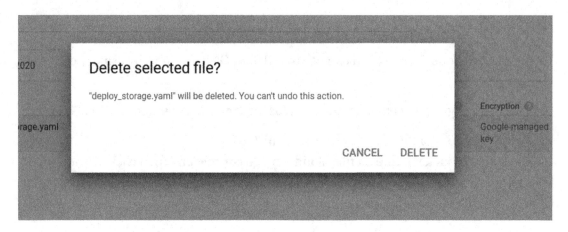

***Figure 9-21.*** *Delete file*

After deleting the file, it will stay visible in the console; however, you will notice that the column of Retention Expiry Date shows the date on which the file will be deleted completely. Figure 9-22 shows the retention expiry date.

| | Public access | Encryption | Retention expiry date | Holds | |
|---|---|---|---|---|---|
| 3:04 | Not public | Google-managed key | 13 July 2020 at 15:53:04 UTC+10 | None | ⋮ |

***Figure 9-22.*** *Retention expiry date*

# Configure or Add Retention Policy

To reconfirm the retention policy or add a retention policy to an existing bucket, click on the bucket name and then click on the Bucket Lock tab, as shown in Figure 9-23. On the Bucket Lock page, you can add, modify, or delete a retention policy.

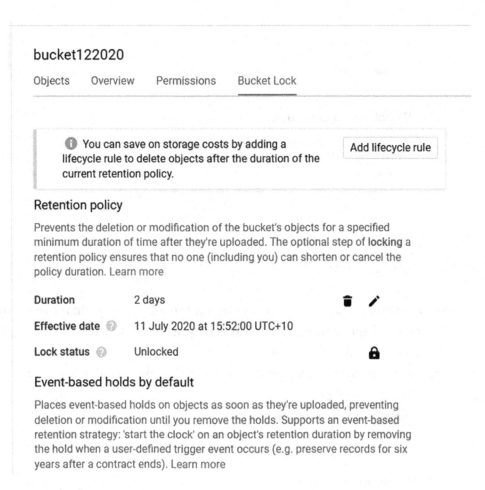

**Figure 9-23.**  *Bucket lock*

# Create Lifecycle Rules

Using lifecycle rules, you can automate tasks like deleting data from storage buckets. To create a lifecycle policy, on the Bucket page, click on the Bucket Lock option and select the Age option.

In my case, I will use 100 days, as shown in Figure 9-24.

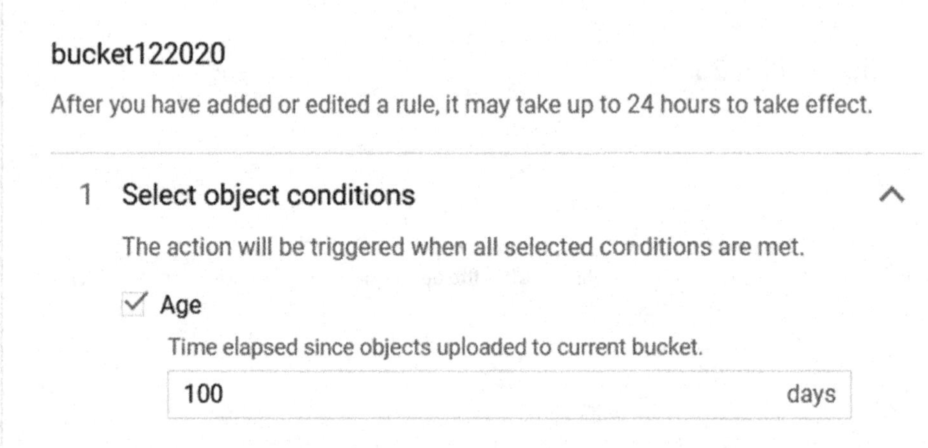

## bucket122020

After you have added or edited a rule, it may take up to 24 hours to take effect.

---

1    Select object conditions                                                    ∧

The action will be triggered when all selected conditions are met.

☑ Age

Time elapsed since objects uploaded to current bucket.

| 100 | days |
|-----|------|

***Figure 9-24.*** *Set bucket age*

In the Select Action section, there are four options; the first three can move old data to a different tier of storage that costs less. This is very useful if you use Cloud Storage to store data that you do not need very often.

The fourth option is to delete, and in my case, any data that is older than 100 days will get deleted from the bucket.

Figure 9-25 shows the Select Action menu.

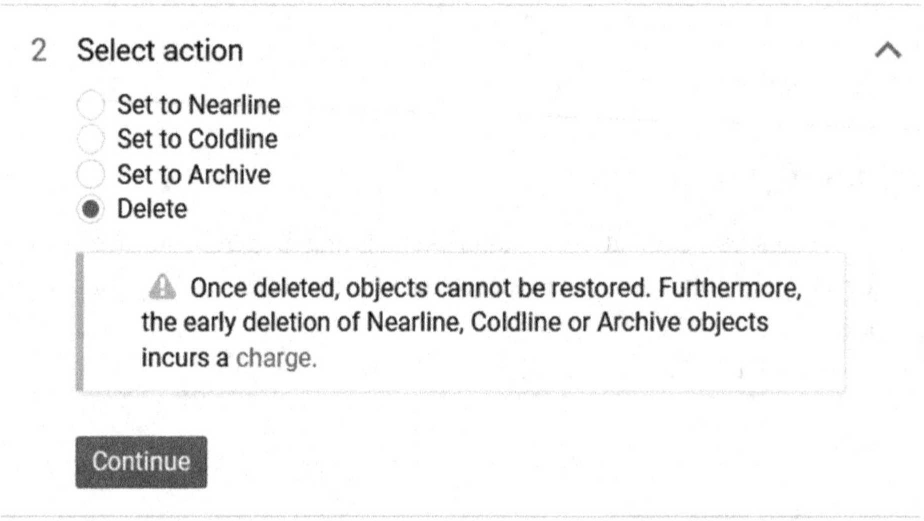

---

2    Select action                                                               ∧

○ Set to Nearline
○ Set to Coldline
○ Set to Archive
● Delete

⚠ Once deleted, objects cannot be restored. Furthermore, the early deletion of Nearline, Coldline or Archive objects incurs a charge.

Continue

---

***Figure 9-25.*** *Select action*

# Back Up Compute Engine Resources

In this last section of the chapter, I will show you how to configure a static public IP address to be used by Compute Engine resources. By default, any public IP address that a VM instance is using is not static, and when the instance is restarted, it gets a new IP address.

This process is not good at all if we are using the instance to host public sites, as public DNS entries use the public IP address to route traffic to websites and applications hosted on the host. Over the last few years, I have seen so many applications hosted on instances and various clouds that become inaccessible after reboot because a static IP address was not configured on the instance.

I hope that this section will prevent you from making this very common mistake.

To set a static IP address, open the VPC network console from the left-hand navigation menu, as shown in Figure 9-26.

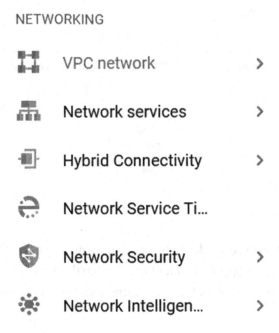

***Figure 9-26.*** *VPC network*

Click on the External IP Addresses section, and you will see all the external IP addresses used by your application. Under Type, you will see if the IP is ephemeral or static. An ephemeral IP will get replaced on reboot, while static will stay. Figure 9-27 shows the External IP page.

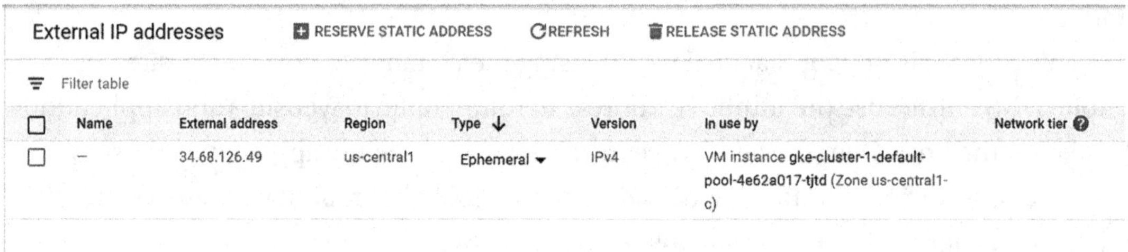

| | Name | External address | Region | Type ↓ | Version | In use by | Network tier ❷ |
|---|---|---|---|---|---|---|---|
| ☐ | – | 34.68.126.49 | us-central1 | Ephemeral ▾ | IPv4 | VM instance gke-cluster-1-default-pool-4e62a017-tjtd (Zone us-central1-c) | |

External IP addresses    ⊞ RESERVE STATIC ADDRESS    ↻ REFRESH    🗑 RELEASE STATIC ADDRESS

▼ Filter table

*Figure 9-27.  External IPs*

You can change the type by clicking on the type of the IP and choosing Static. Then, confirm the change, as shown in Figure 9-28. Please note that a static IP address has extra charges associated with it.

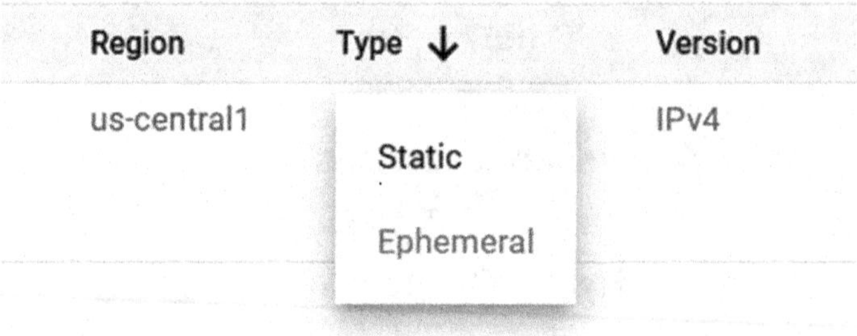

| Region | Type ↓ | Version |
|---|---|---|
| us-central1 | Static<br>Ephemeral | IPv4 |

*Figure 9-28.  Change the IP type*

To create a new IP reserve, click on Reserve Static Address and fill in the details. In the wizard, you have the option to select the service tier type, region, and, most important, the VM instance that will use it. Figure 9-29 shows the configuration page.

←    Reserve a static address

Name *

dockerhost-publicip    ❓

Lowercase letters, numbers, hyphens allowed

Description

**Network Service Tier** ❓

○ Premium (current project-level tier, change)  ❓

◉ Standard  ❓

**IP version**

◉ IPv4

○ IPv6

**Type**

◉ Regional

○ Global (to be used with Global forwarding rules Learn more )

Region
us-central1 (Iowa)    ▼  ❓

Attached to
dockerhost    ▼  ❓

Some of the instances may be disabled due to the 'External IPs for VM instances' organisation policy. Learn more

***Figure 9-29.*** *Reserve IP*

# Summary

In this chapter, we have learned how to back up and restore GCP resources that are using disk volumes for storage. In our case, we covered the process of backing up and restoring VM instance volumes and GKE storage volumes that are used by stateful applications.

In the last section, we learned how to use a static IP address in a VM instance when we host public DNS or if we need a static IP address that doesn't change on reboot.

In the next and last chapter, we will cover troubleshooting.

# CHAPTER 10

# Troubleshooting

In this chapter, we will learn how to troubleshoot the core services we've learned about in this book, but with more focus on using Cloud SDK and gcloud. The main goal of this chapter is to help you avoid common misconfiguration issues with GCP container services.

In this chapter, we will focus on the following topics:

- Basic gcloud commands

- Troubleshooting Google Kubernetes Service (GKE)

- Troubleshooting Cloud Run and Cloud Build deployments

- Troubleshooting GCP Container Registry

- Troubleshooting the Compute Engine resource

## Basic gcloud Commands

Let's start with a review of the most basic commands of gcloud and how to get started after installing it.

## Install Cloud SDK

To install Cloud SDK and gcloud, use the following URL and select your OS platform; as of the time of writing, you can install it on the following platforms:

`https://cloud.google.com/sdk/install`

- Linux

- MacOS

- Windows

- Docker container image

© Shimon Ifrah 2021
S. Ifrah, *Getting Started with Containers in Google Cloud Platform*,
https://doi.org/10.1007/978-1-4842-6470-6_10

# Initialize Cloud SDK

After installing Cloud SDK, start with the following command, which will initialize and authorize your account and configure gcloud with the right project:

```
$ gcloud init
```

To install additional components like GKE kubectl, use the following command:

```
$ gcloud components install name
```

To update a component, use the following command:

```
$ gcloud components update components_name
```

To check the version of your Cloud SDK, run the following command:

```
$ gcloud version
```

To get detailed information about your gcloud environment, type the following:

```
$ gcloud info
```

To access help, type the following:

```
$ gcloud help
```

If your session has expired, or if you would like to log in with another account, you can use the following command and follow the prompt:

```
$ gcloud auth login
```

# Work with Projects

To get detailed information about a GCP project, type the following command:

```
$ gcloud projects describe
```

To change the output of the commands to a table format, run the following:

```
$ gcloud projects describe --format table
```

To set a project and start working with it, use the following:

```
$ gcloud config set project name
```

# Troubleshoot Google Kubernetes Service (GKE)

In this section, we will start by going over the steps needed to connect to a GKE cluster using Cloud SDK.

## Connect to a GKE Cluster

To connect to a GKE cluster using Cloud SDK, use the following process.

From the GKE cluster console, click on Connect, as shown in Figure 10-1.

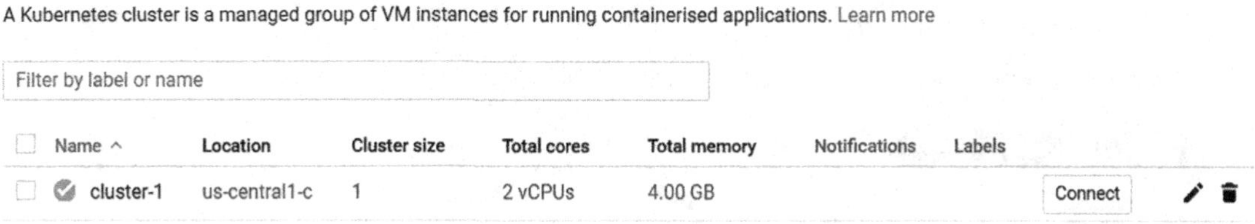

A Kubernetes cluster is a managed group of VM instances for running containerised applications. Learn more

| | Name ^ | Location | Cluster size | Total cores | Total memory | Notifications | Labels | | | |
|---|---------|----------|--------------|-------------|--------------|---------------|--------|---|---|---|
| ☐ ✅ | cluster-1 | us-central1-c | 1 | 2 vCPUs | 4.00 GB | | | Connect | ✏ | 🗑 |

*Figure 10-1.  Connect to GKE*

From the Connect to Cluster page, you have the following two options:

Copy the command into your terminal where you installed Cloud SDK, and authenticate to the cluster.

Click on Run in Cloud Shell, and, using the browser, connect to the cluster with Cloud Shell.

The only disadvantage of Cloud Shell is that sometimes it can take a few minutes to start and connect. Figure 10-2 shows the Connect to Cluster page.

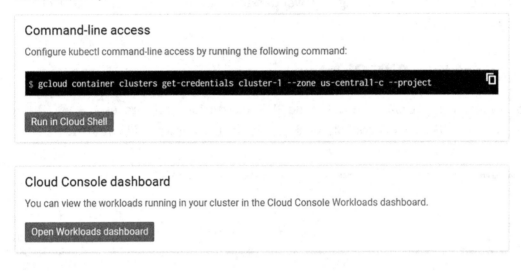

**Figure 10-2.**  *Connect to the cluster*

The following command is an example of the gcloud command:

```
$ gcloud container clusters get-credentials cluster-1 --zone us-central1-
c --project web-project-269903
```

# Overloading

A lot of performance issues in GKE are caused by overloading the cluster with too many deployments. To overcome the overloading issue, I recommend you enable Auto-scaling on the cluster.

To check which workloads are running on your cluster, you can use the Workloads console located on the left navigation menu, as shown in Figure 10-3.

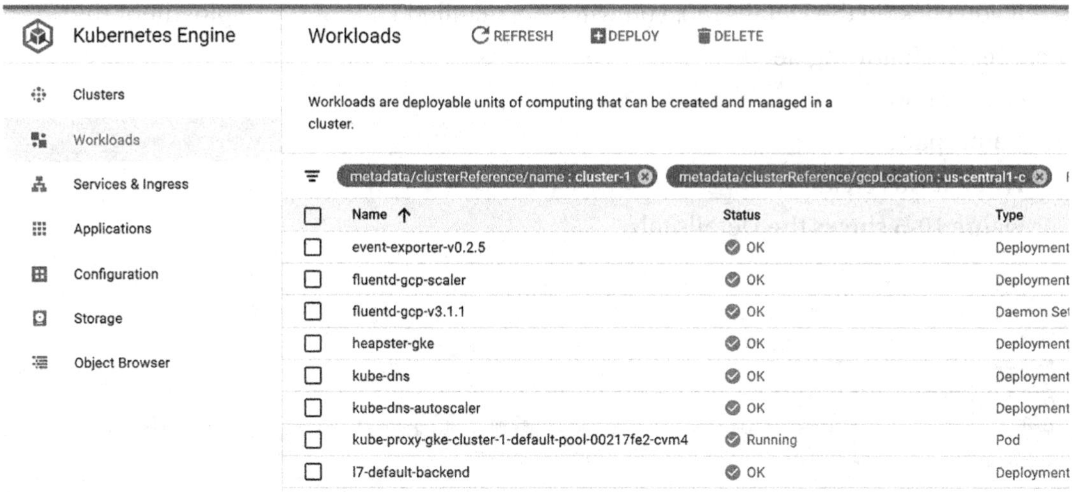

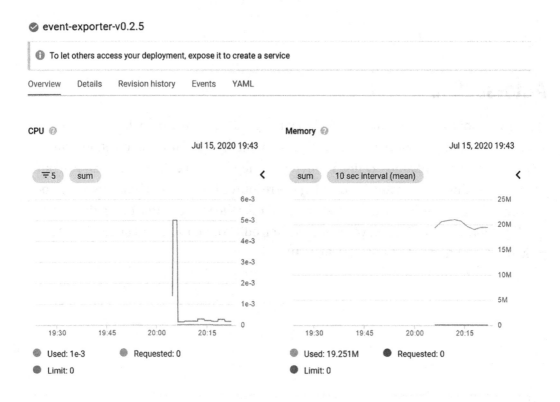

**Figure 10-3.**  *Workloads*

If you click on each workload that is running on the cluster, you will see the resource consumption utilization, as shown in Figure 10-4.

**Figure 10-4.**  *Resource usage*

If you click on the Details tab, you will get a detailed view of the deployment that includes the following details:

Cluster name

Namespace

When it was created

Figure 10-5 shows the Details tab.

| | |
|---|---|
| Cluster | cluster-1 |
| Namespace | kube-system |
| Created | 15 Jul 2020, 20:04:03 |
| Labels | addonmanager.kubernetes.io/mode : Reconcile    k8s-app : event-exporter    kubernetes.io/cluster-service : true    version : v0.2.5 |
| Annotations | deployment.kubernetes.io/revision: 1<br>⌄ Show all annotations |
| Replicas | 1 updated, 1 ready, 1 available, 0 unavailable |
| Label selector | k8s-app = event-exporter    version = v0.2.5 |
| Update strategy ⓘ | Rolling update, Max unavailable: 25%, Max surge: 25% |
| Min time ready before available | 0 s |
| Progress deadline | 600 s |
| Revision history limit | 2 |

***Figure 10-5.*** *Details tab*

# Auto-scaling

If your workloads are slow and you feel that the performance is not where it should be, I recommend you check if auto-scaling is enabled, and, if not, enable it. Running a GKE cluster without auto-scaling is not recommended since the cluster can run out of resources if no one is actively checking the resource utilization of the cluster. Auto-scaling takes the guesswork away and lets GKE manage the resource utilization.

To enable auto-scaling on your GKE cluster, edit your cluster and enable the Auto-provisioning options, as shown in Figure 10-6.

**Node auto-provisioning**  ⓘ

| Disabled | ▼ |
|---|---|

**Auto-scaling profile**  ⓘ

| Balanced (default) | ▼ |
|---|---|

**Vertical Pod Autoscaling**  ⓘ

| Disabled | ▼ |
|---|---|

*Figure 10-6.*  *Auto-scaling*

To prevent issues with your cluster, I strongly recommend you enable all the cluster and pod automation features GKE has to offer. By using automation, your GKE cluster will auto-scale and fix issues that arise as a result of large deployment, updates, and workloads.

# Troubleshoot Cloud Run and Cloud Build Deployments

In this section, we will cover some common practices that will help you troubleshoot and prevent issues with your Cloud Run service. Because Cloud Run is a fully managed service and can be considered as a serverless solution, the main issues that will arise will be performance issues. I have the following recommendations:

- Keep your container images in the same region of your Cloud Run deployment for maximum performance. Pulling a Docker image from a GCR registry in a different region will cause latency in the container startup time.

- Space your deployment accordingly and don't go with the default option. In the Capacity section of the wizard, you have the option to set the memory and CPU allocation, as shown in Figure 10-7.

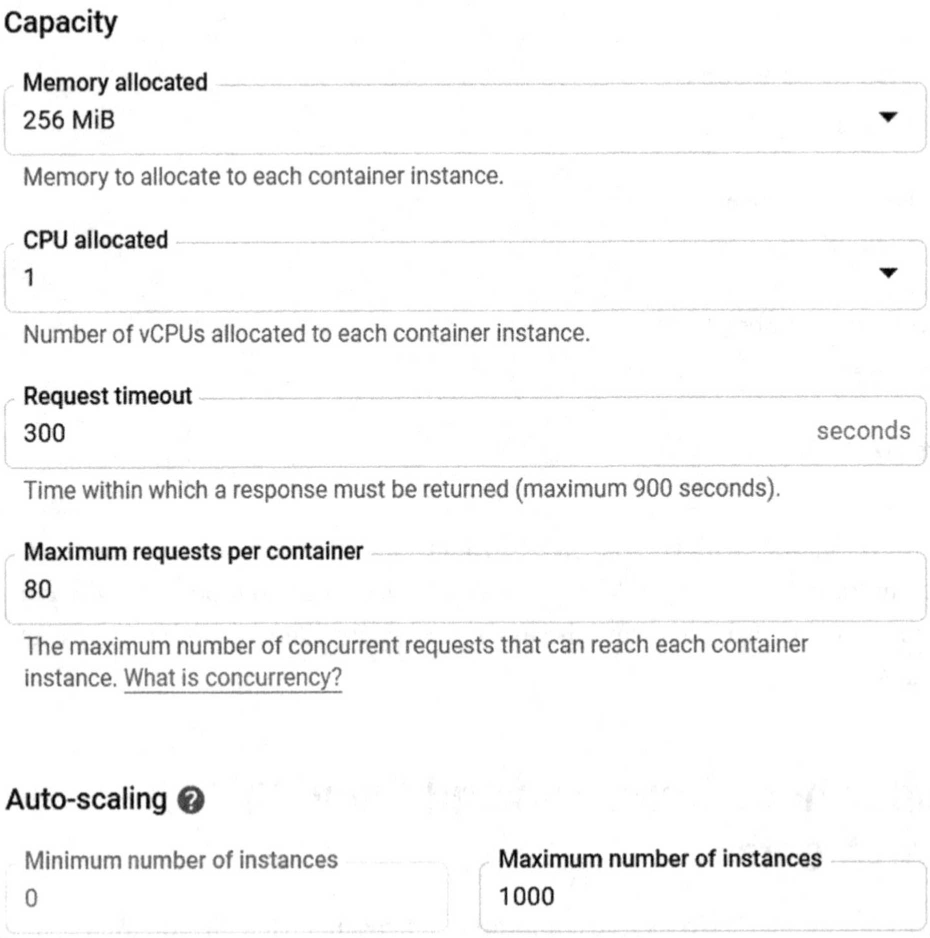

## Capacity

**Memory allocated**

256 MiB                                                    ▼

Memory to allocate to each container instance.

**CPU allocated**

1                                                          ▼

Number of vCPUs allocated to each container instance.

**Request timeout**

300                                                  seconds

Time within which a response must be returned (maximum 900 seconds).

**Maximum requests per container**

80

The maximum number of concurrent requests that can reach each container instance. What is concurrency?

## Auto-scaling ❓

Minimum number of instances                 **Maximum number of instances**

0                                              1000

*Figure 10-7.*  *Capacity*

- By default, Cloud Run is configured with an auto-scaling feature that will scale the number of containers if the load is high, so make sure you review the settings before deploying your Cloud Run service.

# Console Logs

To troubleshoot your Cloud Run application, you can access the console logs from the Logs tab and see what is going inside the container. Figure 10-8 shows the console logs' output.

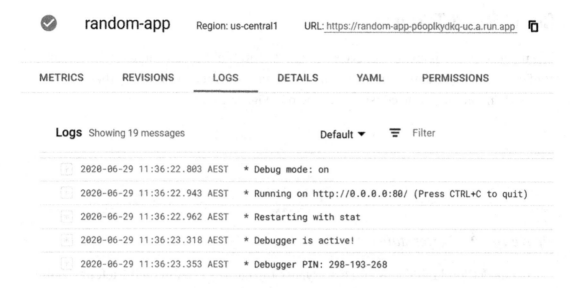

Figure 10-8. Logs

The console also shows real-time logs, and in my case every time someone accesses the application, an entry will appear in the console. In the case of an application issue, these logs can be very useful and helpful.

If you need to troubleshoot RBAC permissions issues to Cloud Run, you can use the Permissions tab to see who has access and which access level he or she has. In Figure 10-9, you can see the RBAC permissions level.

| Role | Inheritance | |
| --- | --- | --- |
| Editor | Web-project | |
| Cloud Run Admin | Web-project | |
| Editor | Web-project | |
| Cloud Run Invoker | | |
| Editor | Web-project | |
| Cloud Run Service Agent | Web-project | |
| Owner | Web-project | |

Figure 10-9. Permissions

# Cloud Build Triggers

The most common issue that I have seen with Cloud Build deployments is the trigger configuration. Make sure your Cloud Build trigger is enabled by checking that the status is set to "Enable" from the console, as shown in Figure 10-10.

| Name | Description | Event | Filter | Build configuration | Status |
|------|-------------|-------|--------|---------------------|--------|
| web-project | — | Push to branch | ^master$ | cloudbuild.yaml | Enabled ▾ |

***Figure 10-10.***  *Trigger status*

To check Cloud Build logs and history, use the History section on the left navigation menu of the Cloud Build console. Figure 10-11 shows the build history.

| ● Build | Source | Ref | Commit | Trigger name |
|---------|--------|-----|--------|--------------|
| ✓ 0b23fdc7 | web-project ↗ | master | 30c7313 ↗ | web-project |
| ✓ f03d1e81 | web-project ↗ | master | 67097b4 ↗ | web-project |
| ✓ 44111ffc | web-project ↗ | master | d72531f ↗ | web-project |
| ✓ d9c2903f | web-project ↗ | master | e4111bd ↗ | web-project |
| ✓ 93702322 | web-project ↗ | master | 6b2b94f ↗ | web-project |
| ✓ 6d6bae66 | web-project ↗ | master | 598394a ↗ | web-project |
| ✓ 6f33908f | web-project ↗ | master | eff48d2 ↗ | web-project |
| ✓ 6c1b8a91 | web-project ↗ | master | b802dd2 ↗ | web-project |
| ✓ 54bbd8db | web-project ↗ | master | 2dc7db2 ↗ | web-project |
| ✓ 8be2c06c | web-project ↗ | master | 2292906 ↗ | web-project |
| ✓ 85f7a2a2 | web-project ↗ | master | 5b26ccf ↗ | web-project |
| ! 62894d0d | web-project ↗ | master | b6a6c02 ↗ | web-project |
| ! 330f7f30 | web-project ↗ | master | e64fc30 ↗ | web-project |
| ! 286b2801 | web-project ↗ | master | e64fc30 ↗ | web-project |

***Figure 10-11.***  *History*

In the case of a failed deployment, clicking on the deployment will show all the steps taken and where the deployment failed. Figure 10-12 shows the build steps of a failed deployment.

```
 1  starting build "62894d0d-dbdb-4251-b8ab-1c79a8e288a5"
 2
 3  FETCHSOURCE
 4  Initialized empty Git repository in /workspace/.git/
 5  From https://source.developers.google.com/p/web-project-269903/r/web-project
 6  * branch            b6a6c02e0616b1c55b82a7595dca8cd981cd5493 -> FETCH_HEAD
 7  HEAD is now at b6a6c02 add
 8  BUILD
 9  Starting Step #0
10  Step #0: Already have image (with digest): gcr.io/cloud-builders/docker
11  Step #0: Sending build context to Docker daemon  57.86kB
12
13  Step #0: Step 1/9 : FROM    python
14  Step #0: latest: Pulling from library/python
15  Step #0: 376057ac6fa1: Pulling fs layer
16  Step #0: 5a63a0a859d8: Pulling fs layer
```

***Figure 10-12.***  *Build steps*

# Troubleshoot GCP Container Registry

The most common issues I have seen with Google Container Registry (GCR) is that the wrong region is set to host the images. Using the wrong region can cause performance issues.

The following three regions are available in GCR.

- gcr.io — United States

- eu.gcr.io — Europe

- asia.gcr.io — Asia

When you tag your image make sure you tag it with the correct location. If your apps are running in the United States, make sure you align the image location with gcr.io.

# Troubleshoot Compute Engine Resource

In this section, I will cover a couple of known issues that you need to pay attention to when working with Compute Engine VM resources.

# Select the Right Machine Family

Many performance issues in public clouds are related to a poor selection of instance type. It is very easy to make a mistake and select a general-purpose instance for running a database server. When selecting your instance, make sure you select a VM instance that is suitable for your workloads.

GCP offers the following three main machine family types:

- General-purpose

- Memory-optimized

- Compute-optimized

Based on the family type and your application type, you can select the best series that will fit your needs. Figure 10-13 shows the main machine family types.

**Machine configuration**

**Machine family**

| General-purpose | Memory-optimised | Compute-optimised |

Machine types for common workloads, optimised for cost and flexibility

**Series**

N1

Powered by Intel Skylake CPU platform or one of its predecessors

**Machine type**

n1-standard-1 (1 vCPU, 3.75 GB memory)

vCPU      Memory

1      3.75 GB

⌄ CPU platform and GPU

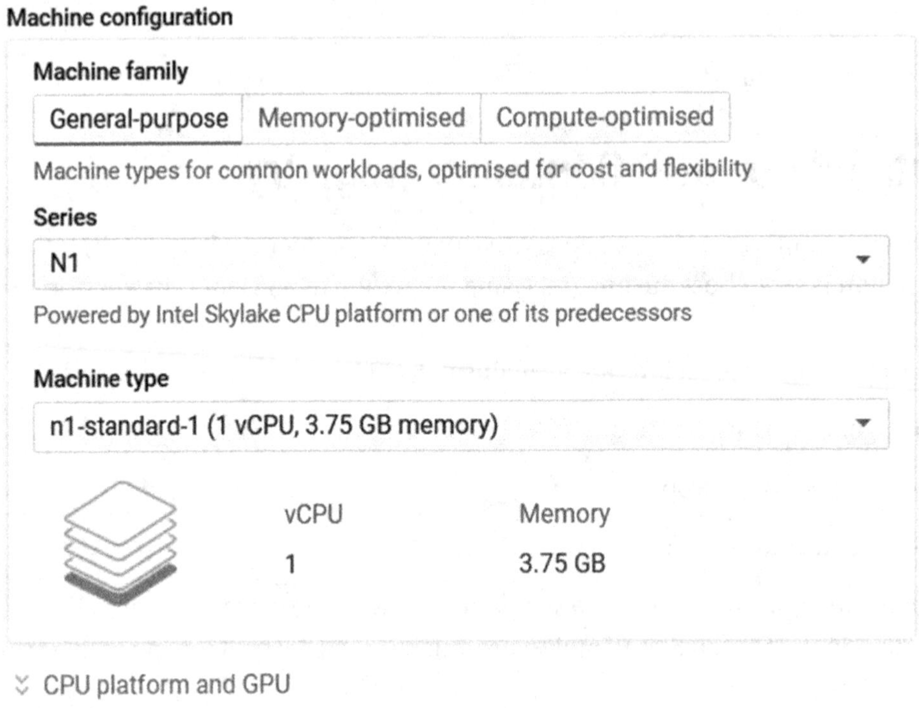

***Figure 10-13.***  *Machine family types*

# Firewall Ports

Another issue that is very common is related to exposing your application to external access over the internet. By default, all ports are closed except remote desktop and SSH for Linux machines. Ports HTTP and HTTPS can be opened from the Firewalls section of the VM during setup or by editing an existing VM. Figure 10-14 shows the Firewalls options.

**Firewalls**
☑ Allow HTTP traffic
☐ Allow HTTPS traffic

**Network tags**

http-server ⊗    dockerhost ⊗

***Figure 10-14.***  *Firewalls options*

# Open Non-standard Ports

If you need to open ports that are different from HTTP and HTTPS, you will need to open them from the Firewalls section of your VPC network. By default, your GCP workloads are protected by a virtual firewall that is attached to your Virtual Private Cloud (VPC) network. To access your VPC firewall, search for VPC network or Firewall from the GCP management console search bar.

Figure 10-15 shows the Firewall console located in the VPC network page.

***Figure 10-15.***  *Firewall page*

To open a port different from HTTP and HTTPS, you need to add a network tag to your virtual machine.

## Add Network Tag

To add a network tag, edit your VM and scroll down to the Firewalls section. In the Network Tags section, type a name that describes your host. For this demonstration, I will type dockerhost and save the VM configuration.

Figure 10-16 shows the Network Tags section.

***Figure 10-16.*** *Network tags*

After tagging the VM, open the Firewall console from the VPC network console. Click on Create a Firewall Rule, as shown in Figure 10-17. Fill in the details and make sure you type the name of your VM network tag in the Target Tags section.

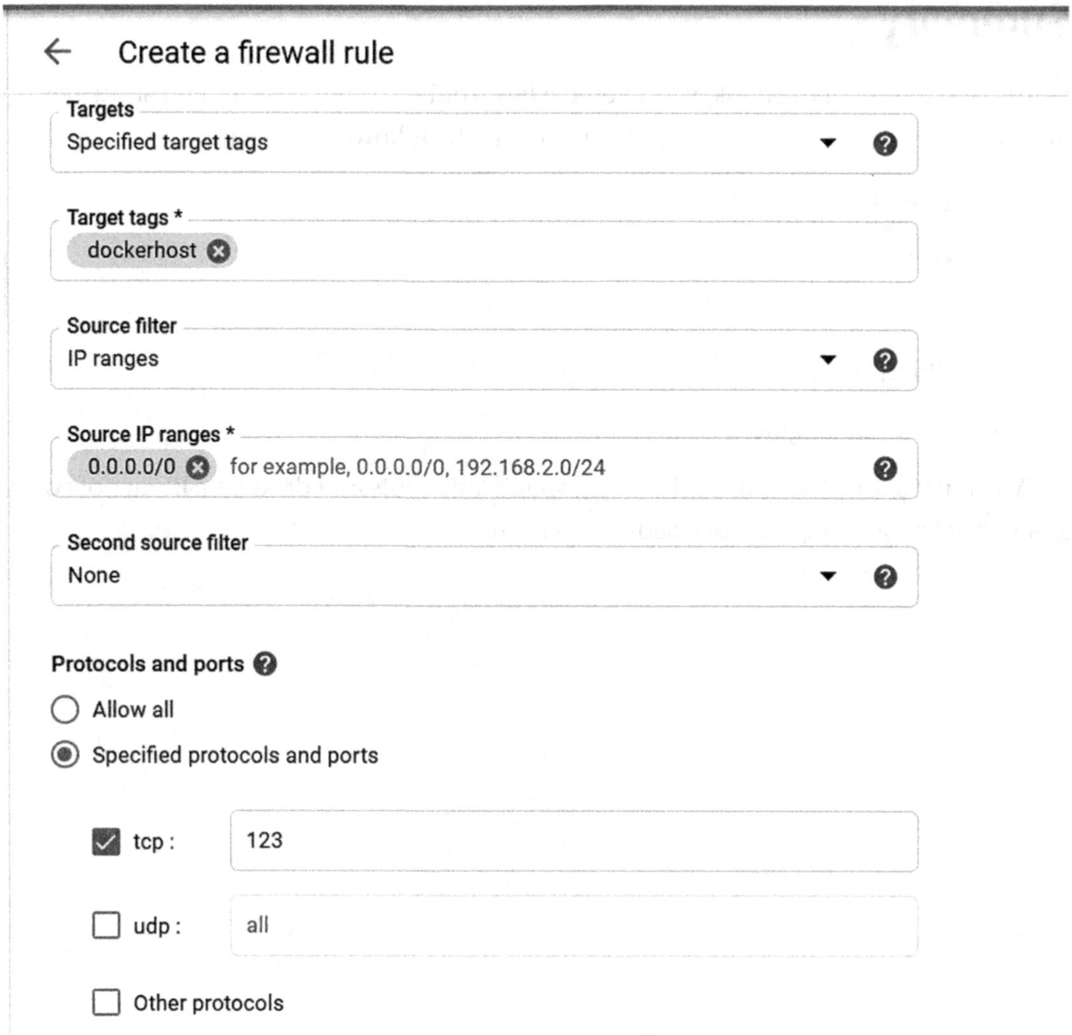

**Figure 10-17.** *Create a firewall rule*

Add the source address; for everything use 0.0.0.0/0. In the Protocols and Ports section, type the TCP port number and click Save.

# Summary

In this last chapter of the book, we covered a few troubleshooting issues and strategies that you might come across and need when using the following services:

- gcloud

- GKE

- Cloud Run

- Cloud Build

- Compute Engine

You must learn how to use gcloud command-line tools and develop a library of code that will help you redeploy workloads and save time.

# Index

© Shimon Ifrah 2021
S. Ifrah, *Getting Started with Containers in Google Cloud Platform*,
https://doi.org/10.1007/978-1-4842-6470-6